Andrew the
next decade was its religious affairs corresp... ...arliamentary sketch writer and a features writer. He now writes regularly for the *Guardian* and contributes to *Prospect* and the *New Statesman*. His other books include *The Darwin Wars* and *In the Beginning Was the Worm*.

'[A] marvellously seamless fusion of personal memoir and politico-cultural survey' *Independent on Sunday*

'[Brown] is a deft writer with a real descriptive talent and a humorous touch . . . this is an affectionate and insightful portrait, offering a much deeper understanding of the country than the usual, often politically motivated, tendency to stereotype' *Financial Times*

'Brown's Sweden is a place of inconsistencies, perplexing omissions, inevitable human frailty and . . . fish. Brown's enthusiastic angling produces some of the most lyrical passages in the book . . . He writes eloquently about the Swedish countryside, the shining lakes, the long summer days . . . It is this ordinary, flawed but hardly pathological Sweden that Brown celebrates in this enjoyably understated book' *Observer*

'Brown's prose is as clear and bewitching as the lake waters which he learns to fish . . . Readers who know the Nordic countries will delight in the author's keen ear and eye for the nuances of language, landscape and social customs' *Economist*

'Deftly weaving rhapsodies of fishing in Swedish waters with political observations, [Brown] has written an idiosyncratic and highly enjoyable memoir of the fall of the New Jerusalem of the Left' *Literary Review*

'His evocations of his early years in the country are miracles of sensuous recollection . . . He describes well the flat-pack rationality of Swedish politics in the Sixties and Seventies' *Daily Telegraph*

'Reveals a darker aspect of Swedish society: oppressed by social controls, frustrated by strict conservatism and moderated by civic duty' *The Times*

'This book is worth looking at just for the fantastic passages on the country's climate and landscape, literary gems in the best tradition of nature writing' *Morning Star*

'A wise respectful and wonderfully written book' *Guardian*

Fishing in Utopia

Sweden and the Future that Disappeared

Andrew Brown

GRANTA

Granta Publications, 12 Addison Avenue, London W11 4QR

First published in Great Britain by Granta Books, 2008
This paperback edition published by Granta Books, 2009

A CIP catalogue record for this book
is available from the British Library.

3 5 7 9 10 8 6 4 2

ISBN 978 1 86207 081 3

Printed and bound in Great Britain by
CPI Bookmarque, Croydon

For Anita and Felix, with love.

Contents

1

The pike summer

Lilla Edet was so quiet a town when I lived there that I learned to distinguish the smells of different trees. There were distinct scents of pine, of spruce, and of the birches whose pollen made tears run down my face.

When I cycled to the square in the centre of the town the creaking of the wheels was the loudest sound. Opposite the school buildings in which nothing seemed ever to happen there was a wide dusty verge between the asphalt road and a meadow where wild flowers grew on tall coarse stems. On this strip magpies hopped and hoodie crows shuffled among the dust and stone chips. I never saw what they ate nor heard a songbird.

In that dry and dusty time I seemed to be cycling everywhere, either to the library, or the lakes in the forests that surround the town. There is never enough water in my memories of southern Sweden. For three months of the year it was all frozen anyway. But even in summer, the thin soil always seemed dry; the brown pine needles that nestled in every crevice of the rocks were hard and sharp as weathered bones. So to look at the lakes, and to breathe their damp exhalations, was a kind of healing. I didn't have to catch anything; not always even to fish. What I needed was to gaze into the surface and, by gazing, to pass into another world, and breathe.

In town, the library was always cool, and smelt of plastic and modernity. I borrowed books about chess, which were easy to read because they were written in clichés when not in algebraic notation; comic books about a cowboy, translated from the French, which taught me more varied and idiomatic Swedish; but I learned most of the language from the library's copy of Brian Clarke's *Pursuit of Stillwater Trout*, or *På jakt efter Stillavattens Öring*. I learned it by heart. If you had read any sentence in that book to me, I could have come up with the preceding one as well as the successor. The promise of fly fishing was that the world I pressed against when I looked at a lake would be deeper and richer than anything I had yet imagined. I wanted to break through there. I loved the illustrations of water beasts that garnished his text. There were delicate line drawings of damselfly nymphs, which are, despite their name, incessantly voracious and shaped like rapiers, with a long pointed tail and a short head, like an elaborate hilt. There were veiled sedge pupae swimming towards the surface, their legs and wings bundled up in a transparent membrane; and dangly midge larvae, feathery at each end, twisting as they waited for trout to seize them. These fabulous monsters peopled my imagination. Some have remained fabulous to this day. I still have never seen a sedge pupa that looked remotely like anything in that book. In real life, they look like tiny, soggy kidney beans.

Clarke's is a rather dogmatic book, written as if to break through to an inattentive and self-confident audience. I read it as an exercise at first, and then again and again, with increasing concentration, as a kind of Zen text, until the words clattered around inside my head like the blades of a helicopter that could lift me high above the valley. I had no fly rod then and there were no trout in the nearby lakes. But my course was set, even though I went on fishing for pike and perch with spinners of every shape I could afford.

The countryside around Lilla Edet has been combed by glaciers from north to south; parallel valleys run through the granite. In the deepest and broadest of these, by the side of Lilla Edet, runs the Göta river, which drains Lake Vänern, one of the largest inland lakes in Europe, into the Kattegatt at Gothenburg on Sweden's south-west coast. To the east of the river lies a chain of deep, clear lakes. They are clearer than they should be, because of the acid rain. The furthest upstream was completely dead: you could see ten metres or more into its depths, coated with white algal slime. Nothing else lived to cloud the water. But two lakes further south, by the bathing place for Lilla Edet, was a lake whose depths were still a deep humus colour, whose margins were full of water lilies and whose weed beds were full of pike.

In Finland, early in the twentieth century, farmers were so poor they ate roach. Bream was a popular, or at least a common, food in rural Sweden; there are poems and songs about catching them in their spawning time – and I suppose they can't taste as bad as roach. Perch were, and remain, a delicacy, found in the best fish restaurants. But when I was poor and hungry, I ate pike.

The hardware shop in Lilla Edet sold red-and-white plastic floats for perch fishing: sturdy, buoyant devices even the most determined fish found hard to pull under. But I hated worms, and switched to spinning as soon as I could. Three or four days a week I would cycle up the vicious dusty hill that led into the woods just east of the town. I had a solid fibreglass rod about five feet long, in mineral green with white streaks, its brass-wire rod-rings lashed on with lumpy twine. With it came a closed-face reel from which stiff coils of 20lb line sprang out. The outfit cost about twelve pounds in *kronor*, which meant I could afford to change the line to something limper and less frightening.

Much of the lake was inaccessible. The eastern shore fell out of the forest in a broken line of granite cliffs ten or twenty feet high and a mile long. It could only be approached by boat. At each end, it was cut off from the rest of the shore by the bogs and streamlets that linked the chain of lakes. But the accessible, western side of the lake was rounded and scalloped with bays between seamed granite promontories. Within the seams were drifts of crunchy pine needles, but most of the granite was bare except for lichen. On hot days the beautiful desolate scent of pine clung to my fingers. There were paths through the forest for part of the way round, but they ran some distance from the water. If I wanted to fish, I stood on granite. Often I was the only person there; perhaps the only human for a mile around. If I caught one fish, it was supper for all of us. Fishing was the only way I could contribute anything to the economy of my girlfriend's family. She was working shifts in the paper mill; but I couldn't get a work permit. It was 1977. Anita was twenty and I was twenty-two. I could have left her to get on with her life. Instead I stayed, and went fishing.

It was almost always a waste of time to cast straight out. The water there was four or five metres deep. The fish were in the warm shallow margins, sheltered by lily pads. Plugs were diffi-cult to cast and expensive, so I used spoons. The Swedish tackle firm ABU made perhaps twenty different types of pike spoon in those days, in six or seven colourings and weights: their cata-logue of spoons, and plugs and spinners was enough to build a whole speculative universe around, like a fly box, except that spinning was more tactile. I could feel the different ways each lure moved in the water, and spent the hours when nothing bit

4

working out patiently which speed seemed to bring the lure most to life. In the end, I settled on a fluttering, leaf-like motion, using an Atom spoon described as 'perch-coloured'. It was copper on one side, and on the other green and black dots mingled in stripes like a test for colour blindness; the larger sizes had a short red plastic tag at the rear that seemed to make a difference. Even through that terrible rod I could feel the twittering of the lure and could tell the difference between the knocks of a perch and the sudden, irreversible haul of a pike.

Very few fish that bit at all escaped. I kept my hooks meticulously sharpened, with a hunter's instinct, and these were simple pike. There are lakes in Sweden where no other species of fish is found, and the Hobbesian war of all against all is complete. Ours was not so savage, but the pike were still overcrowded and voracious. Every lily bed held some. Except on the hottest and stillest days, there was always at least one pike that could be teased or cajoled into striking. Most were not large: they could be coiled, decapitated, into the largest saucepan in the house. Really large ones were fried in fillets.

I cooked them with as much variety as I could, but it was an uphill struggle. In rural Sweden in the 1970s, potatoes marked the culinary seasons. The gradations involved were subtle: potatoes were eaten with every meal all through the year, and they were always boiled in their skins. But in summer, you ate new potatoes, peel and all. At some stage, as the autumn wore in, you reverted to peeling them at the table before eating them. Mashed potatoes were available, but only as a delicacy, from the hot-dog stand. It took me some months to learn the knack of peeling a scalding potato on the end of a fork; my girlfriend's father concluded from this that I was almost feeble-minded.

Some days, when Anita was working the early shift at the mill, I would rise with her rather than stay in the house and cycle to the lake in the hills. The last portion of the ride was downhill, through a meadow, and if I was early enough the mist would still be thick across it, so that, once, everything above my waist was gilded in the pale sunlight, and everything below choked and muffled in white. I freewheeled, as if I were flying through clouds above the surly bonds of earth. That day was bright and still, with the forest calm as a church. I caught nothing.

As the summer wore on, I fished and bicycled with a fierce devotion. As well as the bathing lake there were others on the western bank of the river, further away, but holding the promise of novelty, but their banks were too densely forested and boggy to be fishable at all. I don't want to overestimate the wildness of these woods: they were logged regularly and broken by frequent smallholdings. None the less, it would have been possible to travel from Lilla Edet to Lapland without ever leaving the forest except to cross roads; and, a couple of years later, a pack of six wolves was tracked from Russia, through Finland and Swedish Lapland, and then for a further 1,600 kilometres down the spine where Sweden and Norway are joined until one of them broke off, headed further south, and killed a sheep in a field just outside the town.

There were no such excitements in the pike summer. From Lilla Edet, you could only look north and south to the next bends in the great river. The sides of the valley rose like forested walls, cutting off the horizon, though the eastern side of the river was tamer, with a wider strip of fields. About eight kilometres north, a broad and sluggish tributary joined the Göta; and once at its mouth I lost two spinners and had a tremendous tussle with a large fish which also escaped. This was playing for stakes too high. I returned to the smaller lakes in the enclosing hills.

2

Anna

One day, Anna, Anita's mother took us both for a drive around the coast. That was almost the first time the two women had spoken in three years, even though Anna lived no more than half a kilometre from her daughter. Hans and Anna had been a very respectable couple, and their divorce had been, among other things, a precipitous fall into shame. When I met her, Anna, agreed by all to be the guilty party, was living to one side of the meadow below the church in a low terrace of modern houses faced with dark wood. It was July and there were tall dark weeds in the meadow where the wild flowers had blossomed. In front of her house was a small, neat garden and outside it, by the knee-high fence, a large, unshaven man in a string vest. 'Karlsson,' he said, offering his hand. Then he retreated towards the garage. Anna came down the path, a short upright woman, still dark-haired, who carried herself in a way that struck me as old-fashioned, as if she should be wearing a bonnet. She kissed her daughter shyly and drove us both out in her pale green bug-eyed Saab for a day among the islands of the coast. It was only fifteen kilometres away from the Göta valley, but the sudden open horizons of the coast made me drunk for a week. The large islands are joined by long road bridges that make zooming catenary swoops across the sea, and I felt as if I had swung on them like Tarzan, not just driven peaceably across. Years later I would have a mystical experience there fishing for sea trout, going weightless in the sunset in a little sand-bottomed cove, but it was not so great a liberation as that day's driving around.

It took me a very long time to understand Anna's reserved and dignified kindness. It came from an upbringing that was almost unimaginable among the shiny comforts of Lilla Edet with its libraries and cars. She had been born far to the north in a hamlet so remote that its name just means 'the village' – a scatter of huts among undulating fields in the hills above a river crossing north of Östersund. This is about a hundred kilometres south of the boundary of Lapland: too far north for apple trees to grow, or roses, though quinces will survive the winters, and a cherry tree might. She was born in the middle of the 1930s depression, when very little had changed for poor farmers in centuries. Her parents and all their children lived in one room and a kitchen, on the ground floor of her grandfather's house. They slept on straw mattresses, which they filled themselves. It was a special pleasure to stuff them until they were almost spherical; later they would grow lumpy as well as cold. I asked her once what it had been like, and she said, 'I remember one time, when mother was giving birth, father walked into town to get the midwife, and we all had to wait in the kitchen while it happened. But I can't remember which child that was.' Her mother had given birth to fourteen children in twenty years and then fostered two granddaughters, since their mothers, her eldest daughters, were too young to cope.

The old patriarch – her father's father – and his wife kept the whole of the upper floor for themselves. It contained another

8

room and kitchen. Her father's brother lived in a cottage across the clearing, on the other side of the well. There was electricity for light – one bulb in the middle of the room – but not much else. The family owned a horse, cows, and a few sheep. They grew hay, barley, and potatoes on very little land. Their dialect had a word for calling cows home from the forest where they were turned out to graze, and even in old age Anna remembered how beautifully her mother called, and how the cows would always come for her.

Their richest relative was an aunt who was the warden of the village almshouse. She sewed proper clothes for the children – woollen socks, skirts, vests and underpants with rubber fastenings at top and bottom to keep out the cold when they were old enough to walk to school.

Until then they probably stayed indoors all winter. Vilhelm Moberg, the great novelist, whose subject was the Swedish emigration to North America, wrote in his memoirs about a very similar family:

All I remember from the first years of childhood, before I started school, are the summers. They run together in my memory as one long lovely season, blessedly warm. Were there no winters then? Presumably one had winters in Småland at the beginning of the century, for those are the years in question. But I have no memory of them at all . . . The explanation must be . . . that the children in a smallholder's cabin spent the winters indoors. They were too badly clothed to stand the cold and wind under the open sky . . . they could hardly even look out of the windows, because the panes were covered on the outside with a crust of ice. Life in winter was quite literally shut in: we dozed by the open fire, and slept through many

hours of the night: it was, for children, a quiet
vegetating in the darkness under the low cabin roof. But
in summer the children were set free, across the field and
into the woods. Summer was the time for open-air life,
it was a world where the roof was lifted – for children it
was life under the roof of heaven and in the warmth of
the sun.

The feast of the Ascension was the 'First Barefoot
Day', when we were allowed for the first time in the year
to take off our shoes and socks and run barefoot.

Moberg grew up as a fierce socialist, a republican, and a tee-
totaller: all in their way habits of self-improvement as much as
they were projects for the transformation of society. But they
had transformed society as well, and by the time he died – he
drowned himself, having lost the will to write, in 1973 – they
were the self-evident pillars of Swedish life.

As children, Anna and her siblings had to walk three kilometres to school, which was hard where the path crossed open
ground. In winter the snow would drift, and in summer there
were horses running wild which frightened the children. Even
the neighbour's old ram scared them. But in summer, when
school was over, the children were set free to run in the woods;
they chewed pine resin then as if it were gum, for the taste, but
also, I suspect, because it could numb hunger.

Anna left school at thirteen. Her father, who chose all the
children's clothes, bought her a new pair of beige leather shoes
for the occasion; but six months later, when it was time for the
First Communion, he dyed the school shoes black with boot
polish and sent her to church on a bicycle. It rained. She was
late getting through the mud. The boot polish ran in streaks
down the pale shoes. By the time she arrived, the other children

were already kneeling at the rail, and she could see that all of them had new shoes with clean soles.

One of the children was given a watch that day. Anna got nothing, but hurried home to help with the haymaking. Perhaps forty years later, when Ingela, her youngest daughter, was confirmed in Lilla Edet, the richer parents talked all through the service, and crowded round to film their children for their home movies.

After school, Anna was sent out to a larger farm to work as a milkmaid. All the servants slept in the kitchen there, but when she was fifteen, she was sent as a servant girl to a woman named Martha Jacobsson, who gave her a room of her own to sleep in. 'I often think of her kindness. Her husband had emigrated to America to find work, with another neighbour's husband. They did eventually return, but the children had grown up by then, and she wasn't interested in him any more.'

Martha wanted Anna to do better. She encouraged her to work in the almshouse, and from there her aunt sent her to Stockholm to train as a nurse. After that the church sent her to Antwerp to train as a midwife and to prepare for working as a missionary in the Congo. She spent two years in Belgium, learning Kikongo, and a little French. Her hands always shook when she talked about this part of her life. 'I couldn't manage it,' she would say. Even as a child she had been nervous – 'I had to stay behind in school once because I couldn't recite the psalm verse. I knew it, but when it came time to read it, I hadn't got the breath.' In Belgium it was the same, and just before her final exam she had some kind of nervous collapse and was sent to a convalescent home in Stockholm. I don't believe she ever left Sweden again.

In the convalescent home, she met another neurasthenic, a young man called Hans, who looked a little dreamy, like a thick-lipped version of the young W. B. Yeats. Hans came from a strict and respectable family in the south. As a child he had been dressed in a sailor suit for walks around town.

They got married and moved to the country north of Gothenburg. Hans worked in low-level engineering jobs, helping to tend the turbines of the power stations along the Göta river. Anna worked in hospitals, and had three daughters, the last one after several miscarriages. They were devout, which meant they were teetotal. Provincial, evangelical Christianity was constructed around the absence of alcohol much as Solomon's Temple was built around the empty tabernacle. When they did not drink coffee, they drank water, or red cordials made from rosehips or lingonberries. Their teetotal rectitude had the same faint mustiness of the non-alcoholic beer substitutes that were brought out on festive occasions; it could be sour as black coffee, too.

Every window in their house had curtains framing it: lace ones, tied back at each side, and a band of fabric along the bottom half of the windows, too, in front of the line of pot plants. The tables had embroidered runners down the middle. The bookshelves were decorated with ornaments. Both Anna and Hans worked, but Anna worked harder. The house was always clean and orderly. They ate meat or fish with their potatoes every day.

In their religion, one of the noblest works that a Christian could undertake was to rescue a drunk. Anna, with her medical and missionary training, found it came naturally and she befriended one of the more notorious drunks in town, who had found Jesus and stopped drinking. This was dreadfully hard for him without the love of a good woman to sustain him, and for two years he sought Anna's help. Eventually she yielded; she rescued him so thoroughly that the neighbours started talking. One day Hans came home from work early and found the drunk's car parked outside their house. Catastrophe. Explosion. Anna moved out.

Almost all of their Christian friends dropped her at once and for good. For three months she lived on her own, in a flat by the railway station, wondering what to do with her life or whether just to end it. Instead, she married the drunk, who had waited for her. What else could he do?

Hans, too, was damaged by the scandal. He was a fussy man, energetic like a mouse, with wispy hair, large, pale spectacles and a neatly trimmed dun beard. He peered affectionately at life as if it were a bewildering exam in which he had somehow managed a pass. Released by general consent from the obligations of marriage, he started to respond to personal ads at the back of the *Göteborgs-Tidning*. He found this life of small adventures suited him, and he never really went back to being married.

The three girls stayed with their father. Anita, the eldest daughter, didn't speak to her mother at all for two years. She left school at sixteen and volunteered to work on a kibbutz, returning after four years of adventure with me. The middle sister made a scandal when she was driven into Gothenburg in the back of a rock-and-roll group's van at the age of fifteen. Ingela took refuge in horses: not that she had any, but she read about them continually, even more enthusiastically than she read *Mitt Livs Novell*, the magazine for teenage girls which featured every week a story in which a young single mother found happiness with a safe and reliable man.

Only one family would still speak to Anna after the scandal, and these good Samaritans were foreigners, half-Danish. When I turned up five years later, they also lent Anita and me their rowing boat and I would use it to explore the hidden, southern arm of the bathing lake. One blazing afternoon I rowed Anita round a headland we had never passed on foot, and entered a long channel. At the end was a broad, reedy bay, a place where pike were bound to flourish. Rounded granite like a whale's flank slid into the water at the mouth of the bay. We drifted in a perfect silence until the bottom of the boat crunched gently on the rock. Once we had climbed out, silence surrounded us again. We might have been on an island: the hissing of the line as I cast, the splash of the lure, and the gentle grinding of the reel's gears as I retrieved were all sharp-edged, framed by the silence.

'We could get married,' I said. She rolled a cigarette of Norwegian tobacco and smoked it carefully. The silence held us like a mother. We returned that night with our sleeping bags and a bottle of sour Italian wine. We lit a fire of dead pine branches on the rock and grilled sausages for a treat. The subject was not mentioned again, but we slept deeply on the uneven rock.

Mornings by the lake, the whole world felt enamelled in perfection. The water would be absolutely still, and the mist would trap the metallic smell of the water and the pungency of the reeds. Slowly the mist would curl away, leaving nothing but clarity. It was very cold. All the stiffness of the night would rush on to me as I woke and struggled out of the sleeping bag to make coffee. Every sound was distinct, even the noise the water made as it swirled into the coffee kettle when I pushed it under the lake. You might find the most delicate evidences of rebirth: the shucks of dragonflies and once, lying at the edge of our rock, where the forest began, the whitish translucent skin of an adder. I suppose what Adam and Eve missed most, after they had left the garden, was a world without other people in it.

We returned and ate lunch with her father: boiled pike with dill and new potatoes. About a fortnight later, as we were digging the vegetable patch, she said, 'You're right. We could get married.'

3

Nödinge

That autumn, Anita and I were married in the drawing room of the Danish couple. My father was there, and gave us some money. 'Mixed marriages seldom last,' he said. Hans made a speech afterwards, over black coffee, with tears in his eyes, urging us to take care of each other. Karlsson did not attend. We spent our honeymoon in the little wooden cottage that he and Anna owned up by the Norwegian border. It was a still, warm week just after the first frosts. Cats sprawled in the sunlight on our porch; there was a two-seater earth closet in an outbuilding, and a small lake reflected the embroidered richness of the hillside opposite. The whole valley was full of the sharp smell of turning leaves. From time to time I would laugh at the worried way in which Anna had asked me, a couple of hours before the ceremony, whether I thought I might regret what I was about to do.

After the honeymoon we moved thirty kilometres south from Lilla Edet to Nödinge, a purpose-built suburb of Göteborg: about two thousand flats arranged in low concrete blocks the colour of dog turds on a glacial plain by the river. I found work in a small factory making wooden pallets; Anita was a nursing auxiliary in a small town up the road. Nödinge, the name of both the village on the hillside and the estate on the valley floor below, was so old it was first recorded as two runes, not in letters at all. One of these, *naud*, means 'slavery, want, compulsion', while *inge* means, like its English cognate in place names, '-ing', 'the tribe of'. So this place had emerged into history as the settlement of the tribe of slaves and in the midst of astonishing prosperity it still maintained an air of wretchedness. The prosperity had arrived within living memory; an oral history, compiled in the Eighties, told me that in 1918, when the potato crop failed, people had starved to death in the woods that stretched away eastwards for miles.

One woman, born in 1886 on a farm in the hills, remembered how once a fortnight they would go into Göteborg with a horse-drawn wagon full of stuff to sell from the farm. If they had a big load, they started at midnight; smaller loads allowed them to start at two in the morning. Twice a year, in spring and autumn, the sheets and linen would be taken down to the river and washed. And in the woods there had been a wise woman who set leeches on the sick.

The flat gravelly plain of the Göta made poor farmland, though a factory had been built down here, and failed in the 1920s. After that, people from the village on the bluffs would bicycle to work in factories three miles upriver or four miles downstream.

Things were better in the Second World War. Petrol was scarce, so they had ploughed with horses, and in winter the river, which is half a kilometre wide at this point, froze so hard that they came out on skates to play Bandy on it. It is a game a little like ice hockey, but with more players and a ball instead of a puck. I have seen the whole river frozen once myself, but then it was not smooth, but a choppy sea of ice floes piled one against the other, all tilted facets in the sun like a giant's ploughed field. The cold that froze it smooth enough to skate on must have been terrible. But even in the coldest winters of the 1940s, there was food, and soon after that came the years of unimaginable prosperity.

The Bandy players were the generation who had built the welfare state. Even in the Seventies, hardly anyone in Sweden was more than three generations away from subsistence farming, so that the rich egalitarian country that I had moved to, and which was all the outside world could see, was built by people who grew up with habits instilled by the poor and hierarchical country which survived only in memories. Whether prosperity can survive without the memories and disciplines of poverty is a question I don't know the answer to.

The estate on the plain at Nödinge had been built in the early Seventies, as part of the 'million programme', which may have been the high-water mark of social democracy in Sweden. At a time when the population was about eight million people, the Social Democrats decided to build a million new, modern homes, and they did so, irrespective of whether anyone wanted to live in them. This was the origin of the satellite towns that orbit the emptiness around all Swedish cities. Nödinge was planned to have 1,250 dwellings, housing the overspill of Gothenburg, but the plan was scaled back to 850; and even these were not easily filled. About 250 of the flats had to be converted into day nurseries or sheltered housing for the elderly, which explains why we had had no trouble finding a flat in 1977.

The first thing that struck me was the loneliness. The roads within the estate were all closed to traffic but pedestrians always seemed scarce. The houses might be wonderfully warm, and the spacious kitchens of even the most basic flats were equipped

17

with fridges, freezers, and separate coolers, which worked like larders, to keep food warmer than in a fridge, but much cooler than a centrally heated room. But the public places always felt as cold as November. Even on sunny days I wanted to scuttle through them as if a cold rain were lashing me. I've never lived in, nor could imagine, a place where people talked less to each other. The bottom two floors of our block were taken up by a day nursery, so nobody lived there at all; on the top floor, I believe that in two years we spoke twice to one neighbour, and never to anyone else. This wasn't at all unusual. Lukas Moodysson's film *Together*, which came out in 2000, was set in the early Seventies and filmed in a similar estate to ours, in Trollhättan, higher up the Göta. It has a character in it who pretends that his sink has broken down, so that when the plumber comes he has someone to talk to for an hour. It's a vignette of loneliness that makes perfect sense to anyone who lived on one of those estates.

It wasn't deliberate unfriendliness. People just didn't know how to talk to one another. There was a strong tradition of propriety. It was clearly better to say nothing than to say the wrong thing. There was, in my experience, a great deal of friendliness within families and work places. But when families broke up, or workplaces disintegrated, there was nothing. The idea of relating to strangers for pleasure did not figure largely in Swedish provincial life.

When Anita and I wanted to buy a bottle of wine in our first winter in Nödinge we had to take the bus ten miles to Kungälv. This was the nearest *Systembolag*, the monopoly shop where alcohol could be bought legally, on weekdays before 5.30 p.m. The *Systembolag* in Kungälv had been purpose-built. It was a bleak and largely windowless grey concrete building. There were a couple of large windows at the front but I don't remember that they opened into the shop behind; instead they were used for a display of temperance propaganda. My favourite was a life-sized poster of the human body, with arrows pointing to almost every organ to show what alcohol would do to it, from tingling peripheral neuritis in the feet up through the malfunctioning penis and the swollen liver to damaged brain.

Inside the shop we always queued. The goods were not on display, but listed in catalogues that we read in the queue. These were not designed to sell: anyone who didn't speak Swedish would have mistaken them for bus timetables. The bottles were for the most part concealed out the back. In the more daring outlets, there might be display cases for the cheaper wines, but normally you reached the counter at the front and ordered from a pitying assistant, who would slowly collect the goods from the mysterious shelves in the back.

Nowadays, when you go into a *Systembolag*, which could be in a town as small as Lilla Edet, or even Nödinge, you are given a trolley to push around the shelves. The catalogue is illustrated; the decoration is aimed at selling, not repelling. Everything about the old weighty grey concrete Sweden seems to have dissolved into the air, as Marx might have predicted. Yet something still persists of the old brutal clumsiness about alcohol. Even now, Kungälv resists the lure of joy: driving out from the centre in the summer of 2006 I passed a nightclub called 'Club Hangover'.

Hangovers were usually acquired in the open air when we lived there. In the little park behind the bus station where we waited for the bus back to Nödinge, there were benches where the alcoholics lived. They drank *renat*, the cheapest vodka, whose only merit was that it would not poison them. The full name, *absolut renat*, simply meant 'completely purified'. They were all middle-aged, and looked older: men whose coarsened faces and thick bodies were like a child's idea of the bad grown-up. In winter they lumbered about for warmth, and when they did so their jackets would ride up at the back, exposing numb crescents of white or purple flesh. To be a drunk like that was to have fallen out of society altogether. Anita and I sat primly with our carrier bags in the bus station, trying not too obviously to watch them. Then we went home and drank our wine in a solemn mood, just the two of us, in the flat. I had to carry the empties to the rubbish chute, though. It was too shaming for a respectable Swede to be seen in public with a clinking carrier bag.

All the deserted roads on the estate had floral names. Ours was 'South Clover Path' and at the end it debouched into a sort of East German public space: a square, with shops set into the shabby concrete round two sides. There was a *Konsum*, a shoe shop, a florist, and an employment exchange. There was nowhere to buy drink, or to consume it.

These were the only shops on the estate, though around the back of this square was a small hot-dog kiosk, set in a hole in the wall, where the young men would hang around in their old cars. I don't think I have ever known people among whom boredom was so tangible. It seemed to thicken the air around them until movement was an effort and thought impossible.

All my memories of them are at twilight: the smell of exhaust fumes and tobacco smoke mingling with the smell of sausages and mustard; my workmate Jonny, with his snaggly blond fringe, sitting on the front seat of his ten-year-old Volvo Amazon, reading *FiB Aktuellt*. *FiB* was an abbreviation for *Folket i Bild*, 'People in Pictures', and the magazine had once been something like *Picture Post*, but now all of the people in it were female, and none of them had any clothes on. It was a forerunner of what would, in Britain, become lad mags, but without their ability to pretend that the readers were fashionable and brave.

Jonny had girlfriends sometimes, but their characters remained indistinct to me, as perhaps to him. I remember a pale, pinched face across his living room full of hash smoke one winter evening in his flat. I can't remember anything she said, only the sudden, spiky cold when I walked back home through the darkness, as if the air were full of frost crystals digging into me. He didn't invite me to any more parties; Anita would not have him in our flat. I thought him dull at worst. She thought he might be dangerous.

The walls of our flat were grey wallpaper on concrete: if you wanted to hang paintings or anything else to individualize them only special hooks would do. They were fixed to the wall by three thick needles set in a plastic disk, which had to be hammered in. When the time came to remove them, they had to be pulled off with pliers, leaving behind three neat puncture wounds in the wall.

Faced with all this sterile silence my hair grew ragged and my beard grew melancholy; when I walked to the shops, some of the children would call after me, 'Jesus'. I thought more fiercely about fly fishing when I heard these voices, imagining cool water. In winter I lived still further in my imagination. I studied magazine photographs with blind yearning until they almost felt like real water. I read Brian Clarke again and again, as if the words could helicopter me there.

Deep every winter when the cold really squeezed we would be pushed into a new world where everything outside became as lurid and frozen as the weather inside me. The change was announced by sudden metallic booms resounding through the house a little before midnight. This happened whenever the temperature fell to minus 30° C and the concrete and girders of the flats shrank in loud convulsive shudders. It was like a sonic boom announcing that we had passed beyond earth's atmosphere.

After those warnings, I would dress with special care, putting on long underpants, then jeans, and then a set of overalls when I got up at 5.30. Immediately I had struggled into all these clothes the flat was hot and itchy, but as soon as I pushed shut the door with a scrape and a click and started down the outside staircase, the air felt as if it were full of pine needles that caught in my throat and there was a numbness and tingling on the front of my thighs as I walked across the car park. Such nights were very still. The sky was black as oil and beneath it was the flare of sodium lights on snow. Below about minus 20° C, sump oil thickens suddenly and batteries grow weak. First the car had to be unlocked: this meant heating the key with a lighter and then squirting special oil into the lock. Everything was done in thick gloves. The key would fall, and have to be scooped carefully from the snow. Inside the car felt even colder and darker than the world outside and my steaming breath froze on everything. All the lights and the fan must be turned off to save precious electricity before trying to start. I learned to listen for every undertone in the hoarse thin scraping of the starter motor, and the convulsive heaving as the engine turned over. After the engine started – if it started – I would have to wait about ten minutes while the car warmed up enough for the outside of the windscreen to thaw completely. Otherwise I would be blinded as soon as I started to drive, as my breath froze the windscreen on the inside.

The memory of those mornings is the most painful and poignant of all I have from Sweden. I don't know why. They did not make me miserable or even unhappy at the time. The cold just put up a new series of obstacles that had to be overcome, and made the chores take twice as long. But those mornings seem to me now to have been a kind of grand theatre, as if the whole planet had been hurled into winter just to demonstrate what sadness in the bone is like. That solitary, still, inverted world, where the sky was black and the ground a flaring yellow, comes back to me like a nightmare. It was a world that would only react with endless slowness, although I could still move at normal speed, so that everything had to be fumbled through time and time again and nothing I did seemed to make the shadow of a difference.

The deep chill would not long survive daylight. By half past nine the temperature would have risen to fifteen or twenty below. Such cold demanded cloudless skies and a pale deistic sun. The curious inversion of brightness persisted: the broad flat valley would fill with half-glimpsed sparkles in the snow so that the ground seemed brighter than the sky by day, just as it had at night. Nor had the smells of the world entirely vanished. Close to, the factory still smelled of sweet and acrid sawdust, of the pale machine oil of the nail guns and gritty diesel from the fork-lift trucks.

I call it a factory but it was only a large converted barn in which four or five of us made the pallets on which Volvo marine diesel motors were shipped around the world. There had been an element of deception in the way I got the job: the interview was conducted next to one of the fork-lift trucks, whose diesel exhaust pipe rattled away between us. Leif, who owned the factory, and I were both wearing hearing protectors. When I could hear what he was saying, I probably gave the wrong answers. When I couldn't, or when I failed to understand it, I just nodded and grinned enthusiastically and he heard the right ones. It's a bit like catching fish on a spoon, which is most effective when it is not a detailed model of a small fish but an almost two-dimensional abstract that wiggles with exaggerated clumsiness. You allow the pike to see what it wants and expects and he does the rest.

The language the fishermen speak to their prey is wholly deceptive, but between humans things are more complicated. Leif expected and wanted a fit young man who could speak reasonable Swedish. I was neither when we met, but after three or four months I had become the prey he thought he'd seized in the first place.

We worked from half past six in the morning until half past three in the afternoon, with two half-hour breaks, one at nine and one at noon. The morning break was taken in Leif's house, in a room off the kitchen which had a simple table decorated with one runner and two candlesticks. Our shoes had to be removed just inside the front door, in the small hall which was found in all Swedish houses. It had always been a mark of poverty to have to wear all your outdoor clothes indoors.

There was coffee to drink in small cups, poured black from a thermos which had been put out by Leif's wife, who was also responsible for the plate of open sandwiches, salami or cheese, resting on ovals of dark sweet bread. There were meant to be one cheese and one meat sandwich for each worker. After I'd been there a few months, when I was no longer ravenous and exhausted all the time, I worked out that I had been eating everyone else's sandwiches for the first four weeks.

At noon, Leif would retreat to his house and the rest of us would eat from the lunch boxes we brought with us in a little shed to the side of the main barn, which housed the generator that supplied compressed air to our nail guns. Once I grew strong enough for the work, I ate less at lunchtime, too: usually

I would have two more sandwiches and a thermos of proper, milky coffee. Sometimes I would put out little bits of sandwich for the field mice to eat as they scampered around the galvanized shelves where nail guns, headphone protectors, and boxes of nails were stored. Conversation would usually run out after ten or fifteen minutes. Then I would read before the rest of the shift in the afternoon.

For a long time, I read in Swedish. I had started with Anita's English text books, which concentrated on what was hard about English for Swedish-speakers, and took for granted most of the difficulties that I encountered in the other directions. Then, even before Brian Clarke, I had read a lot of comic books.

I read quite a lot of philosophy and economics that way. I know I read my way through several of Karl Popper's books in these twenty-minute breaks. It turned out to be the perfect way to read serious philosophy, at least for someone as slow-thinking as I am. Every twenty-minute chunk of reading would be followed by a three-hour spell of digestion. By the end of it, I had more or less recovered the faculty of argument I had left behind in my hippie-ish wanderings, several years before.

4

Socialists

For the first six weeks of the job, I would not have believed myself capable of reading or even talking in these breaks. I would stuff my face with sandwiches for the first fifteen minutes of the breakfast break in Leif's house, and then fall asleep, my head propped on my hand, for the second half of the break. Then I would fall asleep at lunch, and again on the bus back to Nödinge, and finally I would lie down on the concrete floor of our living room, beside the cloth-covered cardboard box that served as a coffee table, and fall asleep again. At the end of six weeks I had expected to be sacked, but I was not. Shortly after that, I found that I could stay awake from morning until bedtime.

Within three months the job was no longer physically impossible at all. It remained physically demanding: even on the coldest days I could work in a T-shirt after the first hour because there was so much heat coming off my body. Every movement had become a sort of dance step, though I worked in clogs: there was a quickest and least exhausting way to shoot in every nail and not a day went past without my chasing it.

At the table in Leif's house I began to pay attention to the conversations around me. In winter, the sun would just have risen, or be rising, as we walked to eat at nine, but Leif's curiosity about the world had been up for hours. He was always looking for someone to argue with, an activity he approached as if it were wrestling; as a healthy exercise for friends that must end with his victory. When he was angry, his face would crumple up around his moustache and fleshy nose, until he looked like a homicidal duck.

He was the only member of the Conservative party I ever met outside Stockholm political circles. He had trained his terrier to bark and growl at the command, 'Socialists!' He owned a boat half as high as his house. As a young man, he had been an air force pilot; his story was that he had been thrown out for crashing too many planes. Traces of the jet pilot he had been were still obvious in his driving style, whether he was at the wheel of a lorry or a fork-lift truck. He worked at everything with the same full-throttle approach. He was almost always the first man to arrive in the freezing dark in winter and the last to leave on stifling summer afternoons.

I kept silent for about three months while he wrangled ritually with Rolf, the foreman who had worked with him for years. But one morning I found myself able to speak enough fluent Swedish to disagree with him authoritatively. It was the first time I had managed to talk like an educated man in that language. It wasn't just a matter of syntax and vocabulary, but confidence: I felt as if I were delivering a judgement already written out when I corrected him, and he thought so too.

The paper over which we mostly argued was the *Göteborgs Posten*, a closely printed broadsheet in which, it was said, every subscriber might hope to see their own name at least twice before they died. There were pages and pages of local news for every district it covered, but also a page or two of national and even foreign news. Jimmy Carter was still President of the USA. In so much as any news item stood for the insanity and unpredictability of foreigners, it was the election of Mrs Thatcher. Perhaps it was some mention of her that triggered my rush to speech; but her politics were almost unthinkable in Sweden. To claim that there was no such thing as society would have been like claiming there was no such thing as winter.

The other source of my knowledge of the country was detective stories. Once my Swedish was up to the task, I devoured the novels by Maj Sjöwall and Per Wahlöö, about the policeman Martin Beck and his colleagues. Between 1963 and 1975, this man-and-wife duo produced ten police procedurals set in Stockholm, which sold all around the world. They are excitingly written, realistic about police work, and full of period detail. But most of all they illuminate the lost orthodoxy of the social democratic years. The strangest thing about Sweden, to an English eye, was always its tremendous conformity. It did not matter what the orthodoxy might be: the point is that everyone knew what was acceptable and proper to believe. In this sense, the Martin Beck stories taught me most when they were most absurd, because they exaggerated what everybody then believed about progress and the good society. Sjöwall and Wahlöö were communists and in the Seventies there was an assumption that communism, while it might be imperfect, was at least a form of socialism; and socialism then seemed as completely inevitable as global capitalism does now.

Not all their villains are millionaires. But there isn't a character in their books who is conspicuously rich who is *not* a murderer, and usually of a particularly blameworthy kind. The successful multinational businessman shot in a Malmö hotel turns out to be a crook whose widow is cheating on him with his trusted assistant. The mysteriously murdered businessman from the pleasant suburbs north of Stockholm makes his money from the sale of pornographic films featuring drugged young women. He is murdered in the house of his mistress, who only tolerated him for his money, by his gardener, whose young daughter he had debauched and ruined.

Yet one can also see in their books the worry that affluence is bad for everyone. It is not just the millionaires who are corrupted by their wealth, but everyone in Sweden whose lives have been made worse by the country's success. In part, I think, Sjöwall and Wahlöö were driven to this by ideological desperation, in common with many on the Left at that time. Where would the revolution come from now that the workers all had their own well-furnished flats? One answer was to insist that things were really terrible; and in the later, more operatic books, anyone, policeman or villain, is likely to break into little arias of despair: 'Private citizens . . . were being clubbed down every hour on the streets, or in their shops, or on the tube, or in their houses, everywhere and anywhere . . . The existing system was obviously useless, and even a well-wisher could only say that it just about kept going . . . The so-called welfare state is overflowing with ill, destitute and lonely people who live on dog food if they are lucky and are left unattended to die in their rat holes of houses.'

That was written about a country that was one of the richest in the world, emerging from a hundred and fifty years of uninterrupted peace, and in the middle of unprecedented economic growth, which had just built a million new houses more or less to prove that it could. The tradition of dystopic hysteria has been continued by more recent Swedish fictional detectives, but none has surpassed Sjöwall and Wahlöö, nor matched their furious refusal to admit that things were, for the most part, perfectly tolerable.

FISHING IN UTOPIA

But there was another sense in which their ambivalence about progress was more widely shared. The capitalist prosperity of social democratic Sweden seemed to have come at the expense of all sorts of human kindnesses. Everything old and wooden and ramshackle had been remade in concrete as the country grew richer. It was all more practical, more sensible, and more hygienic, but at the same time dreadfully dispiriting.

Central Stockholm had been almost entirely rebuilt and dehumanized in the Sixties. The process culminated with the whole country changing to driving on the right in 1967. In the years before the night when everything changed, all new roads, and even cars, had been built for the future, when people would drive on the other side of the road, so in the years immediately preceding the change-over, you had the unnerving feeling of being at fault simply for not living in the future. Around Sergels Torg, at the heart of the redevelopment, this feeling persisted long after everyone drove on the right.

The minister of transport who oversaw the change to driving on the right was Olof Palme, who became the presiding figure of social democratic Sweden throughout the Seventies. Palme was prime minister twice, and leader of the Social Democratic party for seventeen years. But dates and facts don't convey his authority. Once he became leader of the Social Democrats in 1969, asking whether Palme was in office or not was like asking whether God existed. For a believer, this is a question that scarcely matters: God is God, whether or not he has the relatively trivial quality of existence, and whether or not he seems to be influencing the world. Similarly, Palme was the leader of Sweden, whether or not he held the office of *Statsminister*.

This was pretty much his view too. When he lost office in 1976, after forty-four years of unbroken Social Democratic government, in and out of coalitions, he and his closest helpers

30

cleaned out the prime minister's offices of all official documents, leaving nothing, even on the bookshelves.

Swedes who hated him – and some really did – had something of the unbalanced daring of teenagers who have discovered atheism. They challenge God to strike them dead, as if this would settle an important point about the universe. What Palme did, and what he didn't, seemed to be significant for the whole of humanity if you lived in Sweden.

To the outside world, in so far as it noticed him, he stood for everything about the country's pious leftist internationalism. Within the country, he symbolized the arrogance and sense of entitlement of the Social Democratic establishment better than anyone else could. The Social Democrats had set out to remake Swedish society almost completely. They had inherited a poor, patriarchal, and formal society, and turned it into a rich, feminist, and fiercely egalitarian one. They seemed to have abolished poverty and war; they had certainly abolished selective schooling and even selective pronouns: when they first took office, Swedish, like French and German, had formal and informal words for 'you', which expressed social position as well as degrees of intimacy; in fact it was extraordinarily rich in hierarchical and impersonal constructions for addressing social superiors. By the time they left, everyone was quite simply 'you'.

As minister of education, in 1968, Palme marched against the Vietnam War at the head of a demonstration in which the North Vietnamese ambassador to Moscow also took part. It was in some ways an odd position for him. He had no illusions about communism, which he opposed from an early age, and was idealistic about the USA. As a young man, in the late 1940s, he had studied there, and then hitch-hiked from New England to Mexico on $300. His experience of life as a poor man in the USA made a socialist out of him, but he remained a faithful lover of America. You might say that he devoted his career in Swedish politics to ensuring that no Swede would ever need to experience the American combination of material poverty and boundless optimism, and that he succeeded so completely that when he died, he left a country where no one was poor and no one had room for optimism.

It suited Swedes and the few Americans who noticed Sweden to suppose that the two countries were polar opposites. The one stood for raw capitalism and murder; the other for socialism and suicide. But in important ways, Sweden resembled the USA far more closely than England ever could. This was most obviously geographically. England consisted of London and a few other cities surrounded by a greyish ooze of suburbia. There was nowhere to get lost in, and hardly anywhere out of earshot of a road. No lakes stretched to the horizon.

This lack of wilderness matters terribly, just as the presence of wilderness matters in Sweden. The countryside is not just a decoration seen through windows. It is much more powerful and intimate than that. The experience of living in a small community with wilderness all round works into every corner of your life and I think it explains some of the affinities between Scandinavia and the duller parts of the Midwest: the strong sense of civic duty; the high value put on worthiness. But there are affinities between Sweden and the Republican South, too, though both sides would deny this. The tradition of warlike Protestantism was once very strong in Sweden. This is a country whose most impressive public buildings derive from an empire that stretched from St Petersburg to Munich, and which ruled Norway as a colonial possession until 1905. The Vietnam demonstration of 1968, still vivid today in the black-and-white photographs of torchlight on snow, pale faces under dark fur hats, teeth vivid when chants ran through the crowd, typified what was most divisive about Palme. He could present the most sensible policies as if they were calls for wild revolution. Pulling out of Vietnam was not, in retrospect, a radical thing to do. It was the only sane choice for the Americans. But to propose it publicly, as the foreign minister of a supposedly friendly country, seemed an outrage against diplomatic proprieties. His combination of self-confidence, self-righteousness and common sense was disconcerting, even at a distance. Within the narrow confines of Swedish politics, it was overwhelming. Anyone could have tidied away the last powers of the Swedish monarchy, as Palme's constitution of 1975 did: only Palme would have looked at the new document and said that with one slash of his pen he could wipe out the monarchy altogether.

He was a class traitor. Neither his success nor the hatred he aroused could be understood without this fact. He had been born and brought up in Östermalm, in central Stockholm, in a high-ceilinged eight-roomed flat, with servants. His mother came from Baltic-German aristocracy and had family estates in Latvia. His father's family had ties to Finnish-Swedish aristocracy. His elder brother volunteered and fought on the side of the Finns in the Winter War with Russia in 1939–40. Olof Palme was just as devoted to equality as his brother was to freedom, though he believed, I think, that at bottom the two were the same, and could never truly conflict.

As prime minister Palme lived in a very ordinary suburban terraced house. One journalist reporting his 1979 campaign was invited in for supper. He found himself slicing a cucumber for salad in the kitchen while Lisbet – Mrs – Palme boiled pasta, and one son made a bolognese sauce. The photographer got to chop parsley. Palme himself perched on a stool in the kitchen and talked about *One Flew over the Cuckoo's Nest*, which he had just seen with Lisbet. 'We get to the cinema together about once every other year,' he said.

This was a life entirely within the aspirations of a teacher or a skilled welder. One of the gradations of equality was that the welder would probably have been paid better than the teacher: it was not until the early Eighties that the great shipyards of Gothenburg and Malmö finally went broke. Lack of ostentation was also one of the traditions of the Social Democratic party. In the late 1940s, the prime minister would work late in his office then catch a tram home. Sometimes the lack of distinction was deliberately theatrical. In the Fifties, when drink was still rationed, customers at the state off-licences, shuffling forward like customers in a brothel where attendance was compulsory, were liable to random ID challenges when they reached the head of the queue. Normally, one could expect to be checked once every couple of years. The prime minister, however, was always selected for a random check, just to show the other customers that it was truly random. Equality meant that everyone had to live up to the obligations of a citizen.

In Palme's case, this was coupled with a really fierce competitiveness, but the object of competition certainly wasn't money or material goods. It may not even have been power. What I think he most wanted was the admiration of all decent people; in an earlier, more crudely nationalist generation of Swedish politicians, this would have meant 'all decent Swedes'. But the happiness and the tragedy of Palme's years was that when Swedes looked round the world, they assumed that everyone must share Swedish ideas of decency, too.

Leif arranged that I should join the union as soon as he decided to make me a permanent employee. We said 'the union' in those days because it hardly mattered which one. They were all part of the same co-ordinated whole. Joining the Timber Workers' Union automatically made me a member of the Social Democratic party as well and ensured that some of my union dues went to fund it. In the Social Democratic years, class became taboo. We might not all be equal in our pursuit of equality, but this was the only difference that could be publicly admitted. Failure to want equality was a handicap to be pitied; it demanded special treatment of some kind; but it was no longer a choice that anyone could make.

This sounds authoritarian, but such uniformity of belief was imposed from within as much as from above. Sweden had once been a very stratified society, with very clear distinctions among and between the nobility, the professional classes, and the poor, but even then it had been one where almost everyone accepted the stratification. Once it became an egalitarian one, equality was enforced and accepted just as much as inequality once had been. Even after the Social Democrats had made quality seem the only sane and rational condition of society, political distinctions existed in every corner of the country and provided the kind of loyalties and divisions that in other countries were supplied by religious differences. But they were distinctions that no longer had much financial bite.

In Lilla Edet, an old-fashioned place, the divide ran down the middle of the main street. On the side away from the river there was ICA, the 'bourgeois' shop; on the west side, facing it, stood *Konsum*, the Co-op, where the socialists shopped. Both of them were small supermarkets, though the aisles in *Konsum* were narrower, and the plastic baskets red instead of blue. Both sold almost exactly the same range of groceries and small bits of hardware but I don't remember that they had a single brand in common. If you bought your split-pea soup with ham from

Konsum, it came in a blue and white package. If it came from ICA, it had an excitingly capitalist, coloured paper label on the tin. Both tasted, as near as I can remember, identical, but I may have been the only man in Lilla Edet to make the experiment and I very seldom went to *Konsum*. Anita's family used to tell a story about a local politician who had, in a hurry, gone into the wrong supermarket and brought something. He spent ten years apologizing for this act, as if he had been caught emerging from a restaurant that sold alcohol. Where you shopped predicted where you lived, what you believed, and even the evening classes you attended; and almost everybody did. There was little else to do on winter evenings

The Social Democratic party was only a part of the power structure. The party and the unions together made up the *Arbetarerörelsen*, the workers' movement, but it extended far beyond working and voting; and you could remain within the movement every minute of your life. You woke in a flat that the workers' movement had built, and owned, and where your rent was decided by a tenants' movement. At work, of course, you belonged to a union. After work, you shopped in a Co-op, paying with cheques from the Co-op bank. In the evenings, classes in everything possible, from foreign languages to handicrafts, were organized by the movement. You read the socialist newspapers, and went on workers' holidays. Nothing on state-run television suggested the world might be different and there was no commercial television.

It was the life of a battery salmon: packed into a crowd in the middle of a boundless stretch of water by a cage of netting that you could not see at all. It just appeared to be part of the sea. Perhaps it was.

Some distance to the right were the net cages of the 'non-socialists', which almost exactly replicated the structure of the workers' movement, and also enjoyed considerable subsidies from the state. There were unions for white-collar workers, organized into a central congress, the TCO, which could be translated with distressing accuracy as 'The Bureaucrats' Central Organization'. Though no one now cares much what the Swedish workers' movement says, the TCO lives on in every office in the Western world, for they are the company that first set ergonomic standards for computer monitors, and the acronym TCO99, found on any monitor you can buy, is their stamp of approval. There were housing condominiums; co-operative networks of small shops and businesses like the ICA, and even parallel evening classes in everything from fly-tying to foreign languages. All that non-socialists didn't have, for forty-four years, was a turn in government without the Social Democrats. Instead they had three small parties who dreamed that they could administer the social democratic state a little more efficiently and a little less arrogantly than the social democrats could manage.

The Social Democrats lost the election in 1976, the year before I arrived in Sweden. The three small parties to the right of the Social Democrats were not really called 'non-socialist', except in their own propaganda. Instead they were known as the 'bourgeois', a word that carried the sort of atavistic horror that 'liberal' carries in the USA today. All of them had been forced by the triumph of Social Democracy to change their names into something that would not frighten the voters too much before they could be elected.

The Liberals had become the 'People's Party', though even in good years no more than an eighth of the people ever voted for them. They were for the most part high-minded, clever, and by tradition teetotal. They represented the respectable middle class, and those who would have liked to be respectable. Anita's father voted for them. It was a way of discouraging his neighbours from drinking.

The Moderate Union Party had once been known as Conservatives. If you changed one syllable in Swedish – and the temptation was hard to resist – they became the Party of Moderate Sexual Union. They dreamed of representing everyone who wanted to be rich. But in the waking world, they represented only those who were already rich, or whose families had once been rich. Ordinary people who dreamed of prosperity still voted for the Social Democrats, or for the Centre Party.

The Centre Party had changed its name from *Bondeförbundet*. It would be cruel and accurate, if unidiomatic, to translate it as 'Peasants' Union', but it would also illuminate the reason they had to change it. To be a peasant, or a farmer, was a term of contempt in urban Sweden as elsewhere. But of all the 'bourgeois' parties, Centre had the firmest roots then. It was the party for hardworking men who did not want to mix with socialists. The kind of farmers who were attracted to this were the same sort of men as would have emigrated to America a hundred years before; and in America they would have been natural New England republicans. They were smallholders and pioneers, who would have been happy to carve their livelihoods from the forests. The hardest Centre Party member I knew – and it was years before I discovered his affiliation – was Rolf, the foreman at the factory where I worked. He had been a shipyard worker in Gothenburg before moving to the country to have a place of his own.

Rolf's wife was a teacher and may well have been a union member, but he certainly wasn't. They hated the Social Democrats for trying to keep down people like them. Rolf hated the unions because they tried to erase the distinction between good and bad workers. He worked harder than almost anyone I have ever known, and he didn't want slackers to be paid at the rate that he was. In a large factory this would have happened, but Leif's wage agreements were entirely personal. No one got less than the union minimum but Rolf got a great deal more.

We were invited back to his house only once: a thank-you for the meal to which we had invited him and his wife after I'd worked alongside him for eighteen months. I remember frilled lace tablecloths, coffee in small cups, and rich white cake.

Rolf and Leif worked side by side nearly every day for fifteen years, but after Leif sold the factory, they never spoke again. It turned out that Rolf, all along, had hated the bosses quite as much as he hated the socialists.

My union, 'Wood', was one of the dozen or so large national unions that together set the wages for almost every worker in the country. I may have been the only member at Leif's for quite long periods: Rolf wouldn't join out of stubborn small-holder's pride, and many of the temporary employees didn't stay long enough to do so; but even so, the union was a pres-ence, and a power, in most of Leif's decisions.

I suppose that at Leif's factory I made about twice or three times what an unskilled factory worker might have made in England. But at the same time, I worked a very great deal harder than my English counterparts, and so did everyone else that I knew. When I was about eighteen I had worked for a month or so in a small engineering factory in Surrey. The work, such as it was, involved lifting camshafts from one box and dropping them into another. It was neither hard nor demand-ing, but as soon as the first box was full the shop steward would walk up and start talking about the war. His stories were extremely long and boring. But it was forbidden to work while he was talking, and he was prepared to talk for as long as it took to knock our productivity down. We were not particularly eager, nor motivated workers, but he made certain that we did no more than half of what we might have achieved in our de-motivated state without him. Screwing the bosses like that was what he lived for, and what they were forced to pay him to do, too.

That could not be imagined in Sweden, no matter how Leif might grumble about socialism. This was partly because it was a much more disciplined society, and partly because it appeared a much less class-ridden one. There really was a sense of common purpose, and a belief that everyone might get richer co-operatively than they could by pure selfishness. I don't mean that people weren't greedy, or personally ambitious. Of course they were. But greed and ambition were mostly understood collectively. One of the things that made loneliness so easy, and so crushing, was the sense that individuals didn't, in some important sense, exist at all.

May Day, the feast of spring, had been taken over as a social democratic holiday, even though it was too early in the year for the weather to guarantee any sense of rebirth. It was once cele-brated in the square in Nödinge when I lived there: Stig Malm, the leader of the metal workers' union, came to speak to us. He was then one of the most powerful men in the country, leader of the best paid, most skilled workforce the country had ever seen. In him, on that weak sunlit day, could be seen the culmi-nation of a hundred and fifty years of industrial revolution: the wrestling of a decent life for the men who worked machines, as well as those who owned them. He didn't look like much. I remember a drooping, coarse moustache and a hoarse, fierce voice haranguing us about the coming wage negotiations. Even at the time, I thought of the open-air ceremony as a form of compulsory chapel. It was an observance, not an entertainment. Our attendance, drab in the spring sunlight, was what gave him his power in society, and he, in turn, gave it back to us.

The crowd was not large but it was earnest. There was a television crew somewhere in the background, which made it seem much larger on the regional news. In any case, there was nothing much else to do on a public holiday; all the shops would be shut as a matter of course.

What was said about the wage negotiations was to a huge extent bluff: none of the workers in the square had anything to do with them. I suppose that those who worked up the road at the battery factory in Nol were in fact members of his union, but their wages would be set, like millions of other workers', by twenty or thirty people meeting in Stockholm from the national organization of unions and the national organization of employers. Malm was one of those men. Later, he would become the leader of the entire union movement.

The national wage negotiations were an annual ritual. They were at the heart of the socialist economy that everyone took for granted. Like any worthwhile ritual, they dramatized real and frightening antagonisms. They had settled a period of industrial strife that looked close to civil war or anarchy. In 1931, five strikers from a timber mill in Lapland had been shot dead by the army. What gave their actions a special flavour of martyrdom was that they were on sympathy strike at the time, in support of other workers whose hourly rate was to be lowered. In Britain, when something similar was practised by the miners' union in 1984, it was known as secondary picketing; in Sweden, the Ådalen strikers became martyrs.

There really was a medieval, folk-religious sense in which

41

their suffering testified to the truth of their cause and validated the subsequent determination never to carry another strike to the point of rioting. Between 1945 and 1980, there was only one big strike in Sweden, among mine workers in the far north in 1969. Otherwise, the rules of labour relations were clear to everybody: once a year the unions' central organization – which also had allies in the Social Democratic government – and the employers' federation would meet to negotiate. They would threaten each other with disaster; then they would come to a peaceful agreement at whatever figure the government thought sensible, which granted everyone rates of pay the employers swore would bankrupt them, and the unions accepted with regret as impoverishing their members.

I had my place right at the bottom of this system, as the union's representative, if sometimes only to myself. The union had not forgotten me after my appointment. The district representative would call around sometimes, and every six months or so I would have an afternoon off for a meeting on union business. This was compulsory: I remember sour coffee and sweet, fluffy cakes while we were treated to a lecture on how to recruit other members during which I tried hard not to giggle. My only real union activity at the factory was ensuring that no one else became active in it. Fortunately, the people who would have liked the union to protect them from hard work were also too idle to dislodge me. My duties as safety officer were more interesting. We wore our hearing protectors all the time, of course; and gloves to guard against the splinters everywhere. But we couldn't have run the place with too much attention to safety.

5

Wood

The timber we used was delivered in two-ton bundles, three or four metres long, that were stacked on open-sided articulated trucks. They arrived from the sawmill, and turned up the drive into the factory. Almost every time the driver, avoiding the ditch by the side of the road, would flatten the mailbox that stood beside it. The drive up to the factory sloped, more steeply as it got further from the road, so that when the fork-lift approached the side of the lorry to remove the timber bundles, these were already at an angle, and threatened to slide off the forks if they were icy, and crash to the ground, smashing the metal tape that bound them and scattering into a thousand planks.

Leif owned two fork-lift trucks: a big six-wheeler with automatic transmission that was fairly safe, and a much smaller, older, four-wheel beast that we drove everywhere. This was the noisy one I owed my job to. Within the barn, it was OK to drive. It could lift a half-ton stack of engine pallets without too much effort, and I learned to drive them out and line the stacks up in a neat row at the top of the barn so that they could be put on the lorry later. The ground was fairly level there, and

43

easy to drive on unless the snow was deep. In that case, the little truck would skate about and we would have to use the big one, which I never really got the hang of because it had so much more momentum, weighing, as it did, three and a half tons. Skidding in that on a dark winter morning was a really frightening experience. I thought for a few moments that I would go straight through the wooden wall of the factory, sideways.

I did once or twice unload the timber lorry with it, but only in daylight and without any snow on the ground. You say lightly that your stomach lurches when you are frightened, and it does. But when the forks engaged with a load of timber from the top of the timber lorry, everything lurched with my stomach, and the seat rose beneath me as the back of the fork lift was hauled into the air by the weight on the front. I was never entirely certain that the back wheels, which steer a fork-lift, would retain enough contact with the ground to do so.

Once or twice, when the big fork-lift was out of order, the small blue one was used to unload the timber lorry instead, and it weighed only a ton or two – hardly enough to counterbalance the enormous bundles of sawn timber on which we depended. The longest planks were three and a half metres long: the bundles were a metre high and a metre deep, with one end cleanly sawn, and the other ragged, as some of the shorter lengths were scarcely two metres. If one of these had to be moved with the little truck, Leif would drive and three of us would hang on to the outside of the safety cage behind him, leaning outwards like wind-surfers, so that the steering wheels would get some grip. Ahead, the bundle of timber would flex each time we crossed a bump, and, as it did so, I thought I could feel the engine housing humping beneath my feet.

Once unloaded, the timber bundles had to be sawed down into usable lengths and stacked on ordinary pallets, and some to be cut down further into V-shaped supports for the transmission. The lower end of the factory had a circular saw set against one wall, with long shining steel runners that fed the wood to it, taking up almost the whole of the side of the barn. The circular blade, about a metre across, was fitted with a handle which the saw man hoiked one-handed into the air, slicing almost without resistance through six or eight planks stacked on top of each other on the runners.

This sawing was easy work. When I started, it was done by a Finn who drank fourteen or fifteen cans of weak beer every day at work. You could smell him before you could see him: he worked beneath a sour miasma of sweat and *Mellanöl* inside a barricade of pallets, stacked with the planks he'd sawn, and when he stood at the saw he was invisible to the rest of us. I don't remember ever seeing him doing anything else but pissing against the outside of the barn by the far door and smoking fat crooked roll-ups in his breaks. He didn't eat with us at either meal break, but remained with his beers by his door into the barn. But between these breaks he sawed five tons of wood a day. He kept this up, winter and summer, for the first eighteen months I worked there, until finally he sank beneath the beer and found himself unable to get up in the mornings. Leif sacked him. The whole factory depended on the saw man. It was the job that I ended doing.

The rest of the workers – three or four people for most of the two years I worked there – had to take this sawn wood and nail it together into pallets. The five types we made differed in the sort of detail that emerges only from the most grinding monotony. I remember vividly only the first I was told to make: it was the heaviest the factory built and the one that required least skill. There were six planks in the base, held together by two thick feet; two thick pine blocks for engine

45

supports, an inch-thick cross-piece where the transmission rested, four side pieces nailed into a frame, and two little reinforcing bits. It was all nailed together. The noise in the barn was like continual gunfire as these nails were banged in by three different types of compressed-air guns. Each gun weighed two kilos, and had to be concealed from close inspection by the health and safety people because we had lightened the triggers on them so they could be pulled at arm's length. I only shot myself badly enough to need patching twice in two years, when the nail hit a knot in the wood I was steadying and twisted into my hand.

A fully assembled pallet weighed forty-seven kilos, or a little over a hundredweight. I had to make seventy-two of them every two days, in nine stacks of eight, the highest flung up about head height before the whole stack was lashed together with wire tape and dragged out by the smaller fork-lift truck. One day would be spent nailing the sub-assemblies together: seventy-two right-hand posts; seventy-two left-hand posts; seventy-two frames and seventy-two plank bottoms. Each had to be fixed together with a precisely specified number of nails, placed in precisely specified ways. Every day I fired around two thousand nails into the wood, trying to place each one exactly where I had fired uncountable predecessors; every day the only break in this monotony came from trying to do everything a little faster than the day before. 'You should start at full speed, and then get steadily faster,' I was advised was the trick of it.

I never really grew strong enough for the work. I was willing enough, and outlasted fifteen or twenty young Swedes whose attitude of sullen entitlement and resentment sat oddly with their enormous, well-fed bodies. One lifted weights for a hobby, but thought it demeaning to exert himself outside the gym or for an employer. But alongside Leif and his foreman Rolf, two men in their forties who had done hard physical work every day of their lives, I would simply run out of strength. When spring came I tried to work ten hours a day, to save for a car, but I found I could make no more pallets than when I worked eight. Shifting three and a half tons of wood every day was my limit.

It was this physical incapacity that drove me back to Brian Clarke. When the demand for marine diesels grew in Australia beyond the rate at which I could build crates for them, Rolf would be transferred to that job for a few days and I would saw out the V-shaped cut-outs on which the transmission rested. The wood for this was thick and unplaned, with a rough splintery surface like flattened chicken skin. That observation more or less exhausted its interest.

I would mark a V on 500 pieces with a pencil: the act reduced to five movements, over and over again as I shifted the stacks from a pallet to my left to one on my right. Then I would feed them into the band saw, little buttocks of sawdust puffing up each side of the blade as I pushed the wood over the sleek steel table. Shrieking and screaming from the blade pressed through my hearing protectors. Pull it back. Turn it round. Press it against the blade once more until the resistance eased for a moment with a sudden clunk. Pull back smartly, and swat away the discarded triangle into a waste crate; in the same movement lift and stack the new V-piece. Swivel left. Pick up another, do it again. Inside, my mind ran round in circles, screaming. This work was not particularly exhausting. It demanded about half my attention to keep up to speed. The rest was fixed on water, on a cool, pewtery surface between water lilies that would stir as something rustled against their stems.

To this day, when I think of the band saw, I see the chipped steel housing of the motor, a thin metallic blue; and behind it the bare pale planking of the factory wall. From the ceiling hang black electric-power lines to the machinery, and the air hoses for nail guns loop in parabolas like jungle vines. I hear the band saw ringing, the banging of the guns, and even the accordion music, slithering out of the radio speaker above my head. But all these things seem misty, as they were at the time, because they stood between me and the lake which shone through them.

In the busy banging solitude of the factory I taught myself to write English. I hardly spoke it to anybody then. I worked in Swedish, I was married in Swedish; I thought and dreamed in Swedish too: it's still the language in which I think of fishing technicalities. But I still read mostly English books, and I wanted to become an English writer. The first thing I bought when we got married was an ancient office typewriter, with its base machined from solid brass, which went on an old desk borrowed from Anita's younger sister. I knew nothing about myself and very little about the world so it was hard to find a subject. But as I worked with the planks, hauling and banging, and building the boxes, phrases would appear to me. If they were good, I grabbed the thick pencil used for marking wood and scribbled them on the cardboard dividers from the cases of nails. This allowed me one good fragment for every 500 nails I fired in. When I came home, the breast pocket of my overalls might have half a dozen of these bits inside it: sawdust would fall from the seams as I pulled out the cardboard strips and placed them beside the typewriter.

6

Misfits

How had I got there? Anita and I had met in the winter of 1976–7 in a Cheshire Home above a small seaside town in North Wales. It was an Edwardian mansion guarded from the road by disciplined and melancholy conifers. We had been sent there, independently, as volunteer nursing auxiliaries, paid around five pounds a week with bed and board.

The home was run by a small, professional, middle-aged nursing staff, who made the decisions that required some medical competence as well as compassion and common sense. The matron was a sturdy woman with red cheeks, devoted to her small grey terrier; the deputy matron was lean, with dark curly hair, married to a senior policeman. They were both qualified nurses, and two others worked under them. All these people lived outside the house. There were also a number of middle-aged women from the town who worked as nursing auxiliaries. The rest of the work was done by a dozen or so volunteers.

The volunteers were housed in the former servants' quarters under the eaves. Among them were police cadets, sent there for a few weeks at a time to learn compassion. There were some Scandinavians – I remember two Danes and two Swedes, Anita

and her friend Elinor – and there were a couple of odds and
sods like me. I had come there at the end of my tether after a
couple of years bumming around pointlessly after being thrown
out of a rather grand school at the age of sixteen. If I could do
nothing else, I thought, I could do good.

Anita and Elinor were already working at the home when I
arrived. They had been sent by an agency they had signed up
to. I was probably the first man they had met in Wales who
didn't expect all Scandinavians to be imaginatively compliant
nymphomaniacs. Of the two Swedes, Anita's difficulty with the
locals was greater because she was in fact blonde. Elinor was
a taller, dark girl, with a long face and the very direct gaze of
someone who had grown up in the deep countryside. Her
father owned the most northerly strawberry farm in Sweden. In
winter, when they wanted to shop, they would cross two miles
of frozen lake to the nearest town, standing on kick sledges,
which would later be used to bring the shopping home. By
contrast with that, Colwyn Bay seemed quite an exciting place
to her, but she was not going to let herself be carried away.

After four weeks of my being polite and friendly and res-
olutely not making a pass at anyone, Anita and I took a sleeping
bag out into the grounds of the home towards the end of a
party at a moment when everyone not too drunk was too well-
mannered to notice.

Some of the residents had been in the home almost since
their nurses were born: George was an old soldier who had
contracted a tropical disease in Malaya, which paralysed him
slowly from the feet up over a period of decades. By the time we
knew him, he could move only his neck. He had an enormous
penis, which would engorge if a woman changed the bottle in
which it lived. I made a joke about this once when Anita could-
n't get the bottle off. I am still ashamed of that. His pleasures

were Everton and cigarettes: once he could no longer lift his hands to smoke with, someone had welded onto his tin ashtray a bracket and a little tube, so that he need only ask one of us to put the lit cigarette in the tube, with the end over the ashtray, and he could roll his head to one side to draw on it.

Elsewhere there was a woman who had survived Nazi concentration camps, but who now had arthritis so badly that she seemed, in her wheelchair, like a praying mantis, with her forearms held in the air, and her wrists cocked downwards. She would gesture with her long fingers by moving the whole limb from the elbow.

Others had had strokes. Two had spina bifida and three more had forms of muscular dystrophy. But most of the residents had multiple sclerosis. Only two of them had any form of mental retardation and they were married to each other and immensely proud. Because of their marriage, they felt far closer to normal life than their fellow residents. They had a little suite to themselves. Almost all the others had single rooms, each equipped with a bell-push to summon one of the four auxiliaries on duty at any time.

Most of our work was feeding people or cleaning up the consequences. We made beds, cleaned and tidied, or lifted people in and out of their wheelchairs and pushed them down to the dining hall or wherever they wanted to go. There was only one electric wheelchair in the home. It belonged to Peter, a tall man who slumped in it like two eggs glued together. The smaller, upper egg was his jowly head, with a few wisps of pale hair around the pointy end. His eyelashes were still luxuriant, and his blue eyes had a determined charm. He had a wide-lipped floppy smile. Beneath this, the larger egg was his torso, with an ample paunch. His arms and legs were spindly; he steered his wheelchair with pale bony fingers on the joystick at his right hand, which was all the force he could muster below the neck. In the absence of muscle, the bones of his arms and legs were all distinct against the skin, but his appetite for cherry brandy remained so he weighed about sixteen stone and needed two sturdy men to lift him in and out of bed or even to turn him over, while his arms and legs tumbled in slow motion orbit after his belly. Placed in the right position and left to himself, Peter could move his arms around the bed by walking his fingers across the sheets so that they would drag the rest after them.

There was only one resident who could not move herself at all. This was Molly, who had been paralysed by a stroke when she arrived, but was still then able to speak and think. Four more strokes had hacked away all her capacities, until when I knew her she lay inert against a pile of pillows, the only inhabitant of the four-bedded nursing room. She could no longer speak or even chew. When she developed bedsores we had to turn her over every two hours; if they rubbed the sheets as we did so, she would emit a hoarse and distant scream although her face remained slack and expressionless.

All the other residents ate in a dining hall, but Molly was fed in her room. I remember the winter sunlight on white sheets, like a Dutch interior, and the silver glittering plait of drool which fastened her mouth to the pillow. I would sit beside her, looking across to the window, with a teaspoon in my hand, cajoling her gently: 'Swallow, Molly,' over and over again. I don't remember any other sound. Sometimes the soft flesh of her throat would hunch together and shudder. She had swallowed. I would collect another teaspoon and start again. This was generally reckoned to be one of the easier mealtime tasks. Once we were a couple, Anita would sometimes join me, and we would sit in the quiet together: 'Swallow, Molly.'

Of course I wondered what the point of all this was. But I didn't doubt there was a point, or that Molly should be treated as valuable and deserving of this kind of care. I knew that. My puzzlement was over how I knew it, or what it meant about her.

I don't think anyone would have kept her alive had she developed pneumonia. But there was no question that she should not be fed, as would happen now in a more modern hospital. Some of the residents were going to suffocate to death, as George would, when the nerves that controlled his breathing gave out, or as Peter would, with his muscular dystrophy. Multiple sclerosis played with its victims. We never knew what lesser disease would kill them; we did not know if, or how, their minds would go before they died. Nor did we know how quickly MS would progress, or whether it would go into remission, sometimes prolonged. The outcome was quite certain, but there was always hope that things could be better next week.

The question of euthanasia was dealt with by treating it as an economic problem. It was taken for granted that certain treatments were a wasteful use of resources that could otherwise go to other people. The official ideology of the Cheshire Homes was highly religious, but though we would have talked about the immense value of human life, no one really thought that life was priceless. On the contrary, every life had a value, which the community would have to pay.

I supposed that in the future all that kind of constraint would disappear, and everyone could afford everything; but you couldn't really call this view of the future anything as distinct or articulated as a thought. In the mid-Seventies optimism was as multifaceted as any other fact about the world. In England there might be hiccups, like the miners' strike or the three-day week, but the general trend of history was quite certain. In the future we would all become more peaceful, richer, and more egalitarian. This was just the way that history had to be.

The presence of terrible diseases didn't make the home a gloomy place. The only sane response to them was the same kind of grumbling cheerfulness that the residents showed us. All of the volunteers drank hard off duty and in my memories someone was always being sent down into the town on their free afternoon to buy condoms, which we called 'cough medicine' in public, so as not to shock the residents or even the older staff.

Most of the residents who could speak at all were extremely grateful to be in the home, and they received our ministrations without complaint, even if it was five or ten minutes after they had rung for help. But one resident, Barbara, felt we should come when she rang for us. Her mind was unaffected by the disease which had ridden her to bed.

If a nurse turned up half an hour after she had rung, she made her disappointment clear. No one else in the home spoke to the staff as if they were servants. Perhaps this had not mattered before, but by the time I was there, almost anyone else's needs took precedence over hers. Sometimes other people really did need more urgent attention than she did. But the Welsh staff felt that their own need for a cigarette break was more urgent than whatever it was Barbara wanted this time.

Anita's contract expired about a month before mine, and she left for Switzerland, where she had got a job as an au pair. After she had gone I was uneasy and at a loose end. Mike, an amorous English volunteer, suggested that I accept an invitation from a blonde, divorced SRN who was one of the locally employed nurses: 'When Phyllis asks you round to have coffee some time, say yes, you'll find it's really worthwhile.' But I liked her, and this made me realize that I didn't particularly want whatever good time she might also give to Mike. When, in due course, she did ask me to drop by for coffee, I answered that my heart, alas, was given to Anita. Afterwards, I suspected that this might be true.

In the meantime, the problem of Barbara came to a head. She developed one of those feverish colds that people call flu: nothing life-threatening, but quite enough to put even a completely healthy person in bed and make them a nuisance to their nurses. Someone – I have forgotten who – was so irritated by Barbara's demands that they tied a knot in her catheter tube so that she was left all night in a pool of her own urine. Everyone except the fair-minded deputy matron knew more or less what had happened; but after Barbara recovered from the high temperature brought on by her soaking, it was generally thought to have taught a troublesome woman a lesson.

I was really shocked by what had happened. I remembered, from my schooldays in Oxford, the figure of Leonard Cheshire descending from a helicopter on the playing fields to talk to the boys. It might not really have happened. Cheshire was an old boy of the school, and greatly revered, but the old boy who climbed out of a helicopter to talk to us might have been John Betjeman, who also came to visit us. We boys definitely thought that flying a helicopter was better than being a poet, though later I was to change my mind. In any case, I felt I had some claim on Cheshire's attention and so wrote to him giving a detailed account of what had been done to Barbara. Of course it never got to him. Some flunky lower down the organization returned the letter to the matron, who sacked me.

That was how I found myself back at my parents' house, writing yearning letters to Anita, who came to visit before we set out to hitch-hike to Sweden together. Where else could I go?

The journey took us five days and nights, with farcical interludes. A dope smuggler gave us a lift from Antwerp into Bergen op Zoom, a resort on the far west coast of Holland, stopping in a forest to check that his samples hadn't deteriorated, leaving us lost, bewildered, and without any Dutch money on the morning of a public holiday when all the banks were shut. By the time we reached Denmark we were completely exhausted, and ended up staying at the farm of one of the Danish volunteers from the Cheshire Home where we lounged in a sunlit apple orchard all one May afternoon, drinking chilled bottles of weak 'Green' Tuborg. It was to be our last moment of public hedonism for almost a year.

We were tired of hitch-hiking, and took the train from Copenhagen to Gothenburg, where Anita's father met us in his car. He drove us up to Lilla Edet so very slowly that I was surprised still to be alive by the end. The main road, up the east side of the river, where we travelled, was four lanes wide, flat, and almost empty. I writhed in my seat, trampling invisible accelerator pedals, while Hans drove the whole way in what appeared to be the fast lane, at 70 kph. In the traffic on the dual carriageway round the city, he slowed down to 50 kph with an expression of prim satisfaction while cars passed him on both sides.

On the main road, when people wanted to pass him, they would drive up close behind, at which point he would veer off into the slow lane and, once passed, resume his stately progress up the middle of the road. This was the way that Swedes were taught to drive. What appeared to be the slow lane was actually an extended lay-by, into which you could retreat if someone wanted to pass you. The real road was the two lanes closest to each other in the middle; the speed limit really was 70 kph and most people, most of the time, observed it.

But I was ready, when I arrived in Sweden, for a wholly new life. In England, I had comprehensively failed the expectations of my parents, and of at least some of my teachers. Then I had failed at doing good. Perhaps I could now try just being good.

7

Under the surface

Deep winter in Sweden is curiously easy to endure. The shortest days of the year in December are much better lit than the longer days to come, first by Lucia celebrations, when girls in white dresses, with candles in their hands and on their headdresses, walk in procession, singing through public places, and then, after Christmas, by the New Year sales, when shop windows blaze and make even the saddest towns look cosy after night falls at half past three. But in February the days lengthen so quickly you can feel it, and you know that tomorrow will cast a clearer light on the landscape of slush and frozen, rutted mud which thaws a little every afternoon and then re-freezes every night.

The thaw is never silent. Our flat in Nödinge had an aluminium railing on the walkway outside, about three feet from the kitchen window, and the measured plinking sound of water dripping on it as the snow melted from the roof was the most agonizing thing I had ever heard in my life for the six weeks that I listened to it. In later years I learned not to listen, but the first spring, I could hear a whole country unfreezing, drip by drip, all day. The first few days, I thought the ringing of the balcony rail meant that spring had arrived. But every night, the snow refroze and the thaw had to start again. For the next three weeks, I thought each plink must mean that spring was on its way – but still the thaw refroze, and spring retreated further. For the last fortnight or so I believed that every plink was telling me that spring would never come. Finally came a day when all the snow had retreated, leaving patches of bare unfrozen dirt. I walked for half an hour up into the hills behind Nödinge, where the map showed a lake, carrying my spinning rod, wearing a black leather bomber jacket against the wind, burning for a fish. When I got there, the lake turned out to be little more than a pond, but very hard to miss – the only pale thing in the landscape among the bare brown hills, dirty blue and green still frozen solid.

I went back almost every day for a week, unable to believe that it could stay frozen. I was perhaps a little mad. Most days I carried my rod and a tin of spinners. Sometimes I would tie on the heaviest spinner I owned and hurl it on to the ice in the hope of breaking through. Sometimes I would throw a rock at the ice instead. One afternoon it rained for hours, solid wonderful rain beating the snow down into mud after months of sleet and snow; with the rain came a boisterous wind, and the next day half the pond was clear of water and there was nothing left of the ice but crumbled chunks jostling and heaving on the waves against the lee shore. I cast for about an hour, certain the fish would greet the open water as ecstatically as I did. My fingers grew very cold. I waked home chilled and fishless, filled with a kind of grim confidence of final victory, like Churchill in the Battle of Britain.

At Easter we left Sweden for a weekend break in Copenhagen. The raw wind in the harbour felt colder than anything I had endured in the winter, and we got lost somewhere on the outskirts of the city and had to walk through diagonal rain for half an hour in the early evening dark. None of that mattered at all. The whole city seemed to burn in a Pentecostal light: everywhere I saw people talking and smiling, drinking in bars or listening to music, even enjoying themselves in public.

The train ferry between Helsingborg and Helsingør took about twenty minutes to cross the narrowest part of the sound: just time to clamber down from the carriage and then run up the stairway to the buffet for the last chance to drink good Danish beer and eat good Danish sandwiches. The woman at the self-service counter, smiling, blonde, implacable, yanked the caps off the bottles when she sold them, with a movement that said that from here on, everything would be clean and quiet and organized and no one would be smuggling drink into Sweden.

Work resumed. Anita had found a job working in a hospice for the senile. It was everything that the Cheshire Home had not been: purpose-built, fully staffed, quite without cruelty – and quite without kindness, either. Everyone in the Swedish home was properly fed. No one was ever struck, or starved, or left with a knotted catheter. They were just left, talking to themselves. If they weren't watched some of them would roll their own shit into little balls, and eat it. But Anita was planning to train as a nurse, and before she could do that, she had to train as an auxiliary, to be qualified to do the job she had been doing for the last year at least.

With two salaries we could begin to think about the future. It was clear that we couldn't afford a car and a child, so I started to take driving lessons since a car was obviously more desirable. I had always loved Fiats – I had been taught the rudiments of driving in my mother's Fiat 500, a tiny car with a hepped-up motorcycle engine over the rear wheels, which she had once driven all the way from Belgrade to London. The clutch pedal had about an inch and a half of travel, and the gear lever about the same amount of play. If you could change gear smoothly on one of those, you could change gear on anything: the fork-lift truck never gave me any trouble after that Fiat 500.

So when I found a second-hand Fiat coupé, this time front-wheel drive, with a 1300cc engine, I bought it, and booked a passage on a cargo ship back from Gothenburg to Middles-brough; my father was at that time a director of the shipping line.

The ferry left the day after my driving test. If I'd failed, we would have been stuck in Middlesbrough, and I was so nervous that I stalled the engine within about two minutes of starting. At that moment I knew I had failed and grew completely calm, able to perform perfectly throughout the rest of the test, just to show what I could have done if I hadn't already failed. I was astonished to hear I had passed. It seemed like the final exam. I was a grown-up now. I walked to the car salesroom from the test centre, drove the new car back to the factory and helped pack up for the summer break. In those days the big factories and so their sub-contractors, too, would shut for three weeks in the summer.

By the time the summer break came round, I had shot in about 12,000 nails a week for forty weeks – nearly half a million of them into various pieces of wood, and three or four into various pieces of me. I looked and walked and talked, at least in Swedish, like an honest working man. I dressed like a working man, in jeans, T-shirt, and a bum-freezer leather jacket. I wore clogs all day for work, because these were by far the most practical shoes for slush and hard-packed snow and because they were so easy to slip off when I came indoors. I weighed less than ever before or since in my adult life, and I was a great deal stronger.

I drove with fluent zany confidence around England, though I felt the whole time that I was on the wrong side of the road. We saw my parents, in Surrey, and then drove down to Cornwall, where Anita's youngest sister was at a language school. On the ferry across a river there, I folded my arms and grinned and thought how extraordinary it was to feel strong and attractive in the sunlight. After a fortnight we returned to Sweden, and I drove twelve hours north, to Elinor's home in the woods, about halfway up the country. We had been there the summer before, hitch-hiking, and gone to a neighbour's party where someone had passed me a vodka bottle containing clear fluid without mentioning that it had been made in the woods. I was taken home in a wheelbarrow, I'm told. This time round we were both abstemious: me from shame, Anita from something less easy to formulate. On the return journey, we had gone about ten kilometres when she told me to pull over, opened the passenger door and was neatly sick in a lay-by. 'Drive on,' she said. I thought she had eaten a bad mushroom until a few days later she told me it was morning sickness. It was impossible to imagine that we might be parents. It was no help that I had been a child in Sweden for a while, in a life that seemed, even then, immeasurably distant.

8

Childhood

My parents were diplomats, and for a couple of years in the late Sixties they lived in a flat on Strandvägen, overlooking the sea in the heart of Stockholm. This was a piece of such overwhelming good fortune that it made no impression on me at all. The building was a monument to gloomy Edwardian luxury, with a hallway of marble and panelled wood. There was a small lift filling the middle of a square stone stairwell. The whole avenue was built in 1895, straightening out and filling in what had been a gentle bay running down from the cavalry barracks, and the lift must have been nearly as old as the flats. It had a rattling concertina door that needed a sharp tug to close, mahogany panelling and a mirror so you could check yourself before knocking at one of the massive doors. The stairwell was one of the most silent places I have ever known. The other tenants, if we saw them, passed us with silent dignity like deep-sea fish.

The lighting, like the lift, was ancient, the product of sixty-year-old technology, with large switches like the ends of boiled eggs. They operated timers rather than simple switches. Once a switch was pushed in, a loud clockwork ticking would announce you had about 45 seconds to reach the next landing. In the quiet of the stairwell, this ticking could be heard as you climbed; and, if you dawdled, the light would be extinguished and the switches would glow red in the dark. It was a little touch of penny-pinching that showed the house had been built for really prosperous people. In summer, the hallway was cool and dark; in winter, comfortingly stuffy. There was a slightly spicy smell of polish; in the yard behind, as summer wore on, a sharp and thrilling scent of fermenting garbage rose to our third-floor windows from the low brick hut where the rubbish bins were kept.

Inside, the flat was the size of a small mansion. We ate in the kitchen, which had room for a full-sized table; along the other side of the flat were four large reception rooms, opening one into the other, which would have held several hundred people. The last was furnished as a sitting room, with boundless views out to the harbour, and on to the avenue with trams running between lime trees below. The future was everywhere we looked. In this room my family watched the grey-streaked astronauts climb down on to the surface of the moon on the first television we had ever owned.

The rest of the time, the television was useless to me. It showed only programmes in Swedish, a language I never bothered to learn, beyond the names of ice creams, and words for 'Thank you', and 'How much?' In so far as we mixed with Swedes, they were happy to humour this disdainful attitude. Some of them, like our Finland-Swedish friends, shared it.

Gregor, the father, was the inheritor of a noble name, a magnificent house, and, all his friends supposed, no brains at all. They had a stone-built mansion in the country, which must have been imposing, but what I noticed most of all was that it had a tidy, closely mown lawn. Houses in Sweden don't have lawns like that. Gardens tend to be no more than cleared plots, which ramble out into the forest or to the rocks around them. Grass grows well enough, but it is usually found growing raggedly in orchards, or in fields for animals to eat. But this estate had a lawn sweeping down towards a boathouse by the sea. I lay there for happy afternoons, shooting balloons with an air rifle, a sport to which Gregor introduced me. He was a lean, kindly man who lived for shooting. He held some appointment at court as the royal elk hunter, but this fact made less of an impression on me than his stalking of an egg.

The frame of the story is still unclear. My grown-up mind supplies a summer evening, friends, vodka swept down with songs between every glass, an overflowing boyish cheerfulness; but none of this was in the story as my parents told it. I can just as well imagine a long sober winter evening, of the sort that I would spend in Nödinge, hunched over a magazine picture of wildflower meadows running down to a river in the Norwegian mountains.

Gregor, perhaps, would gaze at his elk-hunting rifles, shining in the darkness of their cabinet, with the same kind of helpless longing out of season; but not even Gregor would fire an elk-hunting rifle at an egg indoors. No, he shot the egg with an air rifle, across the length of the imposing kitchen. God knows what would have happened had he missed, but he hit the egg straight on, and it exploded. He retired to bed triumphant. The next morning, his wife came down and found the distant ceiling spattered with raw, congealing egg and fragments of eggshell stuck to half the cupboards. She was so angry that the reverberations could be heard in Stockholm: they lived in this splendid house, but there were no servants at all, and Elise would have to clean the whole mess up herself. Gregor worked in a bank; naturally one assumed that he had a position as imposing as his house, but one day someone went in there to cash a cheque and found him serving behind the counter.

This kind of radical equality, in which no one had servants, and inherited wealth counted for almost as little as inherited titles, was how the Swedes themselves expected Sweden to be. It's true there were some very rich families. Across the side street that ran down to Strandvägen beside our house was another block, which was rumoured to hold grand families such as the Wallenbergs. Someone had to be able to pay the prices at the Operakällaren's smörgåsbord. But the idea that these pleasures might be withheld from the ordinary Swede was not debated. People might admit that some pleasures were not affordable. But could they, in that case, be really pleasurable? It was, I think, the entirely sincere belief of most Swedes that any grapes they could not reach must be sour. It made the ones they could reach all the sweeter.

At the far end of Strandvägen, the road splits as the city comes to an end. One branch crosses a bridge to the island of Djurgården. The other wriggles away towards a district of sub-stantial nineteenth-century houses, almost all of them converted to embassies when we lived there, with dining rooms where the brocaded curtains seemed as massive as the walls of lesser houses.

Just beyond the bridge was a little park, too rocky to develop, that rose in the middle to a rounded granite ziggurat. In summer, my younger sister and I would nestle in scoops of the rock that we called thrones, and watch the flocks of little Optimist dinghies with their bright sails manoeuvring in the water below us, out towards Djurgården. One Easter, we nearly died there.

The snow-covered ice down by the boathouse felt smoother than the snow on land. But otherwise it was impossible to tell when we had crossed the shoreline. It wasn't even very slippery, since it was covered in gritty snow and in the overcast day the even sweep of the lake seemed brighter than the wet grey clouds above. We moved carefully at first, shuffling out towards a jetty, which ran parallel to the shore about thirty metres away, where the boats were tethered in summer. But when we reached it, and the ice was still as reliable as before, I decided we should walk across to Djurgården on the other side. We could see over to where the granite bluffs rose about ten metres above the road. On a map, the distance is about 200 metres, but the longer we walked, the further it seemed. The snow, which had been so reassuringly hard-packed when we set out, became thinner and sparser until ahead of us we could see where it broke down into a loose mesh of paler streaks across the dirty grey ice. At some stage, when we were level with the middle of the bridge, or perhaps beyond it, and the ice all round us had been scoured clean by the west wind in from the main harbour, I realized where we were. Our footsteps no longer crunched. They creaked. The whole aching sheet of ice groaned as we moved. We looked at each other, and shuffled cautiously around and then back towards the shore, our speed increasing as the ice grew quiet and crunchy once more.

Back on land, where we could sink safely into the snow up to our ankles and giggle at our own bravery, an angry woman who didn't speak English upbraided us in a way that needed no translation. But we didn't care. We were alive. We were English. We belonged to the only race on earth more arrogant and sure of itself than Swedes. None the less, we didn't tell our mother what we had done. We told her we had played at the edge of the ice. She was frightened at the thought.

We returned to school in England, and did not see Stockholm again until high summer, when we moved out of the city to a house in the prosperous suburb of Stocksund, with a marvellously unrestful garden behind the house where the granite ridges rose like waves to a crest of trees and grassy patches lay in troughs between them. My friend Andy came to stay from school: a freckled, lean child with hair the colour of butterscotch and angry blue eyes, whose parents in Hong Kong had sent him to English boarding school when he was seven. We shot in the front garden with an air rifle, and one day when I was adjusting the target a deer ran out of the trees and across the lawn between me and the gun I had laid down. When the first astonishment had worn off, I felt a burgeoning gratitude that I had not been offered the chance to shoot.

That summer, I would wake up in a moment, as if sleep were no more than a bubble that could pop and leave you wide-eyed, naked to the world. It was always light, no matter how early it was. I slept under a window; the smell of the pale pine window frame mingled with the smells of grass and the sea outside to fill me with the knowledge that I was somewhere else than school. In the cool of the morning, we would eat breakfast on the patio outside the kitchen; and then go and dig worms in the garden before the sun grew too hot.

Sandalled and sockless I would walk down to the shore at about ten in the morning, and not return for lunch until three or four in the afternoon. There was a park running down to the sea, with a shore built of rocks piled together to reinforce it against erosion, then a headland, a small harbour in a cove where a few dinghies were tied up, and a sweeping curve along the road, where we would stand on the revetment and fish. It was a scruffy place that a grown-up in a car would pass in a minute, and notice nothing. But fishing drew me into it: no distance was too small to matter when it was explored with a fishing rod. In grown-up life, a lover's body can grow to become a new continent; the flat suburban reach of sea between Stocksund and the island of Lidingö across the water was for me an ocean, or a world.

The Baltic is brackish, like the waters of an estuary, and grows saltier as you move out from shore. There are herring and cod in the outer archipelago, but within casting range of land the fish are mostly freshwater – perch, bream, pike, and zander. Sometimes we would catch little weavers, a tiny, poisonous, sea fish that lurked under the dinghy jetty and had to be unhooked beneath a sandal. The spines over its gill covers could kill a man, Andy said. We never saw anything of the pike or zander, but once, when I cast out as far as I could from the point of the bay, there was a hard yank on the line, and then, when I reeled in, nothing at all on the end; just a clean-cut ending to the nylon line. It must be a zander, I said. I seemed to know that fish that I had never seen, and scarcely felt. It must be a zander because that was the most strange and terrible of water monsters, a fish that could hardly be caught, that hunted in the turgid dark by smell and feel as much as sight, a fish that could engulf the whole lure in its mouth and bite through the line in the same movement.

Towards the end of the summer, Andy went back to England. The mornings smelled of blackberries as well as fresh grass. The light changed, too, becoming warmer and less blue and otherworldly as the air grew colder.

One day there was a thunderstorm. It was heroic weather for a boy to fish in. I had to screw up my eyes against the rain; waves crashed against the broken granite revetment beneath the road. In the middle of this section there was a mysterious grating – it would be a storm drain or possibly even a sewer, I now understand. What I then knew was that if I cast out as far as possible in front of this, and fished back as slowly and as deeply as I dared, there was a chance at bigger fish.

Against the wind that day I could only cast out five or ten metres, but it was enough. Ahead and below I could almost feel the tiny spinner rising and falling as swells sucked the line into bows. There was a light, urgent susurration in the rod; then it stopped a moment. I twitched the rod back, and felt an alien purpose pull the line to the side. It was a curtain open into another world. When at last the fish appeared, its scales seemed rough as alligator hide. The gill covers were hard as bone, the smooth curves of their sides meeting in a point that drew blood from a hurried finger as I unhooked him. He had scarcely touched the air at all. He slipped back into the lower darkness, huge beyond the reach of dreams.

It was the last summer of my childhood. The week after, I was back in school, and that winter my parents left Stockholm; but the memory of that summer was a great comfort, years later, when I found myself a working man in Nödinge. It told me that there could be real happiness in Sweden, if only I could find the right stretch of water to live beside.

9

Felix

After Anita and I had returned from Elinor's house, the rest of the summer was a time of profusion. I no longer needed to fish for pike, but one blazing day Leif took us out on his boat into the archipelago of granite shoals and skerries that extends for miles beyond the coast. Summer on the west coast is like a carnival that goes on all the way to Norway. Everything floats in a quality of light like mercury. The red-walled wooden houses look as buoyant and carefree as tents. The granite looks gentle as crumpled paper; it is toasty and gentle under bare feet. There aren't really any beaches. Swimming is done from rocks and boats; but owning a boat was as natural as owning a car; perhaps more so for the people who lived near the coast. Leif's boat was magnificent, towering twice the height of a man where it rested, most of the year, swathed in tarpaulins on a trailer outside the barn. Then around Whitsun he would run it down to the sea behind the lorry with which he normally delivered pallets. In a fiercely egalitarian culture which hated ostentation or any sort of nonconformity, boats were the only sort of boasting that was allowed and approved. He would work more on it half the summer, then by August it would be ready for showing off.

The day he took his workers out in it for a day's fishing the others used hand lines, with heavy silvery jigs, almost the size of a fist. I had brought a spinning rod, probably Anita's, loaded with coarse line. At the little seafront supermarkets in every hamlet up and down the coast you could buy cod lures stamped from painted tin plate with a piece of lead the size of a finger welded down one side. They were extremely cheap, since they were designed to be hurled into the seaweed and snagged there. That's what I did with them, anyway. But when they didn't catch the bottom, they caught fish.

Leif motored out for about an hour in his huge boat; we lounged in a way impossible at any other time until he had anchored by two low skerries, a few miles into the archipelago. I cast towards these rocks and let the spoon flutter back in an arc just above the sea bed, sinking as it came towards the boat. It was needless craft. The fish grabbed everything and we hauled until our arms ached and our necks burned from the sun. There were cod, ling, saithe, wrasse and others whose names no one knew or cared. They were fish. All were killed, until the five blue plastic buckets on the deck were overflowing with varie-gated corpses, pale, dulled, and finally smelly.

Leif and Rolf had no conception of fishing for sport. They belonged to the old Sweden, where you warred with nature for everything; and when it showed weakness, you harvested until your arms ached and the light off the salt sea struck headaches from your skull. When I came home with my carrier bags, sick from killing and sunstroke, I had thirty-four fish in them, most of them ballan wrasse, which have a curious pouched stomach that makes them almost impossible to gut. Also, they taste like fermented mud, even when they are very fresh. I stood at the sink for nearly two hours, dragging my knife through the toughening flesh, and tugging out handfuls of smelly intestines with my fingers. There were two carrier bags full of guts before I gave up and threw the rest of the fish, ungutted, into the last bag and threw it all away. It was August; the rubbish was collected in a room at the very far end of our block of flats, and three stories down, so the smell was still tolerable immediately outside our flat when the bin men came five days later. It must have been terrible further along the balcony. I hoped very much that none of the people in the flats closer to the rubbish chute knew I was a fisherman.

In the sleety half of autumn when the sky was the same desaturated grey as the paper on our concrete walls, I began to realize what it would mean to be a working man for the rest of my life and to transmit this fate to my child. The strength drained from my body. I found it harder and harder to lift the pallets that I made, and to throw the last one up to the top of the stack. For some reason, I became quite convinced that I was suffering from TB. When I finally went to see the doctor, he said at once that I was depressed, wrote me a sick note for a fortnight, and gave me some pills. The moment I took the first one, I lay down on the floor of the flat and went to sleep, as boneless and worthless as I had been after the first day's work a long year before.

Apart from putting me to sleep, the pills did nothing. I couldn't drink, and I longed to be out of Nödinge. So I bought a baggie full of grass from one of the boys who worked in the factory – cheaper in any event than drink. After Anita had gone to work, I rolled and smoked one thin, sour joint and then drove down to Gothenburg. The road looked oddly shiny, and I had a sense that there was a terrible wind howling in the corners of my vision, but at least I could not be caught drunk driving. In the basement of the public library I could find strangers to play chess; I played five or six quick games; my last opponent was an

Iranian student who played really dreadfully, and insisted on two rematches. When I beat him for the last time, he looked at me with furious despair. 'This is a stupid game, anyway,' he said. 'You should try playing me at *ping-pong*!' He said this as if ping pong were a conclusive retort to all the insults that exile had ever heaped on him. I felt better at once about my own inadequacies. I drove home slowly and within a week I was back at work, almost as if nothing had happened.

Soon afterwards the phone rang one Saturday morning while Anita was out working a weekend shift. Anna, her voice sounding thick, asked with no warning if she could come to see me. In our kitchen she cried little gasping sobs. Karlsson was drinking, she said, and she couldn't stop him. I hugged her – she hardly came up to my chest – and advised her to leave him. It would be fine, I said: we loved her; all her children did. It wasn't the sort of thing one said in Lilla Edet and I am still glad that I said it.

She went back to Lilla Edet even before Anita finished her shift and threw Karlsson out; he was never mentioned again.

Felix was born at the end of a still cold March night in Vänersborg, about fifty kilometres north of Nödinge. There was a row with the doctor: I had been reading English books in preparation for the event, and expected the hospital to be up with the fashion for parents' involvement in what was going on. This was so counter to the authoritarian culture of Swedish hospitals at the time that the nurse was greatly offended. She left us on our own in the room for four hours with a foetal monitor that neither of us could understand while the labour progressed.

When he emerged, the doctor held him up and said gravely that there was a small cosmetic defect to the baby and for a moment I was really worried. It was a great relief to learn that he meant the little split on his upper lip. Though he did not have a cleft palate, he had a definite hare lip. Immediately that seemed to me the most beautiful shape a human mouth could assume.

When I left the hospital it was full daylight and the temperature had climbed almost to freezing. I drove back as fast as I dared, passing the hump of road outside Lilla Edet at 140 kph so that fear and excitement would keep me awake at the wheel; once I reached Nödinge I slept for an hour then drove more slowly in to work at the factory. In the evening I drove back up to the hospital to visit my family. Until that day, I had been attached primarily to what was not, to the past, and to my own failures. Now I had roots in the future, and in a particular country.

I suppose Felix was about four months old when Anita went back to work. It never occurred to me that I would go on working when I might stay at home and look after him. The regulations then meant that we had a year of fully paid parental leave to split between us, and then another six months with rather less money.

After a summer tour of England to show off our son Anita started to train for more nursing qualifications and I looked after Felix. The pay was almost the same as if I had been going into the factory every day, and the work, of course, was much lighter and more interesting.

I bought a fly rod, too, and learned to use it. One September morning I crunched through the icy margins of a lake while the night was still thinning into a grey mist. By the time the bulging red sun had pulled itself above the pine forest across the water, I was balanced on a broad round boulder. The forest warmed and started to exhale distinct savours of spruce and pine; trout swirled outside a reed bed ten metres away. It took about three hours to catch one, doing everything by the book. When I had landed it, I killed it with a rock and afterwards there was a puddle of cold dark blood on the lapel of my tweed jacket that I was never able to remove. I liked killing things a great deal, just as I liked walking through forests on my own and sheltering under trees when rainstorms caught me. These things made me part of the world I had escaped to. I was twenty-four. I had a job, a wife, a child, and a car, and these achievements mattered; but it seemed to me that they all derived from the man I became in the woods.

I did not fly fish any more that year. The lakes shut for fishing at the end of September, and as the shortening of the days accelerated, I became oppressed by the idea that the earth was not spinning, but turning slowly instead like a gigantic ball, and we on its shoulders were being rolled inexorably, day by day, towards the darkness and the frozen sludge and out of breathable air.

But within the little bright rooms of our flat, with the endlessly fascinating smells and sounds of a baby, this did not seem to matter very much. I probably talked to him too little. When he was about six months old, he had his hare lip sewn up, which meant that we had to spend time in the children's surgical ward in one of the big Gothenburg hospitals and when I saw how some other children there had been born, I realized that the horrors we had glimpsed at the other end of life, in the Cheshire Home, were really nothing at all.

Anna, after a period on her own, had moved back in with Hans, and at Christmas the whole family gathered in their house. We ate a huge boiled ham, warm herring salad, small frankfurters, and potatoes. The windows were fortified with dark and shiny plants; their brass pots gleamed in the lamplight. Nobody quarrelled and there was no alcohol at all. Afterwards

I drove my middle sister-in-law back to her flat in Gothenburg and we chatted about this and that until she said, 'You know, I can't understand people who marry foreigners.' I felt quite a lot of things in that moment, and said none of them. I was so blazingly conscious that I had married a foreigner myself that it didn't occur to me for years that she might have forgotten that Anita, too, had married one.

I was able to attend to the outside world a little, too, and I had begun to write things that people might possibly pay to read. My father, anxious that my mind should not entirely rot in the Swedish provinces, had given us a subscription to the *Economist* and the *Spectator*, and in 1980 I started to sell pieces to the *Spectator*. The first piece I sold was about Swedish drinking laws. It took me about six weeks to write, mostly spent throwing away jokes that didn't work. No time whatever was spent asking questions of other people. So far as I knew, journalism was a purely stylistic discipline. I wrote essays about characters that might have appeared in other journalistic stories.

The mindset into which I cast myself in order to write was doubly artificial. I did not speak English at all in those days, except by a special effort. It wasn't a dead language, but it was a purely literary one, and the books or magazines I read were not colloquial. Few people ever speak with as little adornment as a writer like Orwell or Graham Greene, or even Swift. It takes time as well as effort to reduce all that you want to say to the little you have to say, and working journalists certainly don't have the time. When I fell away from those standards – and as a weekly journalist, I had all the time I needed – it was into the mannered cleverness of the magazines I read, where the important news they had to bring, and keep bringing, was that the writers were smarter than the people they wrote about. Condescension was the breath of life to me.

After a while, this double life stopped being a strain. I had always felt fake as an Englishman, and now in some deep way I was. This let me play the part with much greater confidence. I liked being a conservative of sorts, partly because it was such an outrage to the pieties of the society in which I lived; partly because it seemed to me that the world would go on being run by the grown-ups whatever we clever young people did. The atmosphere at the *Spectator*, which I began to visit about once a year, did nothing to discourage this. The people there were kind, quick-thinking and after lunchtime drunk. I loved all that, and I also loved the fact that they were serious about writing and virtually nothing else.

I thought of them as the wastepaper-basket people, after a phrase in *Goodbye to All That*, when Robert Graves's housemaster attempts to discourage him, with the words, 'And remember: a writer's best friend is his wastepaper basket.' Graves takes the phrase and makes it his own. It becomes a justification for hard, painstaking work: that if you throw enough away, what is left will be good. This thought was always present to me; so was a less true development: that what never made it to the final draft didn't count either. The *Spectator* lived in a dilapidated four-storey Georgian house in Bloomsbury. There was a lot of work done on the ground floor, where the literary editor and the deputy had their offices; quite a lot of work done on the first floor, where the editor's secretary and the editor had their offices, and a great deal drunk in the attic at the top of the house where lunches of unpleasant food were served with terrifying brio by Jennifer Patterson, who became, before her death, a television cooking personality.

The first time I ascended to the top floor I was following the cartoonist Michael Heath, and, ahead of him, the writer Peter Ackroyd, who was then literary editor. Ackroyd was supposed to have got his job when he told his interviewer that there were two things he should know: one that he was gay, and the other that he drank a bottle of whisky a day. He was a wonderfully thoughtful editor. As we all trooped up the stairs Ackroyd ducked into the lavatory on the landing.

'I shouldn't bother going in there, Peter,' said Heath, in a voice like a kindly uncle. 'It's empty.'

Nobody I knew anywhere else in the world would think of a thing like that, or say it if they did. I hoped desperately that I belonged in a world where people not only thought of jokes on staircases, they brought them out in time, too.

Very soon after I started writing for the *Spectator*, they arranged for me to get a Cable & Wireless card, in those days the badge of a real foreign correspondent. It let me send reverse-charge telexes to the office in London. A telex was a cross between a typewriter and a telegraph machine. Instead of sending Morse code, I would type at a keyboard pretty much like an electronic typewriter's, though I don't think it knew anything about accented letters. This would disgorge a roll of punched tape, which then had to be fed into a separate machine for transmission.

It was a serious, expensive, businessman's system, and to have access to it meant automatically that you were well connected. I could walk into the telex office in Uddevalla as a slightly ridiculous figure, but inside I was a superhero, righting wrongs. Once I had the Cable & Wireless card, I was on the lists of Swedish Foreign Ministry as an accredited correspondent, and could talk to anyone I wanted to. Of course, outside the telex office life continued very much as usual in my disguise as someone who wasn't really a superhero.

10

In the woods

We left Nödinge when Felix was eighteen months old and moved to half a bungalow in the woods outside Lilla Edet. If the neighbours never spoke to you there was not much point in having neighbours at all. When the time came to shift the furniture I drove a hired Transit van up the long straight road to Lilla Edet bellowing in my best Joe Strummer mockney, 'This here rock is a revolution rock,' as if my elated position, swaying high above the front wheels, would carry me through the rest of my life.

We had one close neighbour in the woods, the owner of the bungalow, an ancient half-Danish and half-crooked business-man who was dying – I now understand – of congestive heart failure. He wheezed as he waddled, and he had a terrible gur-gling cough, treated with regular applications of low-tar cigarettes. The dark interior of his house smelt overpower-ingly of dog-food, dog, cigarette smoke and old man's undershirt. This made eating with him an ordeal, but some social contact was unavoidable because I held a mortgage on our part of the house. It couldn't simply be rented for compli-cated reasons, which boiled down to the fact that he had no planning permission for the part we lived in. He hoped his married daughter would come and look after him, but until then he needed the money, he said, to finish the conversion of our part. It had started off as a caravan parked in a field as deep into the forest as the dirt road reached, about three miles from Lilla Edet on the western bank of the Göta. Then he had built his own bungalow, a little distance from the caravan, and standing at an angle to it. Finally he swathed the old caravan in wood and turned the intervening space into a crooked shack, where we lived.

It was reasonably weatherproof. There was a fireplace, which on cold nights had to be swathed in blankets to stop the draught rushing down it for no wood could burn unattended all night. The walls and roof were insulated. There was a bedroom for us, a little alcove for Felix, a study for me, with one small desk for the typewriter and another for my fly-tying equipment, and an angled kitchen where we could eat more easily than cook: it had a boxy electric oven with two hotplates on top: you could either have two hotplates on at once, or one and the oven.

The long dirt track through the forest to the bungalow was lined with blackberries in the autumn, and deeper in the woods there were chanterelles growing beside exposed pine roots. In summer I could reach out from the study window at the back of the house and almost touch the leaves of the nearest birch tree; but in front there was a cleared meadow running a hundred metres up the hill to the only other neighbour's house. Across the valley was a clear-cut jumble of stumps and bramble where sometimes we could spot elk or deer grazing but otherwise the forest closed all around. The silence among the trees was very deep; when guests came to visit from England they would get lost within a hundred yards of the house, bewildered by the endless variations on a tiny repertoire of rock and pine; spruce and birch; juniper bushes, sand and ant hills.

When the autumn came, rats moved into our roof space and I began to hate the landlord. He was reluctant to spent money on pest control while they scrabbled around the roof above our heads: they're only shrews, he said. Then one morning I found a trail of crumbly plaster running down from a small fresh hole in the wall above the cooker. The rats were trying to break into our kitchen. I grew hysterical and shouted at him. That night, when everything grew quiet, I was roused from bed by the soft noise of cascading plaster. I padded into the darkened kitchen, picked up a sharpening steel and bashed the little black nose protruding from the wall. I spent much of the night sitting on a chair and glowering at the wall with a carving knife in my hand. I might not be able to do much for my family, but I could by God kill any small creatures that came into the kitchen and crapped in our food stores.

There were also adders in the meadow and one that lived in the rocks at the front of the house, under the heap of sand that had been left when the landlord ran out of money for his building plans. 'It will make a wonderful place for the little one to play,' he said. Felix spent a lot of time playing there, after I had killed the adder by jabbing a crowbar into the crevice where it lived, but I still kept a pair of wellingtons by the kitchen door in case I had to rush out and kill another one. Otherwise, we lived barefoot all summer.

I practised my fly-casting on the meadow for an hour every day. Only the gales that thrashed the oak tree over our bedroom could stop me. Snow certainly didn't. To stand on a crisp February day with the snow half way up my shins and a fly rod in my hand was a sort of liturgical dance, even if there was no one to observe it but a couple of elk. Fly-casting is in any case a way to dance from the hips upwards. Everything depends on catching the rhythm of the line as it loops through the air and this can only be done by feel, one reason why I could often cast better in the dark than when I peered to see what was happening as dusk fell. If I could just get the movements exactly right, I felt as if I were dancing the spring a little bit closer. I had come to feel that I was only really alive when I looked at water, or when I drove towards it.

I started cod fishing again in the autumn, on my own and from the shore. The lakes inland would close around the middle of September and on those that did not the cold grey evening seemed to start at sunrise on an October day. Even the berries were fading then, as if the last scraps of colour were being scraped off the earth in its descent into winter. Only by the black and dark-green sea was there a sense of life.

Fishing anywhere is a form of enquiry. The patient watchful wonder of the fisherman seems to me the root of all science. In sea fishing this mapping and bringing of order from the formless, shifting waves is especially ambitious. Attention broods over the water like the spirit in Genesis, moving, casting, until suddenly all the possibilities are narrowed into one taut line. Perhaps this explains why I have always sought the sea at times of upset and disturbance in my life. The fish comes like an answer, the rod in my hand a divining instrument.

I had a rod well suited to the crude ferocity of the pursuit of cod: a thick blue fibreglass pole with ugly ceramic rings that would hurl a 40-gram lure into the dusk so far I could hardly see it splash into the water. I fished off rocks and round the edge of car parks; the view in front was pretty ugly too. I looked for sites with a deep current close to land and kept my eyes fixed on the water in front of me. It didn't matter if there was an oil refinery or a chemical plant across the bay. The water had for me the same kind of importance as music; and I heard music all the time, by a feat of will. I could not afford a radio or cassette player for the car: to have one seemed to me to entail a state of riches nearly as boundless as possessing a credit card. But I learned, through concentration, to memorize music as I had once memorized Brian Clarke, so that as the winter night fell over the road like sleet, I would hear over and over again a fragment of a Steely Dan song, a descending piano figure and a sprightly bass: 'If I had my way, I would move / to some other lifetime.'

I wasn't interested in sea fish for their sporting quality. In my experience cod feed as voraciously as vacuum cleaners and are about as animated. But their skin was delicately dappled in all the colours that were disappearing in the winter from the land – brown and green and silver – and they tasted delicious. This mattered because the food value of my catch had again become an important consideration. We lived precariously on Anita's earnings as a trainee nurse and what I could earn from writing and teaching English and fly-tying at evening classes, but I spent most of my time looking after little Felix in the loneliness of the forest.

This was not a world in which women played much of a part. Anita took to spending two or three nights a week in Uddevalla, where she was working. It saved a lot of driving and some silences between us. I didn't notice that it was anything more than a practical arrangement. It took me ages to see that the woman who ran my evening classes was making passes at me. It seemed a thing impossible. I was a married man. Evie was a slightly fluffy blonde in her thirties, divorced, with a son of about eight and a cat. She liked to talk. We would chatter for an hour on the phone some days, when I was alone at home. And when I walked into Lilla Edet, pushing Felix's pram, I would stop at her house for coffee. None the less, my first reaction when she proposed a game of strip poker was simple astonishment; my second was to flee, but afterwards I went back to talk about the idea, and three weeks later I was weeping in the car park by an oil refinery, too weak to climb out of the car and fish. How could I have been so stupid? How could I face the rest of my life?

11

The correspondent

Outside the wastepaper basket where I tried to keep my emotions, my life was flourishing. I didn't make money, but I did get myself noticed, which I cared about much more. When a Russian submarine, manoeuvring deep inside Swedish waters, ran aground on a skerry near the naval base in Karlskrona, I managed to make a joke that ran all around the world: since the submarine was known by its NATO code name, Whiskey 137, I insisted that the *Spectator* piece be headlined 'Whiskey on the rocks'. I was amazed no one else had thought of it in the four or five days before the article appeared. That no one else thought very much about Sweden at all was not an explanation that occurred to me. I was already too Swedish for that.

There were endless submarine incursions in those years and they were very good for my business, because the presence of Russian submarines in neutral Swedish waters had the grotesque and inexplicable quality that a really attractive story needs. But after the initial shock of Whiskey on the Rocks, many, perhaps most Swedes, refused to believe that anything bad was happening. They had proclaimed their own neutrality. How could any foreigner really be violating it? The idea of Swedish neutrality, or non-alignment, was central to the country's self-image, as was the belief that it had been preserved by martial valour, even though the country had not in fact fought a serious war since losing Finland to Russia in 1809. What 'neutrality' really expressed was a belief that the country was lifted above the squabbles and sufferings of the world below.

None of the Nordic countries had been involved in the First World War, except Finland, then a province of Russia, which had its own civil war, won by the Whites, after 1917. In the Second World War, Denmark and Norway had been invaded by the Nazis and Finland by the Soviets, while Sweden stood aside. Until about the time of Stalingrad, it seemed to be neutral, firmly on the Nazi side: Swedish volunteers went to fight in Finland against the communists, and German troops and supplies were allowed to transit the Swedish railway system. After Stalingrad, Sweden was decisively neutral on the winning side. This was long and very bitterly resented, especially in Norway. When my parents lived in Stockholm in the late Sixties, we once drove on a long circuit through Swedish Lapland and down through Norway, in a car with Swedish plates. The change in atmosphere was noticeable, even to a child, when people realized that we were in fact an English family even though we had emerged from a car with Swedish plates.

Of course, the Swedes had an entirely different memory of the Second World War. They regarded Norwegians broadly as ignorant peasant bumpkins ('How do you sink a Norwegian submarine? You swim down and knock on the door.'), and they remembered themselves as sturdy, frightening defenders of their own integrity who had helped out the Norwegians in every way they could. Near Sälen, on the Norwegian border, where the Ljöra runs into the Västerdal river, there is now a picnic spot with one of the most important and ridiculous statues in Sweden. It is a conscript soldier, facing the German armies who were occupying Norway between 1940 and 1945. On the bluffs behind are the remains of the fortifications where the Swedish Army would have fought if the Nazis had thought it worth their while to invade the country. Since they could ship their troops through it, and buy as much ore as they wanted, without invading, they never did think it worth the trouble. But it was part of the national mythology that the army was prepared, and might have fought.

The important effect on Swedish society was not whether in fact the army did stand off the Wehrmacht, but whether people believed it did. This particular myth of Swedish neutrality – that the Germans wouldn't dare – gave Swedish society all of the advantages to be had from a war with few of the nasty bits like actually fighting it. There were privations. People went hungry and cold, and were probably afraid. But they were hungrier, much more afraid, and probably colder too almost everywhere else in Europe, while the discipline, the sense of submission to common purpose and all the other things that English people who lived through it remember happily about the Second World War – all came to Sweden without any corpses and without any occupation.

This isn't a moral point. I'm not Norwegian, so I don't think the world would have been a better place if Sweden had been invaded; but it is a disturbing and probably true idea that the pacifist, internationalist social democratic states of late twentieth-century Europe – the ones that were going to show the rest of the world the way to a more Swedish future, where everyone was rich and rational – were only made possible by the continent's terrible wars. This is only partly because the Second World War was so horrible, as well as so decisive, that the survivors determined another war was unthinkable. After all, people thought that in 1918 and they were dreadfully wrong. There is a deeper connection, which might help to explain why some of the most pacifist and well-organized states in history emerged from the rubble of an exceptionally militaristic continent. The kinds of discipline and self-discipline that make a peaceful welfare state possible are themselves the characteristics that made for success in wars between nation states.

But preparations for war are expensive, in time, in money, in other pleasures foregone. Nobody seriously expects Sweden to fight another war, and by the time that submarines started to appear in the archipelago, its armed forces were a joke, though one that only foreigners appreciated. A friend of mine was covering the Angolan civil war in the 1970s, a war in which all the neighbouring countries joined during the apartheid years. Deep in the Angolan bush, he came across a South African tank column, there to assist some faction. 'Who are you? What are you doing here?' he asked, though of course he knew, and they knew he knew. In a broad Boer accent, the officer replied: 'We're the Swedish Army, man.'

None the less, the incompetence of the Swedish Navy when it came to dealing with these submarines may not have been entirely unintentional. It would have been very embarrassing if dead Russian sailors had floated to the surface in front of the world's press corps; and for the biggest and most ridiculous of these hunts, when it appeared that four or five miniature submarines were detected outside one of the main Swedish naval bases in the archipelago, there were perhaps a hundred journalists in a converted schoolroom put at our disposal by the foreign ministry which overlooked the inlet where the submarines were supposed to be. That was a pretty large audience, never to be repeated. After the Swedish Navy had announced that the intruders were trapped, and then, some days later, that they had mysteriously disappeared, no one could take the story seriously any more – the foreigners because they had concluded that the Swedish Navy couldn't, the Swedes, at least partly, because it had never made sense to them that someone would violate their neutrality by force. Wasn't that what neutrality was meant to prevent?

One Swede, however, continued to pick away at it, a rangy policy wonk with plastic-framed spectacles, who called the *Financial Times* 'the pink 'un' to show that he spoke English so idiomatic that hardly anyone in Britain would understand it, and who worked for the Moderate Party, because he was clever, ambitious and greatly loathed socialism. It did no harm that he was engaged to the party leader's daughter. This was Carl Bildt, who, ten years later, would be the prime minister of Sweden, and would do as much as anyone to destroy the country that we had all lived in. He wasn't even a member of parliament, then, I think, but the report he produced on the submarine incursions was a really fine analysis, the product of an intelligent man who understood power and its limitations. We talked for a couple of hours about it and I went away thinking that he was the only man I had ever met in Sweden who could really look at the country from the outside and understand how it appeared from there. Many people still think he has an alien's eye. He left office as one of the most disliked politician in the history of his country, but in the early Eighties his concerns just seemed bizarre. In those days, no one really needed to care what the outside world thought of Sweden, because they thought they already knew.

After I had been selling freelance articles for about a year, my eye was caught by a truly sensational story in *Svenska Dagbladet*, one of the two main Stockholm dailies: respectable, conservative, rather stuffy, but less stiflingly conformist than its left-wing rival *Dagens Nyheter*. The story seemed terrible and wonderful at the same time and it did not bother me in the least that it was written by a judge and not a real journalist. I did not know what a real journalist was. Few, in any case, could have come up with a sentence as gripping, as intuitively right, as Brita Sundberg-Weitman's opening to her piece on the Aminoff scandal: 'There is a country (Sweden) where the authorities can forcibly separate a child from its parents to prevent them from giving it a privileged upbringing.'

The article described a Kafkaesque world in which a child could be removed from its mother by bureaucratic fiat, in which the courts merely rubber-stamped the accusations brought by the social services, and where an eccentric and independent-minded mother whose only crime was arrogance and 'the desire to give her child a privileged upbringing' could find her child taken from her by a snatch squad of social workers sent to a foreign country, while she herself was denied all contact with him, even the knowledge of where he was.

Sweden, the article continued, had far more children in care, proportionately, than any other foreign country: the administrative courts believed anything that social workers told them and so the parents had no defence against malicious, jealous, or incompetent social workers. The statistic quoted by the judge stated that there were more than 20,000 children in care in Sweden. Given that this was one of the richest and best-educated countries in the world, there was either a startling degree of parental incompetence or almost totalitarian arrogance on the part of the state. There was no doubt which explanation she preferred, and she backed it up with a couple of case histories. The most sensational of these was that of the boy called 'Child

A', who had been taken from his mother in the prosperous suburb of Lidingö and was now living under the care of the authorities somewhere in the countryside but officially nobody was allowed to know where. Terrible accusations had been made against his mother – these the judge did not specify – but since they had not been tested by the family court, they shouldn't be regarded as proven, and if they were not true, the mother could only be thought guilty of eccentricity and arrogance.

This article was not published as news, but as a polemic, on the comment page. It was followed by a rebuttal from a more junior judge, who had heard one of the cases against the local authority that had applied to put Child A in custody. This was difficult to follow, since the secrecy laws meant that neither could refer directly to the material in the case. It was obvious that he found the accusations against the mother convincing but he could not explain what they actually were.

So I rang Brita Sundberg-Weitman and she put me in touch with Eva Aminoff, the aristocrat, Finnish mother of Child A. I took a train up to Stockholm to meet her. It was late April 1981 and there were a few snow showers left of the winter. I talked to Sundberg-Weitman first, in her office in the court building, and she showed me a great deal of the dossier from which the court had worked. The matter was complicated because the child had been taken into care twice, as a result of two investigations. This seemed to Eva Aminoff's supporters to be conclusive proof that there was a conspiracy against her. It did mean that everyone involved the second time around was familiar with the material from the first case, which had, however, been dropped after Eva more or less kidnapped her son from the psychiatric hospital where he was being held for observation and took him to Finland and then Spain, where she had stayed until the social services dropped the case against her.

Sundberg-Weitman did not show me the dossier from the first case, claiming that it had no bearing on the second intervention. Actually, it contained the story that explained why the authorities considered Eva Aminoff to be a psychopathic fantasist who was a danger to everyone around her. Her first child had drowned, aged sixteen, in the Canary Islands in the late Sixties – there was a suggestion of suicide and incest; she had then taken a baby from one of the servants and kept it for two years before the social services had removed it; after that the baby Alexander (Child A) had been acquired from a peasant family in Finland, though she claimed to have given birth to him alone on an island in the archipelago. The story was more like a gothic fantasy than anything one would expect in a suburb of Stockholm in the Seventies. All this Sundberg-Weitman disbelieved, and described to me, without any detail, as the lies told by enemies and an estranged husband.

Without any of this evidence, the case against Eva Aminoff in the second dossier did seem thin; there was an alternative explanation for every story in it that seemed damning to her, and each one individually seemed perfectly credible.

I stayed the night in the Aminoff house. If Eva struck me as eccentric and emotional, I put this down to the anguish of a mother parted from her children. I could not imagine any greater pain. When she offered me a bottle of beer for breakfast, I thought it merely a characteristically Finnish gesture. Besides, it was a wonderful story.

An English friend helped me to sell the story to the *Daily Mail*. She gave me one piece of good advice: the paper had lots of women readers. So I sat down and in a couple of hours wrote a piece calculated to make any mother weep at the thought of her family being invaded by soulless bureaucrats. I was paid the miraculous sum of £500. Better yet, there were jokes about

Sweden, based on my story, in the following week's *Private Eye*. It would have become one of the most glorious memories of my life had the story actually been true.

Other papers – none of them Swedish – picked up the story. *Der Spiegel* ran a big piece on the 'Swedish children's Gulag', citing six examples. Olof Palme himself responded by reading all the papers on the disputed cases. When he had done so, he announced that in all of them, and especially in the Aminoff case, the decision made seemed to be entirely the correct one. Clearly this was a cover-up reaching into the highest levels of society.

But, although the big childcare stories went on and on, something about the Aminoff case seemed to put journalists off. Other examples were increasingly chosen to illustrate pieces about Swedish social work, as they became a recognized journalistic form, in which different names, dates, and numbers were used to retell a story by now understood and expected by everyone. I heard nothing more from Eva Aminoff.

I continued to write, mostly for the *Spectator*, where I could plan my deadlines well ahead. I would take the train up to Stockholm, 500 km from Uddevalla, when I needed to talk to people in person. I loved those journeys. My mind has always worked like a river, with the different depths moving at different speeds, and sometimes to different destinations; and on a train journey I seemed to move at the speed of the most powerful currents. Sometimes the result was an intellectual ecstasy, when I would contemplate the problem or the story ahead of me as if I could hold it whole and turn it in my mind, feeling for the centre of gravity, the thing that it was all about. After an hour or more some phrase would come which opened the way to my destination as if it were the most natural movement in the world. At times like this, my handwriting, normally sprawling and jagged, would change so that the loops were round and evenly sized; the ascending strokes parallel to each other, leaning emphatically forwards.

These times are forever bound in my mind with the smell of rotting apples in the stuffy, tepid air. In summer or in winter, the trains were always well heated and quiet. The windows could not be opened. On long journeys there would be four or five people in every compartment who snacked on apples and the cores, thrown into waste bins, would flavour the whole train.

I wouldn't need to write very much on trains. If I had two or three paragraphs that would form the kernel of a piece, I would be quite content, knowing that the rest would grow from them in due time. But sometimes there would be far more. I would sit there with a sense that great waves of understanding were breaking inside me and the hissing and bubbling foam spread luxuriously over the whole world. There was nothing I could not write, nothing that I could not see or understand.

All this ebullience was tethered by the knowledge that someone in London cared what I thought. On the first floor of the *Spectator* offices, smelling of dust, cigarette smoke and old drink, there was a telex machine that would burst into life when I sent it copy. There were competent people who liked my jokes, and who shared my dislocation from the universe. The magazine did not seem at home anywhere in the world, and I liked that. It guaranteed the safety of perpetual exile. To have no roots in the world meant that one could float over anywhere in it, like the inhabitants of Swift's flying island, and call down advice or abuse to the peasants below. This suited my temperament. Less and less seemed real to me on the ground where I was living.

12

The fishing club

In 1983 we had moved out of the forest. Anita found us a flat in Uddevalla, the shipyard town where she was training to be a nurse. It was the first place we had lived that was bigger than a company town: an old port at the mouth of a river valley. To the south of the river were massive bosses of gneiss, making a shoreline of cliffs; to the north was a line of low steep hills, so that the sea was at the end of a long inlet that was almost a fjord. The great frames of the shipyard's cranes were visible from all over town. But there was also a railway depot, a small port, an army barracks, and numerous small industries trailing out along the river valley and the main road east. Visually, it was dominated by three things: the cliffs and the forests around them, the great cranes of the shipyard, and the hospital where Anita worked, a broad red cruciform building, ten storeys high, at the foot of the hills on the north side of town.

From here a broad road snaked up the hill for about a mile through progressively newer and less middle-class districts, till it came to our estate at the point where the town edged up against a scrubby forest. Although it was darker to the eye than Nödinge, being made of grey concrete slabs, the estate seemed much friendlier. Perhaps this was because the flats were newer and more spacious; perhaps because the blocks were only three or four storeys high and arranged around small squares, each of which had a playground in the middle, so that children could be safely turned out to play in company but easily visible. Across the main road was another, less successful estate, where the blocks of flats were arranged across a steeper hillside in longer rows of six or seven storeys. There were some shops and a small library there, but we preferred to go to town for almost all of our distractions.

Down in the centre of Uddevalla, the main road from Norway to Gothenburg ran along the harbour front, a dual carriageway broken up by traffic lights, and in one of the new buildings alongside this road was a small fishing shop where I would spend my free time. It was a great deal cheaper than a pub would have been, had there been a pub. A couple of rangy bearded men worked there, though the work consisted as much in talking about fishing as selling anything. I couldn't buy much, but I could listen. For all my own zeal, fishing had up till then been something I did by myself, or with Anita. No one I knew on land shared my passion, and I certainly wasn't going to waste time by the water talking.

But a few quiet purchases of skins and feathers to tie flies with, and one dreadfully extravagant vice to hold hooks with, meant that I could talk about fishing, and after a month or two get invited to join the local fishing club. It was through the club that I came to the most Swedish house in which I ever felt at home, though nobody lives in it now. To reach it, you have to drive up a dirt road for about twenty minutes from the coast, and then walk a further ten or fifteen minutes through the woods until the path bursts into a meadow by a small lake. In the middle of this clearing, the house, built in 1824, is sturdy and almost square, with three rooms arranged around a central fireplace and a wood store running along one side. It looks spacious today, but it must have been cramped and smelly in the winters when there were ten children living here; that is how many the last farming couple raised before both of them died in 1955.

On three or four little fields hacked out of the forest they kept cows and sheep and planted rye and potatoes. Once a fortnight they walked into town to buy coffee and sugar. All their other food they grew or gathered themselves. Nothing remains now of those decades of effort except a little dry-stone walling, knee-high among the trees, and a stand of lilies which blossoms every spring on the meadow in front of the house.

Two of the farmer's children had tried to keep the smallholding running, but in 1957 they gave up. It was not the last smallholding worked out in these woods: my friend Kristina nursed an old woman in hospital who had lived in the forest on her own until she was ninety, and who kept by her bed a photograph of herself as a young woman leading a cow down a track through the woods.

After Finnish lumberjacks had used it as a winter base for some years, the lake house lay abandoned. Then, at about the same time the hospital was built, the local authority bought it, so that they could rent it to a fishing club.

By then the lake and the well had both been poisoned by acid rain. All of the west coast of Sweden is extremely vulnerable: the soil is thin and sour, one of the factors that gives the forest its melancholy echoing emptiness, and the rain falls for two or three months every year as snow, which all melts in a rush, driving down the Ph levels at the most dangerous time, just before the breeding season starts. This lake was restored by sprinkling lime on the swamps through which the snow melted into it in spring. The well never recovered. From then on all water to the house would have to be fetched in buckets from the lake. But this mattered less now that the house had become a place to play at being in the wilderness.

The members of the fishing club were mostly working class, and they worked for their pleasures as often as they paid for them. My friend Lasse was a welder at the shipyard: in the aristocracy of labour, this made him something like an earl. He was a wild-haired, wolf-like man who worked some evenings in a fishing shop, which is where I met him, for the company and the talk, rather than for the money. It turned out that he lived on the same estate that we did, though his flat was much more extravagantly furnished than our own. He had a sofa that wrapped around two walls, low glass coffee tables, and a bookcase with reels and pictures on it. On some evenings he would have a still in the kitchen, and while we sat on the grand sofa in the living room, a clear liquid would trickle down a tube slung over the top of the open kitchen door and into the glass coffee pot from a filter machine. The filter was filled with charcoal grains instead of coffee and the pot beneath would slowly fill with a viscous, almost clear liquid whose fumes made the eyes smart. He had a hydrometer for measuring its strength: it looked like a large thermometer, with a bulb on the bottom, and a stalk up which were marked degrees of alcohol. When fresh from the coffee pot the moonshine was so strong that the hydrometer would lie flat on its surface. First water was added, until the hydrometer bobbed upright like a float, and then Coca-Cola, until the strength was reduced to about 50 per cent alcohol. Even so, it bit at my throat like an angry dog as it went down.

Everything in the flat was always perfectly tidy. He owned a great deal of fishing tackle, but used little of it. He collected good reels on his shelves the way I collected books of poetry: not just for solace against the winter nights but to admire the way that the parts fitted together: as a metal worker himself, he loved good engineering, and the reels he owned were built to last a hundred years or more.

He once looked at the tackle I had with me, and said, 'Oh, so you've got a polycarbon reel' in the sort of carefully neutral voice you'd use to a child who had wet the bed. Then he showed me a salmon reel which had once been the most expensive in Sweden: it was hand-made from aluminium, with a gearing mechanism so that each turn of the handle brought in more line than it should have done. But what he was really proudest of was the little polythene bag beside it, which contained a tiny worn piece of metal with pin-sized holes in each end. After many years, the reel had started to fail, and he had sent it back to the man who made it. Even though he had stopped making and selling them, he would still service the ones he had made. The craftsman had diagnosed the worn part, replaced it, and then sent the reel back to Lasse with the part that had been replaced, which was what he kept in the polythene bag: it was a proof that there were still craftsmen working the way that they should.

When first I knew him, he did not fish much with the wonderful reel. His tackle was clean but battered; he was one of the two most naturally effective fishermen I have watched. He cast with the least possible effort no further than where the fish were. Sometimes I would stand to one side and just watch the geometric elegance of the curves his fly line made rolling out above the water.

He used very few flies: only those that caught fish. My vest was at that time full of flies that imitated almost every insect that lived on or near the water through all the stages of their development, so that I might have different patterns for the threadlike, crimson larvae of a midge, then for the stiff, hooked pupa, glossy with air as it wobbled gently upwards from muddy bottoms, then a concoction of straight deer hair, humped at one end, to represent the pupa hatching in the water surface, and finally another kind of fly with a buoyant grizzle hackle, like thickened air, to represent a winged midge dancing on the surface – and all these in different colours, because after all, there are something like 2,000 species of chironomid midges in Sweden, and you never know which the fish will be eating. Lasse fished, so far as I can remember, with only one pattern, a hog louse.

His imitation of this unlovely creature, a sort of aquatic woodlouse that thrives in acid water, looked like little flattened clots of fluff tied with the fur from a hare's ear. He would cast out, allow the fly to sink, and then retrieve it in a businesslike, unvarnished way as if all he wanted to do was to bring the fly back to him without fuss, rather than imitating anything in particular, or attracting fish. And then, in the middle of this almost absent-minded process, his rod would bend. He never seemed to lose a trout that he had hooked.

He was not one of the founders of the fishing club: they were slightly older men, all by then retired. By the time he joined it, much of the restoration work on the house had been done. The wooden floors were scrubbed clean and polished, with rugs laid over them; new pine tables and benches were brought in. The farmers had lit their house with candles and later kerosene lamps. Now there were propane lamps to give a mustard-coloured light on autumn evenings. Brazed brass tubing ran to lamps along the walls from the big canisters in the woodshed. There were picky little mantles around the lamps that had to be very precisely adjusted before they would work, and were easy to ruin with an unwisely poked match.

The old house came to seem to me a kind of ideal Sweden. The order that it contained was precious and carefully maintained without being prissy. Even the shortest nights were always dark so far south, and when it was too dark to fish, we would come inside and drink whisky and talk almost until the light returned. After the icy relentless grind of winter, all the extravagance of spring was distilled into the pleasure of the moments when I could slip away from the warm, lit circle of friendship for a moment, and go out to stand on the porch at midnight, half drunk, and pee into a fragrant lilac bush. No one was ever too drunk or too wild to take off his shoes on the porch, and in the mornings, we would spend an hour dusting then sweeping away the evidence of the last night's debauch.

Very few women were ever club members, though many came out to the house to picnic or to stay and some made the curtains, and the runners on the long pine tables. It was a wonderful place for children.

I thought of the lake as my favourite wilderness, although a jogging track, maintained by the local town, ran past one edge. It was signposted, but hardly anyone ever used it. Sometimes I would persuade Anita that she should come, and we would camp there with Felix. We had a tent that smelled faintly of trout blood and mildew as well as the mosquito repellent that saturates all my memories of Swedish summers. It was very small and friendly, and would snuggle down into tiny patches of clear ground between the boulders and juniper bushes that seemed to move every time we left the lake, so that when we returned the place where we had been so happy had disappeared.

When the wind died in the evenings we would set up the little camping stove with the dented frying pan whose fawn Teflon surface could make even hot dogs taste good. We also

cooked trout fillets, rather messily hacked from the brook trout:
they were an intense pinkish red like barely ripe strawberries.
But usually we ate hot dogs, and afterwards swished out the
pans in the water before making coffee. It boiled over every
time, sending up a thick hissing plume of steam and smoke
because we could no longer sit companionably and watch it
together: I would put it on to boil and then stand by myself for
a while, casting across the empty water.

Then we'd drink a little whisky to take the edge off the
evening, before crawling into the tent, one each side of Felix. In
the mornings I would wake at around five in an intense orange
heat as the sun played on the yellowy fabric of the tent and
crawl out, scrunching on pine needles. The very early mornings
were always the most hopeful time for a fish. The water smelt
metallic, and had lost its threatening clarity. Sometimes there
would be splashy rises to damselflies or drifting ants, for the fish
were not at all choosy underneath their calm surface, and, so far
as I could discover, lived mostly on hog lice and other creatures
of the mud. Perhaps they were half starved. It didn't help me
catch them.

In those days I fished as I lived, to a very rigid system. I
would walk into the woods every chance I had, to feel that I was
free, or at least elsewhere; but when I reached the lake, I cast
always the same way, and fished only imitations of natural
nymphs as slowly as I could move them – though sometimes I'd
forget, and catch a fish by accident, tugging a muddler through
the ripples when there was a breeze. What I loved was the grace
of casting. When I cast well, I didn't feel that my rod or line was
an extension of my arm. I felt that my arm and shoulder were
just an extension of the rod and nothing of me outside of them
existed. In its rhythm and passion, it was the closest I will ever
get to dancing. And though the passion is not sexual, there is

something close to love in the detailed, devouring scrutiny that the hunter gives his prey.

In the margins of the lake, I taught little Felix to hunt with an insect net. We would catch nymphs and take them home to study by my fly-tying table. Once or twice there would be a dragonfly larva in the net, compact and hideous like clots of mud with legs and grabbing jaws. I had an immensely complicated pattern to imitate them, carved out of spun marabou with knotted black eyeballs of ostrich herl. I thought it very beautiful.

Lasse had a daughter, a plump, dissatisfied girl named Marie to whom he was devoted. He had actually been married to her mother – unusual in our circle – and was still bitter about the break-up. It was impossible to tell which he resented more: that his ex no longer loved him or that he had ever loved her. He used to drive around town in a beaten-up old Volvo, with Marie by his side, commenting loudly and appreciatively on the breasts of all the women he saw. He loved his daughter, even if it sometimes distressed him that she should be a girl, and therefore destined to grow up into the enemy.

Lasse was not the only neighbour we became friendly with: above us was Kristina, who was harder to get to know. She had large eyes in a handsome, rather haggard face; she worked as a nursing auxiliary in the big hospital down the hill, which was clearly a job beneath her intelligence and qualifications, but there was something angry and defensive about her through which her sweetness only occasionally emerged. She had a son, Andreas, about Felix's age; a quiet, rather clingy boy, who seemed ill at ease in the world. The father was out of the picture, and not to be mentioned.

Apart from those friends, my knowledge of Swedes became increasingly theoretical, even while I was writing more and more about them for the outside world. I no longer taught evening classes, and I would travel as often as I could to Stockholm, and sometimes to other countries, in my life as a journalist. On these trips people were polite and kind but I suffered agonies of embarrassment beside men with real expense accounts. One time in Helsinki my money ran out while I was staying, prepaid, in a grand hotel. I had nothing to eat for the last 24 hours and had to walk a mile down to the boat in a snowstorm before my Swedish cheques were acceptable.

In Stockholm, I had new English friends. Once I had sold a couple of stories, I felt able to introduce myself to some of the people my parents had known there. I was once more someone who might be recognized in their world. Mary and Keith were a couple of expatriates about twenty years older than me who had known each other at Oxford, then fallen in love and married in Stockholm, after their marriages to Swedes had broken up. They stayed, doing various jobs of interpretation and translation; he had half-Swedish children, she had a job at the embassy. None of us were really at home anywhere, or rather, we all three had in common our nationality as foreigners in Sweden, able to go neither forwards nor backwards to living in only one country. They had both married into upper-middle-class Swedish families, quite unlike Anita's, but our bewilderments, hatreds, and unacknowledged love for the country were very similar. We could not look at Sweden in the way the Swedes did, but neither could we block it from our lives in the way that passing journalists or diplomats could do. It was all around us, a dominating enigma. If I had finished a day's work in Stockholm, I would take the tube to their solid Edwardian flat for supper, which meant drinking and talking with hardly a pause for breath until the very last moment before the night train to Uddevalla.

But it was in the summer that their civilized bohemian style was at its richest, when they moved out to an old, Chekhovian house in the archipelago. On a map, or from the air, the sea east of Stockholm, almost all the way to Finland, looks as if God had crumbled biscuit into it; but, being God, he had used granite instead.

On each island is a little open jetty, with a shelter like a bus stop at one end, where parcels may be left. Everywhere is the smell of the brackish, tender sea. It is not as rough and overwhelming as the smells of salt seas such as the Atlantic and the North Sea; but it is still a little wilder than completely fresh water.

The commuter boats were about as noisy, long, and dramatic as suburban buses. There was a kiosk at the front of each long cabin which sold newspapers, and black, slightly acrid filter coffee with sticky buns. Within the cabin, the windows were smeared with condensation. The passengers sat on brown plastic bench seats. On a small deck at the back were folding chairs, and one of the best views in the world. Nowhere was there an open horizon. It was like travelling through a Chinese painting, except that instead of mountains emerging from a featureless mist, these were islands rising steeply from the untroubled sea.

Yet, just as in a Chinese painting, the wildness of the scene, and its strangeness, accentuated the impression of harmony and civilization. The red or yellow wooden houses of the archipelago seemed products of a much more highly developed society than the newer houses of the inland suburbs.

There was a Chinese quality, too, to life out on Keith's island. His house, like the hut of a Taoist sage, was ramshackle, and could be reached only on foot from the jetty, or by a boat moored at the bottom of the garden. He grew a beard there, and learned Chinese calligraphy. He took huge relish in the difficulty of it and in the fact that he would never be really good however hard he worked at it. A respect for the difficulty of art, or anything else worthwhile, was engrained in his and Mary's characters, and the only things they really hated about Sweden were smugness and mediocrity. The Puritanism and melancholy might not be enjoyable, but if pressed we would all have agreed that they were the country's guarantee of worth.

We would sit on the high balcony and look over the water to the fortress of Vaxholm, a mile or so away, across so many invisible submarines. The evenings of the high north make for a terrifying Romanticism and extremes of temperament. People talk of 'putting the world to rights' when they converse, but only in the white nights of St Petersburg or Stockholm, when the extended daylight has a measurable effect, does it seem to the talkers that the world is coming right as they speak.

It was in the late spring of 1984, in Mary and Keith's Stockholm flat, that I started to read the unexpurgated dossier on the Aminoff case. It was three years since I had first written up the story, and I had lost touch with Eva Aminoff, but one day at home I got an excited telephone call from her, saying that Alexander – Child A – had escaped and had run away to Finland, where she had gone to meet him. On the same day I caught the train to Stockholm, and then took one of the big boats across the archipelago to Finland.

These boats almost constituted a fifth Scandinavian country, one in which all distractions had been removed from the business of getting drunk. They held several thousand passengers distributed across eight decks; I never counted the bars. At the entrance to the men's lavatories stood waist-high porcelain funnels, for the convenience of those customers who could not reach the lavatories before vomiting. You could buy drink in all the restaurants, outside the casinos, and in the most expensive duty free shops in the world. This was, for most passengers, the point of the trip, since on the mainland at both ends, the sale of drink was a state monopoly and everything possible was done to discourage people from actually buying any.

Eva and Alexander were staying with an old friend of hers in an old-fashioned flat: we talked in front of a window shaded by plants whose long straight leaves fell across it like bars. Alexander proved to be a lanky adolescent who claimed to have made his escape by building a raft in secret on the island where he had been held and then paddling across to the mainland and hitch-hiking to Stockholm, where he had managed to find his mother.

We talked for three hours. During his time on the island, he said, he had not been allowed to go to school nor to maintain any contact with the outside world. When he fled, he had left all his clothes and possessions behind. He asked me: would I collect them for him? The foster father would almost certainly beat me senseless if we met, but perhaps I was brave enough to try. He solemnly signed a piece of paper asking me to do this. Eva was very excited by the thought of being proved right before the world. She would be remembered, she said, as the woman who changed the law in Sweden.

When I caught the night boat back with my story I was so disturbed by what I had heard that I drank myself into a stupor and woke in my cabin after the boat had docked in Stockholm, emptied itself of passengers, reloaded, and turned around for a day cruise to the Åland isles. A terrible hangover gradually receded as the boat moved unhurriedly around the archipelago. I seemed suspended between land and water, between apocalypse and shame. The horizon was a golden haze, mercifully still. When I left that weightless, slowly turning world, and disembarked in Stockholm eight hours late, I was forced to acknowledge my feelings: I didn't entirely believe the Aminoff story.

I hired a car and drove out to Strängnäs, where I found the house that Alexander had been staying in. It was indeed on an island, but there was a perfectly good causeway to the mainland. If that had not been enough to discredit the story of the raft, there were ten dinghies and sailing boats tied up at the lake. I spent the afternoon talking to the foster father: a straightforward-seeming, forceful man, who greeted me in a perfectly friendly way and showed me Alexander's diaries and some of his school reports. It was immediately clear that this had not been and could not have been a prison. Alexander had attended school on the mainland, travelling back and forth by bus on his own. His mother had written to him. He could at any time have written back or phoned; in fact she'd asked him to, but he would not. The diaries and letters, read in the light of reality, made it quite clear that Eva was delusional, and that her son, when he arrived, had also had difficulties with reality.

I drove back to Stockholm, bewildered as to how we could all have got it so wrong. I had made an appointment with Lennart Hane, Eva's lawyer, to see the files in the case, so that I could refresh my memory of it before writing; but when I got to his office late that evening he had gone, and his secretary simply handed me the dossiers that the social workers had compiled. The case was over. The Aminoffs would obviously never return to Sweden until Alexander was eighteen. No one had a reason to care.

There were two dossiers, about four centimetres thick in total. I had already seen the later one; the other, which made sense of it, was new to me. Both came as Xeroxes of typewritten originals, marked by close attention from at least three hands. Some pages had broad strokes of highlighter, which Hane favoured; there were neat, pencilled annotations that I think must have been Sundberg-Weitman's, and then Eva's own angry notes in scarlet ink. The more I read, the more obvious it became that the truth was in the bureaucratic typewriting, rather than the red ink.

By the evening of the third day I worked out that almost everything I had ever believed about the case was untrue. I had spent three days going through the papers in the plain grey cell that was my workroom, just off our bedroom in Uddevalla. There was a table, a typewriter, a telephone and a bookcase. A window above the table gave a view of the enclosed playground, around which four three-storey blocks of flats were arranged. When I finished it was a quiet May evening, as safe as life was supposed to be beneath the shelter of the helicopter.

The story had only seemed credible because everyone who told it, and who told it to themselves, had felt in different ways entirely alienated from the country that they lived in. Swedes or not, they felt themselves strangers in Sweden. To be expelled from respectability, from the consensus, was like being thrown out of a space station. There was nowhere else to go, no gravity, no natural orientation. We had tumbled, giddy and unanchored, through black space, believing anything, trusting only the other outsiders.

From next door, Anita asked when I was coming to bed. In a moment, I replied, and for a few moments fiddled with the papers, neatening the pile on my desk. I had an urge to pick up a pen and dig it into something, writing as if I could press down through into the truth. Instead, I picked up the telephone for the last time that day. Brita Sundberg-Weitman had read all these papers years before me and concluded that Eva Aminoff was more credible than all the witnesses ranged against her. I think I found this more distressing even than the story of evil and madness in the dossier. I now had all the evidence anyone could need to show she'd been mistaken – though I knew, I suppose, that these mistakes could not have been innocent. She must at first have wanted to use the case to make a point about the evils of the social democratic state. Later, it would have been impossibly humiliating to admit she had been wrong.

I wanted our conversation to be friendly but it writhed around this hook. Whenever I checked a disputed or suppressed fact with her she would claim either that it was unimportant, or that it was too unlikely to be true, or that the court should never have taken it into account. 'But, Andrew, how could you believe a social worker?' she asked, breaking into her excellent English. Her tone suggested that I'd confessed to beating my own children while drunk and locking them in the attic. Later, I asked some final detailed question about what she'd known and when. I am no longer co-operating with you on this story, she said, and hung up.

It had been forty-five minutes since I said I would be coming to bed in a moment. When I came into the bedroom, Anita was pretending to be asleep and I pretended to believe her. A week or so later, I went back to England, and the *Spectator* published a long article of mine admitting, if not unduly emphasizing, what a fool I had been about the Aminoffs. What a fool I had been about my own wife and son while I was working on the story remained a mystery to me for some months more, and when I saw it, I thought of it for years as yet another example of Eva's extraordinary capacity for destruction. She was unscrupulous in offering stories her victims might want to believe. But we had to want to believe them ourselves. In 1965, after a drunken quarrel, Eva had reported her then husband to the police on a charge of attempted murder. Adolf Aminoff had told the investigating inspector (who concluded the story was nonsense) that his wife believed there were only two sorts of people in the world, authors and idiots; and this was also what I had believed.

13

England

For one or two weeks each summer, Anita and I visited my parents in Godalming. Surrey, the county of stockbroker-Tudor houses and horse-brasses in pubs, seems to me the place furthest on earth from Sweden. Instead of the vertiginously changing seasons everything is frozen at room temperature in an unchanging drizzly light. Even the soil of clay and sand is dead. Nothing looks modern or artificial; nothing is in reality old or natural. Only the trains to London were honestly disgusting: they smelled of grit and grease and childhood misery, as if every one was carrying me off to school.

My parents lived in a house with high-ceilinged rooms in which everything was tasteful and calm. It was filled with exquisite, impenetrable manners from which Anita hung as if they had been barbed wire. It all seemed part of the natural order of things. I scarcely noticed that I was shuffling round in the mud and rats of the family trench system, or that every night in our bedroom I patrolled to the other side. I talked all the time there, inexhaustibly showing off to everyone, but no one would ever say anything important out loud. Unspeakable things unsaid rang in my ears all day. I wanted to get back to the whisperings of the forest, and one year I took my fly rod onto the Surrey lawn, where I cast again and again over the roses (the back cast flew over the gravelled drive) until after two or three hours the sweat running down my arm reacted with the black foam plastic handle of my fly rod and I developed terrible eczema. My fingers swelled and bubbled like melting plastic. Anita looked up from her book in our room. My God, she said – she has a lovely smile – they look like crayfish claws; and that is what we called them for the next five years. The claws did not stop me fishing, of course. They merely convinced me that I must spend an extra forty pounds on a fly rod with a cork handle, made in Norway.

Every time we visited my parents, things were worse. After a while I no longer needed to touch a fly rod to bring my eczema out. Touching anything in Surrey would make my hands swell and itch. I rubbed my blistered fingers on the rivets of my jeans until they bled and this would stop them hurting for a while. And I went fishing. Quite close to where my parents lived, at Willingshurst, there was a lake where Brian Clarke had fished in the early Seventies. It figured in a chapter called 'Early experiences of practising what I preach'. He had caught three fish, one after another, as he saw them moving along the edge of the lake towards him and immediately deduced what they were eating and how to cast the right fly so that it was waiting for them as they swam by, without offering them any chance to see him. Then he had gone to a smaller lake in the woods and caught several more by spotting the faintest glimmer in the dark water, and, realizing that this meant a trout four feet under the surface, had seized a midge-pupa half an inch long. After that, he could cast out his own imitation and wait for the gleam to come before hooking the fish.

I never saw such things in real life, but I watched for them with such fanaticism that I must have missed innumerable fish whose signals would have been obvious to anyone who had not read Clarke's book. For some reason the easy, selfless predatory instinct, which in Sweden had guided me to all those pike, deserted me whenever I held a fly rod in my hands. Whatever my technical accomplishments as a fly-caster and a fly-tier, I was blinded, when I was trying to catch fish, by the idea that there was a right way to do it, the way that Brian Clarke would have done it. So it was with very high hopes that I took Felix to Willingshurst, when he was four and a half.

I had made him his first fly rod that summer, spreading my threads and glues and varnish bottles over the polished mahogany dining table in my parents' house. The rod was a perfect child's wand, built with as much magic as I could summon. It was only two metres long and the grip was thin enough for the smallest hand. I had anguished for half an hour in the shop between scarlet and viridian silk to whip on the lightest rings I could find. Even with a reel and line, it weighed virtually nothing.

At one corner of the smallest lake in the woods there was a little concrete outwork; it probably concealed the mechanism that kept the water looking natural. There we sat, with our legs dangling over the edge, each wearing, like uniforms, waistcoats made up almost entirely of pockets to hold everything that might help to charm a trout: there were fly boxes, spools of nylon in differing thickness, tubs of unguent to make the nylon sink, and grease to make it float. None of these helped Felix to cast, though he loved the dressing up. There were trout feeding quite close to us, but in the end I laid my own rod down and cast his line out, telling him to watch. The line lay across the dark water like a stroke from a calligraphy brush. At the end, it vanished and the meaning was clear. I was almost blind with apprehension. I knew a trout was mouthing at the fly. I knocked his rod into the air with my forearm so the fish was hooked. 'There! You see?' I said. 'You caught a fish!'

We killed it, of course. There is still a photograph some-where of the two of us crouching in front of a laurel hedge in my parents' garden: Felix holding up a distended, gutted little battery trout. We both are smiling because we know it is expected of us. But I can admit now, nearly twenty years later, that he has never really liked fishing. Sometimes I say that he has never seen the point of fishing but in some sense he has seen the point of it all too well.

Later that summer I returned to England alone, and when Felix asked in the car when Daddy was coming back from this trip I could not answer.

I could have stayed and become a Swede, I think. I never wrote anything longer than magazine and newspaper articles in Swedish, but if I had applied myself I might have found some kind of literary language there. I certainly could speak in my own voice.

But ambition was an essential part of my unhappiness. If I could function at all as a grown-up, I wanted to be one at whom the whole world marvelled. And London, in turn, seemed marvellous to me, stimulating and sating a thousand appetites. In the days before Ryanair, the cheapest way to visit the city was to book a package holiday for a week, which would give me a hotel room and a flight for less than I could otherwise pay for a return air ticket. The hotels were ghastly, plaster-boarded warrens in Bayswater or Earl's Court, where the doors clicked shut with Yale locks as soon as I shuffled away down the corridor to the shower room. But they were also the anterooms to paradise. One night, newly arrived in a fourth-floor room in Earl's Court, I lay on a narrow bed smoking by the open window with a glass of whisky balanced on the window ledge. I could smell the city more distinctly than I could hear it. I could see nothing but the sky just before dusk. When I drank the whisky, slowly but all in one go, I felt as joyous as a falcon; hovering on an uprush of delight, I realized that I could never be happier or hungrier.

London did not seem to me the least like England. It was a city that filled all horizons: a third, unconquered country in my life. Even the small lonelinesses of life in Sweden seemed to burn away there. I believed I had found a place where I was understood and liked for what I did well. Of course, this place wasn't a geographical entity: it was an alley off Grub Street that would lead, I believed, to the glorious freedom of the Republic of Letters. Well, anyway.

Anita and I never consciously agreed we were divorcing until long after it was too late. Instead we came to one of our terse agreements that she would come over to England when I had established myself in the trade sufficiently to support them both, although this may have seemed an impossibly distant goal to her. But I did slowly claw myself a niche in London. I even found a flat in Bayswater, no more than a bedsit really, in a cobbled mews. I wrote to her from there once, on a May morning when I felt happier than I had done in years. I hadn't seen her since the New Year. I thought we should split up, I said; I didn't think we any longer could really help each other. There had been too many silences for too long. In the second paragraph I said that I had found someone else, although, I explained, this was not the reason.

I never posted that letter. I remained superficial. I felt so proud of my own honesty and courage in writing it that I never managed to show it to the woman whose vivid yellow hair on my scarlet pillow had inspired it, nor to post it to Anita. Instead, I wrote, and this time posted, a short note saying that if she still wanted to come, she had better do so quickly.

I told the woman with the yellow hair that I had to leave her. I tried to leave her. I went back to Uddevalla to organize things with Anita and we all went out to the lake house to camp for the last time. I don't think we ever quarrelled there. The pressure of other people's domesticity was too much. All our friends were divorced except us, and the lake house had become a sort of shrine for some of them: a place where they could build a house where people didn't quarrel and betray each other. So when we came back for the last time as a married couple, we were quiet and tender. But when we came to embrace, I could only kiss her. Afterwards, I walked down to the lake. I could see across the water a grove of birch trees and their reflections, all very empty, all very clear. It was still evening, almost as bright as daylight; but the sun had long gone and with it the warmth of the day, the air had a blue metallic tinge as if it had changed places with the lake. Nothing disturbed the water; not even the memory of yearning. For a long time I had been home in exile but now I couldn't get back.

She and Felix came over in the early autumn. Until the catastrophic experiment was made of having him live in England, Felix and I had talked to each other in such a seamless mixture of languages that I hardly noticed they were almost all Swedish. He was sent to an excellent school but was quite lost there; for one thing, everyone spoke English. Anita was desperately unhappy in England, too. She knew that I didn't love her. I didn't know that I didn't love her and was correspondingly cruel. They returned, for good, to Sweden before Christmas and I did not see her again for six years.

She remained friends with our upstairs neighbour Kristina and her son. He and Felix were much thrown together, especially after I moved to England. Kristina and Anita used to go out to the lake house together for weekends with their sons, though none of them fished. On one of these trips they found themselves sharing the lake house with a man who had been a member of one of the local drug rings, known as the moped gang for their method of delivering amphetamines. He was off the pills now, but still crazy, and at some stage in the weekend, he picked up an axe and threatened the women with it. Somehow, they talked him down. I don't know who did it: both of them are quite brave enough, but when I heard some of the story – months later – and understood that I had not been around to protect anyone I realized for the very last time that I really was divorced.

Some time after that, Lasse and Kristina got together. They had a daughter, and eventually moved to an old house on a hill to the south of Uddevalla, where Kristina had grown up, a part of town so peaceful that Lasse once saw a beaver walking down the road outside. At the top of the hill above their house is a place where elk can be seen, and in winter deer stalk daintily down from the woods to eat at their bird feeder.

In the autumn of 1985, when my marriage collapsed like a building blown open, so did my political ideas and any sense that I might have found another home inside an ideology. A Conservative think tank hired me to write a report about Ray Honeyford, a Bradford headmaster who was in trouble for writing rude things about multiculturalism in principle, and Pakistani Islam in practice, in small-circulation magazines. It seemed outrageous to me that a headmaster should have to moderate his opinions because of the opinions of parents. If he didn't know more than they did, why was he the headmaster? That was pretty much Honeyford's view, too. He saw himself as bringing enlightenment to a rather benighted corner of Bradford.

The difficulty arose in the first place from the fact that Bradford's Conservative council was not very interested in enlightenment values if they upset the voters. The leaders of the mosques opposed Honeyford because he wanted girls to do PE and objected to their being taken back to Pakistan to be married; a small minority of white left-wing parents opposed him because they thought he was a reactionary. I thought them unscrupulous and silly, but his backers in London were quite as unscrupulous. The pamphlet was commissioned by the education sub-committee of the Centre for Policy Studies, which was on the outer rings of the Thatcherite orbit; its members were either heading for outer darkness and the House of Lords, or working their way in to real power. But no one knew who was which and the hatreds within it were terrible. In particular, the chairman of the committee, Alfred Sherman, who had started his political career as a communist machine-gunner in the Spanish Civil War and carried this attitude to his opponents, even after he had become one of Mrs Thatcher's closest advisers in opposition, now had nothing but a consuming hatred of everyone to sustain him. He hated socialists, lefties, Muslims, and foreigners, obviously. But none of them could provoke the furious, despairing contempt he lavished on the 'Finchley Woman', as he called the Prime Minister. If he started talking about her, he could not stop, and business would be suspended for five or ten minutes while he denounced her for a coward, a traitor, and the thief of his precious revolution.

I quite rapidly discovered that there was absolutely nothing, as things then stood, that would enable London-based politicians to help Honeyford. He was employed by the Local Education Authority, and if they, along with a majority of his parents, had turned against him, the best outcome he could hope for was a sizeable pay-off. Had he been the kind of outstanding headmaster and free-range intellectual that the education sub-committee wished to pretend this might not have been a problem. He could have found a job elsewhere, and continued to write. But he was only a good headmaster, and a decent man, and the members of the committee knew this. They were never going to find him a real job; they certainly didn't think he was a first-class metropolitan intellectual, as they so obviously were. They wanted this to be a great affair of principle: I remember at one meeting, a woman arguing that Honeyford, then suspended from his job, must not take the proffered settlement from his employers, because he was close to a nervous breakdown, and if he did crack up, this would make a really edifying story about the wickedness of the loony left.

Under the circumstances, I found it hard to deliver a pamphlet that would satisfy everyone and when I finally produced one saying that the matter was complicated, and even if Honeyford had a perfect right to say what he did, and even if he was correct as to policy, it was difficult to see how a democratic council could impose him against the will of the local voters, the sub-committee dissolved itself rather than be responsible for publishing the pamphlet. With that resignation, Alfred Sherman lost his last foothold in policy-making circles. Later I came to suspect that this had been the point of the whole exercise.

Honeyford eventually took the money, as was inevitable, and retired to Bury. For some years he wrote opinion pieces for the

Daily Telegraph; later his opinions grew less useful and were published only as letters to the editor.

I had other things to worry about. But the rapt, humourless vindictiveness of almost everyone involved came as a great shock to me; a reminder, perhaps, of how long I had been away from my expensive schools and how successfully I had forgotten them. Obviously, I wanted to be a person at the hub, and not on the periphery; one of the disposers of the world and not one of the disposables. But now that I had been both, this division didn't seem desirable to me, merely inevitable. I had mocked Sweden for failing to live up to its own ideals, but I had always supposed these were ideals that everyone shared. I had not considered the possibility that some people could *want* a less equal society. I assumed that most people thought like I did, that inequality grew naturally out of human nature and was something to be overcome so far as possible. No one in Sweden, I thought, would have treated anyone quite as savagely as poor old Honeyford was treated; or, if they had, they would have been a little bit ashamed, and not thought of themselves as especially clever for it. It was perhaps the first kind of admiring thought I had had about the country in months, a seed waiting in the darkness.

In the years that followed that autumn of catastrophe I learned slowly how to be a real journalist, writing about different subjects. First was a book about the police, in a part of East London that seemed to me at least as foreign as Sweden had ever been. After I had finished that, the *Independent*, then just starting, hired me. Since neither I nor the editors had any clear idea of what I might usefully do, they made me the religious affairs correspondent and I turned out to be quite good at it. The first few years of the paper were about as much fun as anyone could ever hope to be paid for.

I remember the Archbishop of York leaning against the battlements of Windsor Castle with me, looking across at the chapel of his old school where it rose from the valley mist, and complaining that another Etonian, then editor of the *Sunday Telegraph*, had clearly not been taught history there, or else he would not write so foolishly about the Church of England; I remember a dark-haired woman with huge eyes sitting against the light in a pub called the Angel; I was sometimes so eager to get into the office in the mornings that I would run up the concrete steps from Old Street tube station as the sharp smells of the cobbler's shop in the underpass receded.

14

Murder

It was a murder that first brought me back to Sweden as a stranger. Olof Palme was shot on the street in the middle of Stockholm as he walked home with his wife from the cinema on the night of Friday, 28 February 1986.

His funeral cortège passed through Stockholm for an hour that seemed to last that whole brief day. It was an atheistic ceremony – you could hardly get a more atheistic celebrant than a progressive Lutheran bishop – but it was organized as a piece of theatre by the party, which bound a tight bundle of order and grief that was profoundly religious. While the procession circled the centre of the city I walked among the quiet crowds, who kept their hats on against the chill and rubbed at their tears with gloved hands. I remember deep drums beating like inexorable waves. In one of the quiet streets a little back from the route of the cortège, I stopped to weep myself. I had not liked the idea of Palme, and had written some remarkably silly things about him, but the tears ran out of me as if I were crushed by the icy sky.

When Palme had been transport minister, the narrow, curving streets of central Stockholm had been straightened and reproportioned to suit cars; their dark and decorated houses were replaced with giant concrete shoeboxes which seemed light and clean and curiously hopeful in summer, and in winter funnelled the cold wind into your eyes. The old part of town had been full of bars, known as restaurants. In the new creation there were only alcoholics in the parks: shouting men and raw-faced women, beyond the bounds of decency; we supposed that most of them were Finns.

To the south of the centre in the Old Town, the narrow streets and massive palaces and court buildings of the oldest bureaucratic state in Europe seemed unchanged since the seventeenth century, when the Swedish empire stretched from southern Germany eastwards into Russia. To the north, the heavy brown rows of mansion blocks, monuments to nineteenth-century prosperity, ground against the stony sky like molars as they rose up the slope to the wind-whipped district of Siberia. To the west, where Lake Mälaren opens into a bright, heart-lifting harbour, after its constricted rush past the parliament building, the mansion flats are more spacious, too, and brighter. This is Östermalm, where Palme grew up, the district of foreign diplomats and aristocrats, who might as well have been foreign for all their contact with the stream of public life around them.

Sometimes when I weep, I can continue thinking, as if my mind were still, working among the tears like a research submersible. I thought then that I was not weeping for Olof Palme; that perhaps no one in the crowd was doing that. We wept for each other and for all the futures that would never be; all the past that could not have been real, for if it had been, this could not have happened. The country we had lived in was cracked open like a roofless house in winter.

After Palme's death, Sweden became, for a while, a foreign

country to itself. Until he was shot, the country had seemed to be focused on the light-grey modern centre which his cortège wound round on its way from the city hall to the graveyard: a clean region of government buildings, libraries, railway stations, department stores, employment exchanges, insurance companies, hotels and social security offices, each very like the other. Now it was apparent that a terrible, disruptive power lurked outside these ordered precincts and held them at its mercy.

No one knew whether the killer had come from within Sweden or from outside. There was a feeling of foreignness everywhere. It could have come from the outside – Palme's foreign policies had made him enemies practised in assassination. He was the UN's mediator in the Iran–Iraq war. He supported the ANC; some people thought the South Africans had had him killed. There was a theory that the Kurdish terrorists of the PKK had killed him. Croat fascist terrorists had operated in Sweden in the past. His murderer might have been a single Swedish madman – there might even have been a conspiracy of madmen.

Lisbet Palme, who had been grazed by a bullet, had glimpsed the killer as he ran away. He was pale. He wore a dark jacket and he knew the city. After the shots, he dashed up a narrow staircase to the next parallel street. There he could have reached a waiting accomplice in a car. He could have simply run through the streets – almost empty at that time on a February night.

Palme had no bodyguards, and there were hardly any police on duty. It took five hours before enough were found to put up roadblocks; the (married) chief of police was off in the countryside having a dirty weekend with one of his subordinates and could not be reached. On the other hand, the murder was so far outside their experience that it could hardly had been planned for. You might as well have asked them to defend the prime minister against pigs falling from balconies. The murder rate in Sweden was astonishingly low, at around a hundred a year. The last political assassination had been the murder of Gustavus Adolphus III, at a masked ball in 1792; and, while the police spent years with no idea who might have killed the Prime Minister, it was clear from the start that the murderer – whoever he was – had almost certainly been a stranger.

Nor were there any real terrorists who had a grudge against Sweden, even if some groups were active there against their enemies at home. There was nothing like the Baader-Meinhof gang in Sweden. The grim incompetence of the Palme investigation was forelit, rather than foreshadowed, by *The Terrorists*, the very last of the Sjöwall and Wahlöö books.

Sjöwall and Wahlöö's terrorists are a sinister and ridiculous amalgam of Spectre and global capitalism; their leader is, of course, a white right-wing South African. They are hugely professional and have been hired to assassinate an American politician – a sort of Ronald Reagan figure – when he visits Stockholm. Only the collective genius of Beck and his team defeats them, by working out where they will plant their bomb, which will be detonated by remote control, and then arranging with Sveriges Radio to delay its live coverage by fifteen minutes, so that by the time the terrorists in their hiding place see the cortège go past, the police have cleared the area and damped down the explosion with sandbags.

The contrast of this cold-blooded efficiency with the panicked and incredulous inefficiency of both the police and Sveriges Radio when Palme was assassinated twelve years later could hardly be greater. But there is another, even more unreal element to *The Terrorists*. After the plot against the American senator has been foiled, the book's Swedish prime minister is murdered, almost casually. No one in the novel is greatly affected by the death of the prime minister. There is no suggestion of the convulsion of grief and self-reproach that affected the country when Palme was assassinated. At the precise moment when a sense of irreparable, adult loss overwhelmed the country in real life, the fiction retreated to childish omnipotence. The fact that it could shows what made the real loss so awful – that an assassination had been something so unthinkable in that it could be played with in daydreams without consequences.

Sjöwall and Wahlöö's killer is a girl who symbolizes the alienation of late capitalism and doesn't do much else. The action opens when she is arrested for carrying out an accidental bank robbery by mistake. She had walked into a bank and asked for money, since she had heard that banks are places you go to when you need some. She is eighteen, and a single mother, but has not been much troubled by the details of the capitalist system – such as how you get money – up till now. As a child of nature and keen gardener, she is wearing a pruning knife at her waist. (This touch, by the way, is completely credible. Knives were used for fighting nature and sometimes worn around town by perfectly respectable people.) But the bank has instructed its employees to react to robbers simply by handing over the money and alerting the police. This, say the authors, is because it's cheaper that way than to have to pay compensation if an employee is heroic and gets shot. So when the gormless Miss Lind shuffles barefoot to the counter with a knife at her hip and asks for money, meaning a loan, the cashier presses the hidden alarm and starts filling a carrier bag with bank notes, while the unwitting robber looks on, wondering if all transactions will be this simple in the future. In due course, the police arrive, the girl is arrested, the banknotes are scattered all over the floor.

She wanted the money to visit America, where her boyfriend and father of her child, a Vietnam deserter, has disappeared after being promised safe-conduct to visit his parents. The perfidious American authorities have jailed him instead. When she later discovers he has hanged himself in an American jail, she decides to shoot the Swedish Prime Minister, and does so, assisted by the uselessness of the police detail guarding him.

That uselessness is the last fragment of realism in the book. On confessing, she is given the longest aria yet, in which she denounces all grown-ups: 'Everybody lies. It's terrible to live in a world where people just lie to each other. But everyone believes they have to lie to make it in this life, and when those who are most important tell other people what they must and mustn't do, then things must be like this. How can a villain and a traitor make decisions for the whole country?'

Yet *The Terrorists* preserves, in the way that only popular culture can, many of the things that everybody knew before we knew better. It is very difficult for anyone to recapture the sense that people had in the Palme years that the future was both inevitable and largely understood. It is perhaps most difficult for those who lived in the expectations of that future, for they had also to live through the subsequent disillusions, and this is a process which is irreversible. The future, when it arrives, changes the past as well, and cuts us off from the past that we actually lived in, which could only make sense from the vantage of a future that has disappeared.

In the future that actually happened, Palme's murderer was never officially found. It seems certain that he was in fact Christer Pettersson, an alcoholic and speed freak, who had murdered a stranger with a bayonet in the early Seventies, served time for it, and been released.

That it should be an ordinary random criminal somehow

makes the whole story more humiliating. Most of the conspiracy theories that grew up inside and outside the police investigation required that there be powerful foreigners who were so offended by Swedish policies that they decided Palme must be swept aside. After all, two Swedish diplomats had been murdered abroad in the late 1940s for their work for peace – Raoul Wallenberg, who disappeared after falling into the hands of the secret police in Hungary, and Folke Bernadotte, assassinated in Cairo by the Stern gang. But no sinister foreigners, it appears, cared enough about Palme or Sweden to think him worth murdering.

Christer Pettersson was tried and convicted of the Palme murder in 1988, largely on the strength of Lisbet Palme's identification, but later released on appeal – because she had understood from the police that he was guilty before being asked to identify him. The murder weapon was never found. On his release, he was paid compensation for wrongful arrest, money that he proudly and publicly spent on drink and drugs. So long as the gun could not be found, he could confess that he had killed Palme without running the risk of any kind of legal retribution. From time to time he would announce that he might have done it, but was too stoned to remember; or that he *had* done it – but then he would withdraw the confession. His motive, had he needed any motive for murder towards the end of a thirty-day amphetamine binge, is supposed to have been to avenge the prison sentence imposed on another notable Stockholm criminal, who had attempted to bomb the national tax authority's offices. Pettersson died in 2004 after a drunken fall off a park bench. The revolver with which he probably shot Palme was retrieved in 2006, after a gigantic effort, from the hydro-electric scheme into which he had thrown it, but by that time it was impossible to recover any evidence from it which would link him to the crime.

15

Downturn

In the summer of 1989, I returned to Sweden as a rich man – or at least a man on generous expenses – for the first time. Pope John Paul II was touring Scandinavia, and I was part of the entourage of journalists who followed him. In all his travels around the world, I don't think anyone ever saw him in a more alien environment, even though it was just across the Baltic from his Polish home. In Tromsö, in the very far north of Norway, the Catholic population was almost entirely made up of Vietnamese boat people. He celebrated mass for them, a couple of hundred people, in broad daylight at ten in the evening. There was still snow on the mountains and after the service was over, the Norwegian foreign ministry took us out on a fishing boat into the fjord, where we could jig for cod with hand lines and eat our catch freshly boiled on the deck afterwards. There was not a whole lot else to do in Tromsö, even though it has a university and a brewery, both of them further north than the northernmost point in Alaska. When we returned, the more adventurous of us went off to dance in a nightclub where the curtains were tightly drawn to keep the daylight out, and then there was time for an hour's sleep before flying on to Finland.

In the city of Turku – Åbo to Swedes – a walkabout had been arranged from the station to the Cathedral, and the streets were hardly even lined one deep. The spectators were neither hostile nor reverent. They were benevolently bewildered as to what the point of a Pope might be. As I sat next to a delightful woman from Finnish radio in the cathedral, listening to the papal homily, she whispered to me '*feel*' and put my hand on her thigh. 'I never normally do this. But I have put on stockings and a garter belt, just to show what I think of his views on women!'

We arranged to meet that evening in Helsinki, but I rang her from my hotel and said I was ambivalent about the whole thing because I was married. This was true. I had found a pretty, intelligent English woman. When you're a young and moderately fashionable journalist, the world seems full of pretty and intelligent women, but this one liked fishing and Felix, too, and was prepared to devote time to both of them.

When the papal tour reached Stockholm, I went out to Keith's island and we all sat, as we had done so often, on the balcony to talk. When I told them I had remarried, Mary asked, 'What colour are her eyes?' She was curious as to whether I had noticed: no wonder I loved them both. Keith had recovered from a bad depression brought on by a false diagnosis of liver cancer and was planning to abandon Stockholm altogether, and live either in France or on his island. We talked a little about the economy. There was a right-wing social democratic government in power, and it had started to chop a little at the gilding on the social democratic state. Down in Uddevalla, the shipyard had finally been allowed to go broke when the state subsidies ran out in 1985; and in 1987 Felix and Anita, along with almost everyone else in town, stood to watch as the cranes were dynamited, and crumpled to the ground.

Everyone in town then thought that there would be a factory along to replace it.

Keith was more concerned about pensions than anything short-term and particular such as the shipyards. We had known for years that they could not compete with foreign industries. 'When I get old, I will have two Swedes working for me,' he said, meaning that the ratio of pensioners would soon be unsustainable. But he said it with relish, confident that it would be a problem for the workers, not for him. Indoors, the television was full of the Tiananmen Square protests, so I drank the good whisky that Keith had brought back from Scotland with a clear conscience. Unless the Pope was shot, nothing that I wrote that week could possibly get in the paper, and now that I was on staff this didn't bother me at all. It was an early June evening. The light never entirely left the sky above the sea. We talked as if life could go on forever.

The next day I, who had once saved for six months to buy a £50 mail-order fly rod from Cardiff, walked into one of the grander shops in Stockholm and paid for a £250 American rod with a credit card; it wasn't even for me, but a present for my wife. I was rich precisely to the extent of my most avaricious dreams. In Uppsala the Pope preached in the great round hall of the university, trying to summon Sweden back to its Christian roots as part of Europe; later he went out to the grassy mounds, which are all that remain of the pagan capital there, and preached again. It was difficult to tell which religion felt deader, or further from the Sweden all around me. Only among immigrants, and especially Croats, was he popular. At a party I met the senior Roman Catholic priest in Sweden – I can't remember if he was even a bishop – who had maintained a strong Birmingham accent even after eighteen years in the Swedish provinces. This was disconcerting when he spoke Swedish.

Almost his entire flock were immigrants or their children; Sweden was such a homogeneously Protestant country that in 1938 there were more Jews than Roman Catholics there, and there were not many Jews. Among the ethnic Swedes, only a few intellectuals, who wanted to distance themselves as much as possible from Social Democracy, became Roman Catholics and this was a gesture so baroque it was mostly, politely, ignored.

Sweden, it seemed, was still entirely unmoved by the convulsions in Europe beneath it. The autumn before, I had been in East Berlin in the last week of its separate existence, where I had seen quiet women in late middle age praying and going on hunger strike in a Lutheran church, while plain-clothes police lounged around the porch to intimidate them: tall, beefy young men in leather jackets and the only trainers that could be seen anywhere in the East. Their piety and courage had shaken the regime; it might never have collapsed without them. It was difficult to imagine any member of the Swedish Lutheran church in that context. They lived in another Europe: psychologically, the Baltic was wider than the Atlantic Ocean.

In the autumn of that year I was in Poland, writing about the role that the Church had played in the collapse of Communism and trying to give up smoking when the phone rang in my hotel room in Warsaw. Keith was dead. He had woken in the flat on a Saturday feeling funny; by the time that feeling had turned into what looked like a heart attack, it was too late, because no one likes to work on Saturdays and it took a couple of hours for a non-urgent ambulance to arrive, even though they lived in the middle of Stockholm. So he never saw the end of Social Democracy in Sweden. But he had been saying that it was inevitable for so long perhaps he thought its inevitability could be postponed forever. Almost everyone else did, then: it is always a shock when something that can't go on forever just stops.

The rout started with a financial crisis. The *krona* collapsed even though interest rates had been screwed right up to defend it. Until then it had been understood that politics worked with a sort of ratchet mechanism: governments might change, but the progress was always in the same direction. The Social Democrats and their allies developed social democratic policies, and the Conservatives and their allies conserved them. After the crisis, everyone in the country would have seen the point of Keith's joke about his pension: 'When I get old, I'll have two Swedes working for me'.

In the late summer of 1991 the news that things had stopped had not reached Lilla Edet, in any event. There was still a bus station where drink could be delivered if it had been ordered 24 hours previously from the *Systembolag* in Trollhättan. At one end of the bus station was the kiosk that sold sausages – grilled or boiled – with sweet mustard and mashed potato slightly flavoured with nutmeg. At the other end was the newsagent's stand where the passing of time was marked only by the changing billboards for the celebrity magazines, which had a curious stately innocence. No one outside the country would have heard of the celebrities in them, who never did anything very scandalous. Once every three or four months there would be a headline about a popular singer: 'LILL-BABS' NEW LOVE', and even though I hadn't seen the place for nearly ten years, I was reassured to see that the kiosk was still going, and that Lill-Babs had just found love again.

I had been sent over to cover the election campaign. In

Gothenburg I rented a little car and as I drove around I passed almost everyone else on the road, to show I was a foreigner now.

Given the extraordinary emptiness of Swedish roads, it had always seemed one of the distinguishing features of the country that people did not speed. In Denmark, this makes more sense because the country is crowded. Finland, though also empty, seems full of rally drivers. Norwegian roads are often terrible, so that it would take Finnish courage to speed on them. Only in Sweden would you find people driving in cars that can do 180 kph on wide, empty roads at 90 kph because that was the speed limit.

This was a puzzle, because there weren't that many speed traps away from the frontier. In Norway, where the speed limit was even lower, the police took a sadistic and profitable pleasure in trapping Swedes as they hurtled across the border at more than 80 kph. Norwegian drivers, rendered light-headed and lead-footed by the freedom of the Swedish roads, were busted in turn all down the main road from the frontier to Gothenburg. But off in the back roads you were more likely to hit an elk than a speed trap. What kept us honest was the thought that the police had helicopters that watched the whole country for evil-doing drivers.

After I had passed my test, and bought our first car, I always knew that the helicopter brooded over my freedom and my adulthood, like the eye of God, ensuring I never enjoyed them to excess. Everyone had a friend who had a friend who knew someone who had been caught by the helicopter, and the loss of licence was a terrible punishment. Part of the problem was that once you started breaking the law on these wide empty roads, there was no natural limit to your speed. If you trusted your own judgement, rather than that of society, you might as well drive at three times the speed limit as just over it. When a British officer, Captain Simon Hayward, was caught smuggling a huge quantity of drugs into Sweden in the late Eighties, he was tracked by the helicopter as he hurtled up the road to Stockholm. That was easy to understand; what was hard even to believe was just how fast he drove. I would have thought it physically impossible to travel at twice the speed limit, not because it was, but because it was unthinkable.

Beneath the helicopter we were undeniably safe. Driving at legal speeds with the seatbelt on in a car that was thoroughly tested every year, the only thing that could kill you on those roads was old age. It was not just the roads: all Swedish life was meant to be conducted with the same stately security as one drove. There were to be no accidents that really damaged life. The blows of unemployment, illness, or simple inadequacy were all cushioned as if by airbags. Equality was to some extent a shibboleth; but security – *trygghet* – was something people really wanted, both for themselves and for others.

But in the elections of 1991 *trygghet* had disappeared and the whole country was on the edge of panic. There had been race riots in some of the smaller towns where employment had stopped. A psychopathic sniper shot eleven dark-skinned men at random (one died) over a period of seven months in Stockholm and Uppsala, using a rifle equipped with laser sights. When he was finally caught, he turned out to be a foreigner by origin, half-German and half-Swiss, who had been teased as a foreigner growing up in a Stockholm suburb because his hair was black, although he was otherwise impeccably Aryan.

In the election campaign two protest parties, one nice and one nasty, arose from the backwoods: the nice one was the Christian Democrats, who had been a fringe party for thirty years, representing people such as my father-in-law. They were against drink and the sexual revolution and in favour of foreign aid. For those three decades they had continued as a joke, never getting more than 2 per cent of the vote. Suddenly, they were in parliament. More than that: they had three seats in the Cabinet and a chance to put into action their favourite policy – a subsidy paid to mothers to look after their own children, rather than one paid to the local day nurseries so that the mothers could go out to work.

But the real shock was the emergence of a vulgar party: 'New Democracy', founded by a couple of successful businessmen, one – Ian Wachtmeister – born to money, and the other entirely self-made. Bert Karlsson was a record producer who had become rich from understanding unfashionable taste. Earthy, sentimental, and garish, his music and his politics were everything that polite Sweden reprehended. If Sweden had had chavs, Karlsson would have sold them whatever their hearts desired. His first money had been made from the ludicrous but genuinely popular undergrowth of dance music from which Abba emerged. Young men, and the occasional woman, dressed in ridiculous matching outfits would play music in which a sickly organ or accordion melody was strung across a rigid beat. They would tour incessantly at weekends, in summer to the open-air dance grounds that are found in almost every town. These were people for whom winning the Eurovision Song Contest was a dream of sophistication and success. I couldn't stand the music myself, but it would be wrong not to acknowledge it as a sort of folk art, full of hideous vitality, that prospered because people loved it.

Karlsson had started one of the first amusement parks in Sweden, *Sommarland*, a land-locked miniature Blackpool in the middle of nowhere, or the middle of Småland, which is much the same thing. I drove for three hours to find it, but on a Sunday it was, of course, closed. No one liked to work on Sundays.

It was hard to know what New Democracy stood for, but what they were against was clear enough: taxes, foreigners, bureaucracy, idleness and unemployment. The party imploded before the end of the parliament, but before then a great many certainties had disappeared. Carl Bildt had risen in opposition to be leader of the conservatives. Now that he was prime minister and leader of the coalition, the government privatized everything not nailed down. The postal service went, and the railways. The Swedish government had never actually owned very many of the industries it controlled: only some of the shipyards had been nationalized in the late Seventies as a last measure to stop them closing. Welfare benefits were now shaved: a worker had to be sick for three days before drawing any sick pay. When I had worked in Leif's factory, a day off sick, self-certified, would earn us 90 per cent of our notional wages, but the income tax was then so steep that this sometimes meant in practice more cash than if I had gone to work. The Bildt government also encouraged private schools and day nurseries. Dogmatic socialism was replaced by a dogmatic distrust in the power of the state. In some ways, this period looked like Thatcherism: inequality increased as a fact, and was accepted as an ideal. The slogan of the times, launched by the Employers' Federation, was 'Bet on Yourself', and while this was meant to encourage self-employment, it also reflected a rising individualism, and a sense that if the Devil did grab the hindmost, this was no longer a problem for the foremost, or even those in the middle.

Yet the Bildt government did not have quite the same bitter and corrosive character as Thatcherism. It did not turn on its own civil service as she did. Though it exposed the country deliberately to the outside world, negotiating an entry to the EU, there was no counterpart to the British hatred of 'Brussels', even if the Swedes had in many ways actually given up far more of their independence to the EU than Britain had. Thatcherism was in part a reaction to decades of despair among the ruling classes of Britain – the sort of civilized Etonians with whom the *Spectator* was associated – at the discovery that they no longer ruled anything. But the small bureaucratic and political establishment that ruled Sweden kept its confidence through the economic turmoil of the early Nineties. But by the end of that decade the country no longer seemed safe, prosperous or tolerant and even if at its core it still was those things, the progress towards ever-greater safety, prosperity, and tolerance had come to be a pious affirmation, not a historical fact.

16

The trout summer

None of this made much impact on the outside world. In the summer of 1992, I returned for a family trip, with my English wife and two-year-old daughter and Felix, who had been staying with us. With Anita and her new husband we all risked a trip out to the lakes by the fishing-club house: a picnic with brook trout in the woods.

The brook trout lived in the deep pot outside an apron of land by the second and smallest of the club's three lakes, more than a mile from the nearest road: not wilderness exactly, but a very long way to hurry over a rough track with a rucksack on your back containing fifty litres of water and a dozen sluggish trout, which was how the club members brought the fish in. We who did this felt we'd earned the right to eat those fish. Often it was easily claimed. One afternoon my friend Lasse and I caught thirty-four of them, mostly on a fly I tied to resemble a caddis house made of pine needles. That's what the caddis we watched in the margins made their houses from. Only later was my smugness at this careful observation undercut by the notion that the fly dropping slowly through the water could be mistaken by an artless fish for a hatchery pellet.

That lake was where Anita and I had our last quarrel, sitting on a bench in pine needles where we had used to camp. It was a perfect Swedish June, with the sun striking buttery lights off still clear water. The only vivid colour was in the bays where water lilies flowered. The rest of the shoreline was composed of granite, lichen and pine needles in endlessly differing browns and greys. The same colours ran up the striated bark of the pine trees whose needles were beginning to acquire the sated, dusty green of summer. Only the stand of birch trees was still pale. I couldn't catch a trout and she had forgotten her matches a mile away. So we quarrelled in front of everyone about how to boil coffee on a camping stove. I said you should let the froth cover the entire surface before whisking the kettle away to brood. She claimed that the coffee must never boil at all. Her new husband, a mathematician, closed the argument with perfect logic. 'Me, I never let it near the fire,' he said. Laughter delivered us back to the afternoon. I wouldn't say we've been friends, but we've never been enemies since, and I'm grateful to both of them.

Later, I walked around the main lake in the sunlight with a naked daughter on my shoulders and when she peed all down my back that, too, felt like a kind of forgiveness or home-coming. We took her to meet Anna, who welcomed her as an extended granddaughter. She had moved to a flat thirty kilo-metres upriver, near the hospital where she worked. She greeted my new family as if they were her own, and somehow, without a word of language in common, managed to com-municate with them. For years afterwards she would write slow, loving letters in a sprawling hand about the seasons seen from her window that were full of a gratitude and love for nature, which was all that really remained of her childhood religion:

It is so sunny and beautiful here this evening. I have been sitting on the balcony for a while, and soaking up the warmth of the sun before it disappears behind the large and heavily leafed poplar. It grows statelier, broader, and higher every year. The rustling of the wind in its leaves is delightfully cosy, and it gives a wonderful shadow on hot summer days.

How lovely and full of memories this summer has been. Thank you for coming to visit us all here. It was all so overwhelming when you arrived that I forgot many things I had meant to show you and say. We are delighted, and remember the day through rosy spectacles.

Time rushes so swiftly away. The summer has shut its door; the migratory birds are gathering in huge flocks before their long journey; the evenings are dark and the rain whips our windows. Inside it is warm and quiet, with our memories hidden.

Thank you for your lovely letter, for the pictures; thank you for Felix being able to accompany you and he so loves the time he spends with you. I haven't seen him yet [since his return] but I have spoken to him many times on the phone. He seems happy and well before his new school starts. Now he is in a secondary school and the workload grows just as the pupils do.

The flowers you gave me lasted for a fortnight. I think of them with pleasure. I take care of the bag and the table covering. They will last a long time. One day last summer I was waiting for the bus together with some children and grownups. A nine-year-old girl started to talk with me. She thought I had such a lovely bag. I told her who had given it me, and that you were

all on holiday here. *Jaha* she said: old ladies ought to
have flowery shopping bags.

But she was exhausted by a lifetime of work, and took retirement a couple of years before her full pension kicked in. No one
realized at the time, but she was for a while nearly as poor as she
had been as a child, though at this time her children were far
away; two daughters lived in Gothenburg, while Ingela, the
third and youngest, had moved back to Östersund and married
a cousin who still lived in the same village that Anna had come
from. She was crazy about horses, and he kept them.

After a while, Anna, too, returned to live up there. She had
never really liked the south and she missed the landscape of her
childhood.

Anita had two more sons with her new husband and Felix
grew up in school in Gothenburg. They were prosperous and
ambitious. Life was more interesting, not always in a good way.
The Social Democrats, who returned to power in 1994, did
very little to reverse the policies of the Bildt government. Only
the Christian Democrats' policy that mothers should be paid to
look after their own children was immediately abandoned. The
Labour movement threw itself behind EU entry, and convinced
a sceptical public to vote for it; the new social democrat prime
minister, Göran Persson, who had got his start as the mayor of
a small provincial town, rather than a policy wonk's job in
Stockholm, symbolized this change when he built himself a
large country house south-west of Stockholm, and started to
mix socially with the local aristocrats. It was a long way from
Olaf Palme living like a schoolteacher.

Physically, the country became much less safe in the
Nineties. Violent crime increased by about 40 per cent over the
decade; rape by about 80 per cent. Drunkenness came back into

fashion. Felix, growing up in Gothenburg, learned there were parks one did not walk in after dark. A generation of flamboyant gangsters and businessmen, not always easy to tell apart, moved through the newspapers.

I was too busy to notice much of this, living in Notting Hill and reading, sometimes writing for, glossy magazines full of advertisements for a suddenly fashionable drink. These showed people with sharp cheekbones in soft focus, beautifully, dressed, vigorous, young, and electric with hope and sexiness. They drank some elixir as clear as spring water from clear sparkling bottles that never made them drunk, only more vivid and desirable. The name of this elixir was somehow familiar to me, even though it, too, had been shortened. *Absolut renat*, the gut-rot that the alcoholics drank outside the bus station in Kungälv while Anita and I waited primly for our buses, had now been re-branded. Instead of *renat*, which the drunks had called it, the smart people now drank *Absolut*.

17

The world intrudes

Helsingborg, a flat town at the southern tip of Sweden, only four kilometres across the Öresund strait from the battlements of Elsinore, was bustling in the sleet of December 1997. It was the first time I noticed fat people in the streets, and the first time I saw a McDonald's in Sweden. It had always been a visual shock to return to England, and see that everyone was shorter, darker, fatter and dirtier than in Sweden. But when I saw the McDonald's in Helsingborg I also saw, for the first time, that the Swedes around me were now shaped like the English, though still taller and for the most part more blond.

Perhaps the hamburgers in McDonald's were exactly the same as those in Clock, the Swedish chain that it bought and replaced. But the message that they brought was completely different. This thing in a bun was no longer just a slab of fatty mince topped with processed cheese. It was succulent, flavour-enhanced international capitalism, glamorous in the same way as *Absolut* vodka.

At the same time, the glamour was seeping the other way. Where once Swedish culture, to the British middle classes, meant sex and Bergman, now it meant Ikea. A British paper had sent me to do a novelty story: Ikea had started to sell flats and they wanted to know whether these came flat-packed and ready to assemble. In fact, all that Ikea was doing was marketing. It's not a company that makes the things it sells. The flats were built by Skånska, another large Swedish firm trying to turn itself into something global – the superior little 'o' would fall off the 'a' in its name as this process continued – and Ikea merely had an experimental counter selling leases to the block. I don't think the experiment prospered, but it was great publicity while it lasted.

There were now shopping malls along the outskirts of the city, which looked like any of the prosperous parts of the USA. Advertisements seemed to be everywhere. They were even on the television, from which they had been banned in the old days. The flats that Ikea were showing still seemed, from the inside, like places I might have lived in. The people in them moved around their polished floors in slippers or socks; the colours were chosen to avoid undue excitement; across the windows little lace curtains hung from brass rods about the height of a plant pot. The ideal window of a respectable worker's flat would conceal the inhabitants behind a fortification of sombre, glistening pot plants. There were knick-knacks everywhere, and the retired couple to whom we spoke had the mixture of gratitude and pride that characterized their generation.

The young woman showing journalists around belonged to the future of credit cards and insatiable hunger. Neither gratitude nor satisfied pride seemed emotions that came naturally to her or her peers. It might come as a surprise that credit cards were part of the future as late as 1997, but only a couple of years before it was reported for the first time that the government was issuing credit cards to ministers. This followed a scandal when a prominent Social Democratic politician was forced to resign after she had been discovered putting private treats on her government credit card. To older social democrats, credit cards still seemed rather immoral.

In May 1998, Felix graduated from his high school. His family all came to watch: it is a very important ceremony. The students dress in traditional costumes – white trousers and jackets, with little peaked caps – and nowadays drive slowly around town in the biggest cars they can find, which are garlanded for the occasion with freshly cut birch boughs lashed to the radiators and flowers round the radio aerials. While these cars with their yelling freight lumbered around the centre of town, lurching over tramlines, blowing their horns, Felix marched us around the town he thought of now as his. There had been only one place to get a decent cup of coffee here, just as the covered market had been the nearest place we could buy fresh garlic when we lived in Nödinge, thirty kilometres away; it may have been the only place on the coast between Malmö and the Norwegian border where there was fresh garlic for sale. Now Felix and his friends had a choice of half a dozen coffee houses a short walk from the school, and there was fresh garlic on much of the food we ate.

It poured with rain throughout the ceremony, but Anna glowed under the lemony light of a big golfing umbrella. I don't think I have ever seen her look so completely happy. She had been ill earlier that year with heart trouble, and it had been a great effort, not entirely wise, to come down for the ceremony. But only complete incapacitation could have stopped her. She kept saying that Felix was the first member of her family ever to graduate from high school. I asked Anita, quietly, how Anna had reacted when her own new husband had been made a professor of mathematics. Oh, she said, that was good, too, but Anna didn't really distinguish between a professorship and a graduation. All were one dazzle of impossible achievement on the horizon of her world.

The only problem for the happy graduates was that they had no jobs to go to. In 1977, the year I came to Sweden, there had been 1.1 million industrial workers in the country – a quarter of the employed population. Even then there were more than twice as many people employed in the service sector, but the country didn't feel like that because there was still a socialist belief that the only real worker was a man using his bodily strength and skill, and everyone else was merely playing at employment. But in the next thirty years, two-fifths of the industrial jobs disappeared. There are only 686,000 industrial workers now, and nearly five times as many service jobs. 'Work' is something done in shops or offices, and with keyboards instead of nail guns.

At the same time as skilled industrial work has largely vanished, so traditionally professional jobs have been industrialized, and lost the protection that the unions once granted. Some time in the Nineties, employment just dried up for middle-class children. About half of Felix's class headed off for Norway to become migrant workers. They gutted fish in the Lofoten Islands, or worked in canning plants. Some became warehouse workers, adept at twirling fork-lift trucks. Felix came to England and spent a summer working in the warehouse of a toyshop down the road from us. His friend Oskar, who wanted to become a journalist, did manage to get into the University of Journalism, in itself a considerable feat; but he is nearly thirty now, a father, and he still has never had a permanent job though he has been making perfectly good radio programmes for years now.

This nomadic life is a direct consequence of the legislation that was meant to stop workers being exploited in temporary jobs: the 'Law on the Protection of Employment'. It rules that anyone who has been doing a temporary job for a year must be offered a permanent one. So Oskar, and nearly everyone he knows in his business, is always sacked eleven months into the job, or hired on a short-term contract that is not renewed. The law contained provisions to stop this: if a company has hired a temp and then not made them permanent, it is forbidden to rehire them for three years or so.

The effect has been that radio journalists have to move all around the country at yearly or six-monthly intervals, working for different stations. Obviously this looks like a trick played by the evil capitalists on the trades unions, who had lobbied for laws that would make it harder to sack permanent employees, but that can't be the whole story. No one would pass a law like that without some understanding of how it would work. Since it would be politically unthinkable for the Social Democrats to pass a law with the avowed intent of making workers *less* secure, they had to sell it as a law to preserve the security of employment, while intending that it should produce a generation of workers grateful for any employment they could get.

Felix left Sweden after school and went to university in Belfast, a place foreign both to Sweden and to mainland England. With the distinct shock one gets when national stereotypes come true, his new friends discovered that he had never in his life hit anyone in anger; he found that some of them had never met anyone before him whose parents were divorced. There was only one among his Swedish friends whose parents were not.

With no more family ties, I had no reason to visit Sweden much in the next few years. There were occasional travel pieces, but they felt completely wrong. Sweden had always been a country from which tourists left, rather than a destination. It was hard to imagine mass tourists who would enjoy the discomfort, the silence and the mosquito bites which seemed to me an essential part of enjoyment in the country. Then there was the problem of luxury. I had lived too long in Lilla Edet to suppose that the countryside was a place in which food or drink might be savoured for any price less than completely ruinous. Finally, the assumption of servility and inequality that lies behind any kind of service industry was not something that I could easily imagine Swedes adopting. It was not a matter of unfriendliness, particularly, that made this so: more a strong expectation of reciprocity. You got what you were entitled to, no more, no less. That is not how modern hotels can function.

The bright modern country of rich gangsters and alcohol advertisements did not seem different enough from the rest of the world to be worth visiting for long. However much I had loathed my life in the forest outside Lilla Edet, and bridled under the yoke of solitude, it had also taught me to write thoughtfully. This is not a skill a journalist often needs, and in my busy years in England it had pretty much atrophied. I found, when I wanted to write books, that the only way to be able to think deeply was to retreat to a place with pine forests and running water, as far as I could go and still have electricity. I wrote much of one book, for which I needed to understand the elements of molecular biology, in a boarding house in the Julian Alps in Slovenia, walking for two or three hours a day after I had finished my thousand words; but in the summer of 2005 I wanted to work on a novel. Hunting quickly on the Internet, I found a *stuga* – a cottage in the woods – with electricity and not much else in Swedish Lapland. I hadn't realized until I came to arrange the journey just how very far north

I was going. It took a week for my letter confirming the booking to reach the owners; in fact it arrived the day after I did, and my own journey had been circuitous. I had wanted to take the night train which continues to Kiruna, a mining town on the plateau above the Arctic circle; I had done this twenty years earlier and it had been the strangest and most exciting journey of my life, rivalled only by a trip, years later, into the guerrilla-controlled mountains south of Bogotá; even though, on the Swedish journey, nothing outwardly interesting happened at all. But when I came to arrange it this time, I discovered the night train had vanished. The railway system had been privatized, and it was no longer possible to take any passenger train up to the high north. Instead, I would have to drive, or fly, or take the bus. None of these modes of transport had the transforming quality of the night train, but this, it turned out, did not matter. I managed to spend part of the journey on a sleeper to Östersund, though I had to stay up till midnight before the train could leave, and in the grey thin morning, I found the bus I needed in the station car park.

18

Getting away

It was a double-decker bus, with wing mirrors that protruded on stalks and between them, above the driver's head, a row of bug-eyed headlamps, extinguished at half past seven in the morning. It had been light for five hours. We drove northwards on a wide empty road through the forest. Soon everything brightly coloured or square-edged was far behind us. There were no more fields with ripening crops, nor any other patches of yellow or red. All I could see were low green and brown hills beneath a huge sky that was blue and purple and grey. When the road passed by the side of lakes the horizon would suddenly recede and then the most distant hills were a deep greeny-grey, as if they were made half of sky and half of forest. This monotony continued; it could have continued for days, since the forest extends unbroken for 800 kilometres across northern Sweden and Finland. But after six hours I climbed off at Sorsele, a town on an island in the middle of the Vindelälv river. There are no other towns for fifty miles in any direction; but here are 1,500 people, two supermarkets, a few shops, a library, and a branch of the state-owned off-licence.

When you enter a supermarket, you leave geography behind.

Like airports, they are all the same place with the same lighting, equally distant from the world around them. But in Sorsele, the countryside kept breaking through on to the shelves. There was canned tuna from Alaska, canned sweetcorn and fresh garlic; but at the meat counter there were cuts of elk and venison as well as beef, and half-litre tubs of reindeer blood for cooking with.

I must have looked out of place as I browsed for supplies, for a tall elderly man with a cast in one eye pushed his trolley up to mine and started to talk urgently but without haste about setting nets under the ice in winter. He just wanted to share what was at the top of his mind. In the background I could see people turn their carts sharply when they caught sight of him. But he seemed reasonably sober and terribly lonely so I listened and his discourse expanded. He lived fifteen kilometres out of town, on the river. He had started mining at sixteen, when he'd learned to set charges by hand in holes he had made with a hammer and spike: when he told me this, he mimed the invisible hammer blow. We stood between the stationery and the canned vegetables but his hand was somewhere else and in another time.

The mines where he had worked had shut down decades ago. He was only seventy-one, he said; he wanted to be taken on as a teacher at a new mine. He didn't want to be paid – he had his pension – but he'd love to teach the mining skills he had known all his life; besides, his wife didn't like him hanging around the house. He seemed to recollect himself then, and wished me a courteous goodbye.

I had arranged to stay on a farm about five kilometres downriver, reached by taxi along a metalled track through the forest. I had hoped to be somewhere entirely self-contained, but I turned out to have rented an annexe, with a bedroom, a bathroom, and a kitchen with a table where I could set up my computer. I had travelled here to work on a story that had become unreachable: I supposed that I, too, was setting nets under an imagination that had frozen.

The next morning, after a shower, I sat for minutes on the spare bed, just listening to silence ringing in my ears. There is a sort of concussion that persists for three or four days when you leave behind the sound of motors, for even when cars seem inaudible there are almost always electric motors whirring all over a modern house.

Behind the farm the road I had come along rose up a fairly steep hill through replanted forest and I walked up there before breakfast. It was so quiet that I heard the crunch of my shoes on the loose surface but also, after each foot lifted, a second noise of displaced gravel shifting back into the depression that my heel had made.

At the top of the hill was a small, shallow pond that had killed all the pine trees around it, so that they stood with grey, peeled trunks and blackened limbs as if they had all been poisoned when in fact they had just drowned. A little beyond the dead lake the north side of the road opened up into an enormous logged clearing, with about every hundredth tree spared, so it didn't look as awful as a clear-cut; but it was still a desolating sight.

In that vast silence, not oppressive, but inescapable, everything I could see felt alien to human concerns. A human being made no more difference than a midge. We might be happy for a while here, but we could never belong, and in the cool shadows of the forest there is almost always a sense that whatever elusive spirit does belong there wishes us no good. In the early years of the twentieth century, children who had to walk long distances to school would do so with their coats turned inside out to ward off the trolls. The word conceals a whole taxonomy in folklore – the *vätt*, the *näck*, and even the *tomte*, now shrivelled to the comic status of a leprechaun – but these creatures as they appear in folk tales display towards humans almost exactly the indifference, blazing sometimes into cruelty, that peasants show their animals, and sometimes on an isolated farmstead I have wondered whether we are the tamers of the forest, or its pets.

Such thoughts recurred as I worked through the next few days, and walked by the quiet reach of the river past the farm. From the table I could watch the rain gurgling off the gutters of the main house and falling past the window boxes, when I was not counting the mosquitoes patiently waiting on the screen window. Most days there were thirty at least. Towards the edge of the clearing where the farm stood there were two purpose-built *stugor*, or cottages for holidaymakers.

Late one evening, everything grew still on the broad smooth flat of the river here. I stood on the sandy bank, looking towards the far shore, about half a kilometre away. There were rises clearly visible out on the stillest water; I heard noises and excitement downstream on my shore, and found two middle-aged couples from the cottages in the grounds loading a little motor boat with fishing gear and bickering happily while they did so. 'Where do you want me to sit?' asked a rather fat wife. 'On your bottom,' replied another voice. I asked whether any of them knew what was rising, and they suggested *sik*, a sort of white-fish. They were going upriver three or four kilometres to spin for pike in the pool below the rapids.

The next morning, I saw them again. They had caught ten pike from the boat and were now going to lay a net on the far side of the river from the farm. When they returned, they had four fine *sik*, a small pike and a small perch which, one of the husbands – a short, round, bearded, gleeful man – was carrying carelessly, with its head cut off, and tiny streak of bright red blood running over the white flesh and green flanks. 'They get so tangled in the net it's the only way to get them out,' he said.

The wasteful fecundity of the river fascinated him: 'The river is full of pike,' he said. He pointed to a set of large iron hooks, high under the eaves of the barn. 'There,' he said, 'they used to store the spatchcocked bodies of the pike all summer, sheltered by fine mesh so the flies couldn't reach them. They would dry in the sun and the wind, and all winter you would eat little bits of dried pike, as a snack, or with a beer. But no one bothers nowadays.'

The next morning, as I wrote at the kitchen table there was a bang on the door, and he presented me, grinning, with a paper plate of three newly fried perch, bulging like yellow pillows, and dusted with gold where the butter had burnt a little; also a polythene bag full of little ones, smoked with their skins on so they had gone the dark green of pine forests. I was almost dumbstruck. I explained that I had had breakfast, and would put them in the fridge. But before I could do so, I had to eat one, in my fingers. It was just perfect. I knew I had to go fishing myself, and when the rain stopped, a little after one, I decided to chance a walk to the rapids.

I had been walking for about forty minutes when the first car to pass me stopped and a young man gave me a lift to the point where the path down to the river leaves the road. The path across the clear-cut soon vanished into chilly woods all bright after the rain. I walked down to the rapids on one of those narrow, irregular, descending Scandinavian paths that look as if they have been carved by water and maintained at night by busy trolls: stone, moss, damp earth form successive sections, and everything is veined with pine roots. A noise of rapids could be heard, and after about ten minutes the path came down to the glorious smooth reach just before the whole river vanished into five or six hundred metres of white water.

Downstream, the path soon brought me to a locked wooden shack with a porch and an inverted rowing boat on the ground in front of it. This was where I had the first shock of the day. I was congratulating myself on not only performing a thorough toilette with jungle oil first thing this morning but remembering to put the bottle into the pocket of my Goretex jacket – yes, that one, the pocket with the zip open and nothing in it. I must have gasped in horror: I certainly had to spit out a mosquito immediately afterwards.

So I changed into my waders down by the river, where there were slightly fewer insects than under the trees, assembled my rod, threaded the line, and then stood quietly for a while, watching the river from beneath the trees. I had been able to see another boat at the foot of the rapids from which people were fishing, but by the time I had tackled up it had vanished, and I saw no one else the whole time I was there. Not that I was looking for them. I was looking for fish, and wondering where in this crazed frothing wilderness of water they might be. It is almost always the wildest parts of these big northern rivers that hold the trout and the grayling. They have more oxygen in hot weather than the placid stretches, and the bottom is so irregular that the rocks will always provide shelter while plenty of food rushes helplessly past in the adjoining currents.

Grayling are rather delicate fish, a purplish black on top, and bright silver everywhere else, a colour that is only really visible in the air: in water it is so perfectly bright that it becomes invisible by reflecting the weeds and gravel all around them. Any writer might try for a style like a pane of glass, but only a very great one could find a style as luminously invisible as a grayling's skin. The body is streamlined, with a fine wrist before the forked tail. The grayling has one superb extravagance – a long dorsal fin shot through with purple lights that dry to turquoise in the air. It is almost as high as the body beneath it is deep, so that when you see a grayling appear in clear water with its dorsal fin flaring it seems as if the river were waving at you a banner made from the Northern Lights.

A few hundred metres below me there was a long stone bank curving out into the water – this was built to narrow the rapids when the river was still used for floating timber. On my bank there was the usual jumble of boulders sloping into the river, most of them about the size of an armchair and difficult to walk across. I looked across them, then up towards a small island close to land. I was wondering how best to reach the hard current in the middle of the rapids, and thinking that if this were a normal river, there should be fish in the stretch where the two streams from each side of the island reunited beneath it; and as I watched this, I distinctly saw some tiny splashes in the choppy little waves there.

I picked my way out across the rocks until I stood on a flat-topped underwater rock at the foot of this run, able to cast upstream to where the two currents joined. I couldn't actually see any flies in the air, but in that kind of water it was a safe bet they would be sedges – little drab delicate flies that look like moths in flight, but on land settle with their wings folded to form a long narrow ridge that conceals their bodies entirely. Their wings, under a magnifying glass, are covered in tiny hairs, but if you want to imitate them you must forget all such refinements and just make a fly that is dark and narrow, and will float through any waves. I put on an especially small and scruffy one of these, and from the first cast grayling made little splashes at it with a discretion that quite concealed their real size.

The first one took me five minutes to persuade to land and was the largest I had ever caught. I slipped him back into the water, as a thanks-offering to the Vindelälv, and on the next two casts caught two more, only a little smaller, which just about hooked themselves: I saw nothing, but just found them there when I lifted the line. I thanked the river, but I didn't want to presume so I changed my fly; and changed it again, and again, and again, until I found something else that I could see and that the fish appreciated. Then I caught two more, which I put back, and kept the next one. I had been fishing for three hours, and for part of that time I felt completely human – looking down the river, into the clear water, with a grayling that I knew I would eat knocking furiously on my rod, I felt this was about as close to happiness as one could come and know it.

When I came back to land the forest air was muggy, and full of midges. By the time I had climbed out of the clear-cut I could feel my whole face streaming sweat, like a baked tomato just before it bursts. I trudged on the three kilometres home. It was easier once I was up on the hill, for the breeze cooled me down a bit. But I was carrying ten or twelve kilos the whole way, and none of it was flat.

It took an hour to walk home with a full pack. I fried the grayling fillets in bacon fat, with dill. I could not have spoken, even if there had been anyone to hear.

The rain returned next day. I worked. My senses refined. The less there seemed to be to see and hear, the more clearly I could apprehend what there was. For days I had seemed to be struggling through a bog in my work, measuring progress only in exhaustion. But at least I could attain exhaustion. It seemed to me, from where I sat with nothing to watch but the swallows, that trying to work as I normally do with a telephone and an Internet connection was like trying to think in a cloud of mosquitoes. In the evenings, if I didn't fish, I would walk by the still reaches of the river. One day I realized that my story had almost reached a point where it moved by itself without needing to be pushed every inch.

That evening, I spent an hour by the river, being hardly bitten at all, slowly overwhelmed by the silence. The various ducks and divers out in the main stream seemed restless and boisterous, though they seldom called; they were constantly splashing and resettling on the water, seeming to jostle one another. Right on the far bank at the other end of the old ferry route, I could see a white blurry sausage and a dark one and hear the occasional hollow noise of a wooden boat being moved around. The noise was much more distinct than the sight. After about half an hour of this, the blurry sausages spoke – there was a child there, too, and their voices, at normal conversational pitch, carried right across the river. I remembered an earlier evening walking on the shore when a car had driven along the gravel road and it seemed so loud and distinct I supposed it was a train.

19

Seeing the *vätt*

After I had been staying for a while, the Vinblads, who owned the farm, started to make small friendly noises. I had approached them cautiously, with a nonchalant display of harmlessness, as if we were creatures meeting in the forest. I had been visibly conscientious about cleaning and sweeping; I borrowed their washing line when I needed to dry the clothes that I washed in the kitchen sink; I waited for them to speak.

They were both short and firmly built: Sture, the husband, had an expression of mild, amused determination and a handshake that felt like rusted iron pipes. His wife, Ulla, had short ash-blonde hair and a face – kindly when she talked to me – that filled with brutal determination when she thought. Some people look vulnerable when their thoughts are elsewhere. Ulla seemed to leave behind a face of stone, like an effigy on a tomb. But whenever we talked she was considerate, thoughtful, and easily amused, and when she learned that I planned to walk into town to go shopping, she offered me a lift, and on the way told me a little of their story.

The farm had belonged to Sture's parents; he and Ulla had bought it from his widowed mother in 1970, after she had a stroke, and lived there ever since. For twenty-five years, Sture had worked full time, mostly as a logger, and farmed in the evenings. Then in 1995 he'd had a heart attack – it was the stress, Ulla said – and after that the work had become impossible. So they had sold the cows and built the annexe where I was staying, and, later, the two *stugor* in the grounds.

Ulla had brought up six children – that was all she told me then. They had eleven grandchildren; one of their children lived in the valley; two in Sorsele, two on the coast, and one in the far south. She only thought of the son who actually lived in their house as living 'here'. The two in Sorsele had 'moved away', though it was only by a few kilometres.

On the west coast of Sweden, 1500 kilometres, more or less, from where I now was, I'd had a friend who could distinguish between the different dialects of adjacent fishing villages – except that no one nowadays spoke in anything but television mulch. In the high north, this seemed to be less true. Ulla and Sture both spoke a dialect that, at least to my ear, had all the word endings missing, and the vowels were shifted towards the back of the mouth. I remembered winters further south, when snot would freeze hard on my moustache and I imagined Swedish as a language pinched and chopped off by the cold, arranged so that you spent as little time as possible with your tongue exposed. But here were differences too fine for an outsider to notice. Ulla came originally from the Skellefteå district, about 150 kilometres away, on the Baltic coast: when she took Sture to meet her parents in the early Sixties, and her father and grandfather talked to each other, Sture couldn't understand a word of their dialect.

They were puzzled that I didn't have a car; I don't think they believed that I wanted to walk as much as possible, and I couldn't see any way to explain to them that three or four hours' fiction-writing counts as a reasonable day's work, when their own definition of work was so different. Ulla offered to dig out an old bicycle for me from the farm's abundant store of broken-down machinery, so that I would not have to walk the whole way to the water; and at about five o'clock one afternoon this was produced. I think it was younger than me, but not by much: an ancient, upright, foot-braked lady's bike with swept-back handlebars and flecks of rust all over the cream skin. But there was a baggage carrier, on which my rucksack fitted. I rode it around the yard, upright and wobbling like the schoolmistress in *Butch Cassidy*, and then piled everything on the back to explore the path to the bottom of the rapids, which led, I was told, from another settlement upriver. The road along the shoreline that I would have preferred to follow doesn't exist for the fairly obvious reason that it would be destroyed by the floods every year.

So I pushed up the hill, feeling like a superannuated Vietcong. It was a very long hill, even with a bicycle to help. But nearly at the top, I turned left to Stridsmark (battlefield), the hamlet at the foot of the rapids, and whirled down a succession of switchbacks, very upright, with my cap wedged down hard, rejoicing in the rush of air on my bare arms in the sunlight.

After a couple of kilometres, I braked where the road petered out at a house and barn. A man with hair like drying hay, and browner, yellowing teeth set widely and at irregular angles, was fixing something with a spanner. He wore trousers, sandals, and nothing else. He had a full, hay-coloured beard, a large, pale stomach bulging over his jeans, and blue eyes that were very bright and deep. He looked at me as if I were strange and possibly mad.

I asked where the path went to the rapids. He looked as if all his suspicions had been confirmed. He said nothing.

I asked again, recalibrating my accent to the flutingest BBC Swedish I could manage.

'You can't get there,' he said.

'But I'm sure there's a path,' I said.

'Well,' he said, 'in that case, it's the path from beyond the barn. But it's a good two kilometres, and it's very bad.'

He studied my expression.

'Well,' he said, 'maybe a kilometre and a half.'

But something inside me rebelled. I determined to go home, and not to wear myself out fighting through another tangle of mosquito-infested undergrowth. I wheeled the stately bicycle around and prepared to mount.

'Did you come from town?' asked the farmer. His manner suggested that if I had, it was the funniest thing that had happened all week.

No, I said. I had come from the Vinblads' farm. He absorbed the disappointment. I cycled slowly away up the gentle rise, and, when it became less gentle, dismounted and pushed.

The rain returned, the next day; bright puddles formed in all the declivities of the road. In the pauses when the drizzle died away, I bicycled down the valley, away from town. This stretch of the road, or track, was where the earliest settlement had been built, when the first farmers and trappers pushed up the river in the 1670s and built a 'Lapp chapel' on the island of Sorsele. Before that time the whole valley was pure unsettled wilderness. Now, of course, every tree you see, in all the apparently endless forests, has been replanted or allowed to grow by man. There are only a few scrappy fringes of primeval woodland on the borders of Russia and Finland, deliberately preserved.

Coming down one little slope I saw an animal so red and snub-nosed that I thought it must be a lynx; otherwise, the forest seemed empty. Reindeer and elk left tracks on the sand when they came down to the river to drink; the local paper had stories about bear and even wolves. But most days I did not see any animals at all.

I told Ulla that I thought I might have seen a lynx. She was delighted. In all her years up there, she said, she had only seen one once, and that had been a hundred kilometres away, where the mountains rise out of the forests towards Ammarnäs. But she knew there was supposed to be one hunting this stretch of the river. There were also red deer there, she said, which the farmers kept alive in winter by putting out hay, since deer can't scrape down through the snow for food as elk and reindeer can.

She gave me a lift into the library so that I could look the mysterious animal up. It was an airy modern space that seemed unusually warm, with a huge chamber off the hall for hanging outer clothes in winter. There was a display of children's books in Turkish as well as glass cases showing the utensils used by peasant families in the early twentieth century: wooden plates and spoons, but also a washing-up brush made of birch twigs lashed together like a little broom.

I knew that my younger sister-in-law, Ingela, who I remembered as a fourteen-year-old girl with big teeth, big glasses and a passion for horses, had been married, unmarried, was now living somewhere in Östersund, so I poked around on the Internet to see if I could find her. It was a shock to find her mobile number on the first search page I tried. 'What are you doing in *Sorsele*?' she asked: 'Counting trees?' I promised to visit her and her new family on my return journey.

I found an encyclopaedia and discovered that the animal I'd seen must have been a fox; a lynx would not have had such a long tail, even as a kitten. I told Ulla this as we drove back. It was a shame, I said, that the beautiful story could not be true.

She seemed to accept this. It was perhaps a way to chip myself off from the undifferentiated block of tourists.

We went together around the junk shop, where clothes, books, and ancient plastic gadgets were all sold second-hand. It looked like a collection of all the unwanted Christmas presents in the country. I imagined that each of the regular customers must have owned something in it at least once. As we drove back, Ulla said that she must take me some time to see the church. There was also, she said, a very beautiful woodland graveyard.

In the morning I wrote in my diary, 'Today it is raining and looks as if will get rainier and colder all day. I hate it that the days go past, and that this must come to an end. I want to spin here like a capsule far above the earth, just watching.' But around one-thirty that day the drizzle evaporated, leaving the skies grey and cold enough to wear a jacket over a flannel shirt even when cycling. I piled everything on the bicycle and set off for the river. I seemed full of strength, and determined to walk down to the very tip of the rapids. But I found that the other path led through a fresh, rain-soaked berry bog. It would have been fun in waders. It smelt deliciously fresh, but soaked me from halfway down my calves, and grew at last quite impassable.

So I returned to the first place, and stuffed my soaking feet into dry waders, swearing loudly in English at the empty river. There were no rises. I decided to catch the fish down at the bottom of the river, where they feed on the larvae, or nymphs, of flies. I waded carefully out to a run I had spotted at the very start of the rapids, put on a large and hideous bead-head stone-fly nymph, and caught nine grayling, all returned, and none much above the minimum size. Still, nine grayling in three hours is not bad.

Just as I was sitting down to peel off my waders and put on my soggy cold shoes again, a middle-aged man and his son picked their way over the stones towards me. He was lean, blue-eyed, with a short red beard: the son was taller, clean-shaven but for a blond goatee about four inches long, and a habit of tipping his chin in the air to stroke it. The son had a fly rod and waders; the father wellington boots and a long spinning rod. I was feeling exhausted as we chatted – I thought this was the effect of flickery sleep patterns in the light – and making silly mistakes in my Swedish. Then I happened to look up at the spinning rod, which was about my eye level where I sat on a rock with my waders round my ankles, and saw on the end of the line a curiously misshapen silver and metal fish about ten centimetres long. It was so huge to my eyes, accustomed to dry flies the size of my thumbnail, that I burst out laughing. He stiffened like a terrier and demanded to know why I was laughing.

It looked so big, I said, in comparison to the flies I had been using.'

'I made this myself,' he said. 'I have caught more than 500 trout on it, thirty of them weighing more than five kilos.'

He looked ready to fight for the honour of this little wobbler. I was impressed by the metalworking skill that must have gone into such a thing, and I told him so, as his bristling subsided. I realized his whole life turned around such things, as mine might turn around my writing.

Once I had cycled home I was slumped over the remains of a plate of meatballs, as exhausted as if they had been fired into my stomach like grapeshot, when Ulla banged on the door. Would I like to come out with them and lift a net this evening? If so, I had to come now, because this was the rotting month, and the fish would be spoiled if we waited until morning.

I didn't understand the urgency until we were all sitting in their fibreglass dinghy. The outboard motor had been Sture's fiftieth-birthday present, sixteen years ago. He sat at the oars, and Ulla at the engine. I sat in the middle with a camera and we set off across the calm river at its widest point. After about ten minutes we reached the empty detergent bottle bobbing on the surface that marked the end of the first net. These were gill nets, long sheets of clear nylon about a metre deep, which are left out to hang in the current and entangle the fish that pass. They choke there and are almost all dead by the time the net is collected, or as near to it as makes no difference. If the net had been left overnight, they would have spoiled in the ruthless fertility of summer.

Sture rowed the boat backwards up the line of the net while Ulla lifted the cord on top of it, and peered down the mesh for tangled fish. If she found one, she lifted a stretch of net on board, and pushed the fish and pulled the net with her broad hands until it came free, when she flipped it into a plastic bucket. But in the whole length of the first net there were only three small *sik* and a perch; when I saw that some were still alive, I pulled a Leatherman tool from my belt to use as a priest and clubbed them on the head with it. In the second net there were only three plump perch where a shoal had passed in the night. These fish seemed much more wrongfully (and unexpectedly) dead than the ones I had caught myself.

As we stood afterwards around the gutting table, in the usual cloud of small bloodsucking bugs, their eldest son Per walked up in jogging shorts and a T-shirt, as if there were nothing there but air. I had watched Ulla negotiate with a couple of Polish tourists while a mosquito moved slowly along her forehead under her woollen hat making ruminative pauses, and she just didn't seem to notice at all, though I twitched trying not to brush it off.

I was introduced by my distinguishing characteristic: 'This is Andrew. He puts back the fish that he can't eat!'

Walking up to the house with a bucket of headless, gutted fish to smoke, Ulla pointed out the potato patch. The plants were nearly a metre high, and some were flowering. They were going to pull the first ones today, and promised me some. This was about two months later than one eats the first new potatoes in the south, but these had only been planted on 13 June, less than six weeks before. The light is so strong and continuous in the north that plants never pause in their growth for a moment.

Later we sat in their kitchen drinking rosehip tea and talked. Hugo, the Norwegian forest cat, made up to me in the most shameless and flattering fashion. He placed his front paws on my thigh, and stretched his neck right out, twisting it to expose new bits for scratching, and at the same time rubbed the back of his head against me. 'Is it true,' Sture asked, 'that in England it gets dark at night in summer?' He asked the question as if summer dark were unknown in about half the world.

As a young man he had worked on logging crews in the woods in winter; out there for a month at a time in a steady thirty below. 'We used to burn wood in the evenings, and then it would be beautifully warm – 20, 25 degrees inside the cabin with ten men there. But the cabins were badly built, and when you woke the next morning to make coffee, there would be ice on the water bucket. Of course, once you were out in the woods and working, you don't feel the cold.' Did the chainsaws mind the cold? I asked. No, they were reliable. But the tractors were always breaking down when it was more than thirty degrees of frost, so they used horses instead.

Ulla's father, who was eighty-five, had been in the Stockholm paper because the first meteorite to land in Sweden for a century had struck right in front of him, leaving a charred circle in the grass. But he was a remarkable old man in other ways, a dowser, too. He could dowse not just for water, but also for electric cables buried in the ground. Here Sture mimed the leaping of bent copper wire in his father-in-law's hands as he walked over a cable. Then he said that his wife had a gift of her own.

'Oh, *don't*,' she said.

No, he said, really, she could see the *vätt*.

It took me a moment to recognize the word: the *vätt* are forest trolls who lurk around dwellings as if on their way to domestication.

'I don't like to talk about it,' she said, meaning that she loved to, but was afraid of mockery. 'Even as a child, I had feelings about them, but I didn't want to tell anyone, because they would have thought me silly. But when we moved out here, there was clearly something in the barn. There was one cow that would be milked overnight sometimes when no one was there. Once I found a trail of milk drops going back into the woods from the barn, but even before I saw that I could feel there was a path to the woods. I told Sture not to park the tractor there, but he just laughed. The next day, the big back tyre was flat and he had to take the whole wheel into Sorsele to mend it. But when they got there, there was no puncture. The tyre was fine, and so was the valve.

'Then, about three weeks later, he parked the tractor there again, behind the barn. That was the most convenient place. Again, Sture came out the next day and found the tyre deflated; but when he took it into Sorsele there was nothing wrong with it. After that, he's never parked the tractor there again, even if he doesn't completely believe me. But a few years later, forgetting, he parked the snowplough there at the end of the winter. When he came out to look at it, four of the long split

171

pins that hold it to the tractor were missing. They were heavy steel things' – she held her hands up – 'about twenty centimetres apart.

'Sture came in and said, "Someone needed those," meaning that they had been stolen. He was going to order fresh ones. But I told him that he should move the plough, and this time he believed me. Three days later, two of them were back where they should be.'

Sture took up the story. 'I found the other two a couple of months later, behind a big slab of sheetrock that was resting against the wall in the barn. I know I didn't put them there.'

She looked at me. 'Andrew doesn't believe us,' she said.

No, no, I said. It was just the way that these stories took place in a world of tractors and cotter pins. But still, I said, there was no reason why the *vätt* shouldn't adapt to a world of refrigerators – after all, Hugo had.

She rose to make more tea and as she walked across the kitchen, her hips seemed stiff and high. It was the first time I had ever seen her look tired, but after that I could not forget that she was also old.

Back with fresh rosehip tea, Ulla told another story. She had been lying in bed one morning at about five when she heard a great bang at the front door and someone come into the kitchen. But she was tired and didn't bother getting out of bed. She thought it must be Per. When she came down, the fridge door was open, and the front door, but no human had been there.

Once, she had actually seen one: a little grey man, about so high – her hand a couple of feet above the table. The grass had been high, then, but not yet cut. The long wooden frames on which the hay is dried stood empty in the meadows. She had been on the tractor on the big meadow down the road (she used a dialect word for meadow, and Sture said 'in Swedish', so then she used the word I'd understand).

Just as she drove past the frame on her tractor, she saw from the corner of her eye a little grey shadow standing on the top pole. She stopped the tractor, and looked again. Three times she stopped and restarted the tractor. Each time, when she looked at the pole, the creature was there. She was sure he wanted something. But what? At last she thought that he must be warning her. So she drove straight back to the farm and told Sture that they must get in the hay on the big meadow at once.

She told him why, and he believed her. So he took his tractor down, and they made hay of the whole field: the storm came over the hill just as they placed the last few forkfuls on the stack. Then it rained without stopping for a fortnight. In this short summer that would have lost them all the winter hay.

This meeting seemed to her unequivocal proof that the *vätt* were benevolent spirits, happy to exchange favours with humans.

Did we have such things in England, she asked. No, I said. We have driven the wilderness out, and ploughed it over, and gardened it for a thousand years now. Nothing like that could live there any longer. I looked out at the bright evening. It was twenty past eleven and time to go to bed.

The next day, Ulla took me to the graveyard. We were supposed to be shopping, but she said she wanted to show me the sights of Sorsele, and so she drove from the supermarket to the church; but when we reached it, she continued over the bridge, to a spot where she said there was a beautiful forest graveyard. She drove past slowly, me making the right sort of noises: it just looked like a sparsely forested slope with unusually regular outcrops of granite. 'Sture and I will be buried there,' she said. 'We have chosen a spot. It's just up there. We had a little boy who only lived four and a half hours, and he's there.'

She continued a few hundred metres until we came to a junction. A road ran off, completely straight, into the scrubby forest on our left and she slowed down to turn round. 'You can get to the rapids down there.' She said. 'Lots of the fishermen go that way.'

As we drove slowly back past the graveyard, I asked when the child had died. 'In 1965. He was our second child . . . We could stop,' she said, as if the idea had just occurred to her. 'I want to check the grave is all right.' I caught her eye and rather wished I hadn't.

At the gate, she turned left and walked down a straight, asphalted path. I walked for a while through the upper regions, photographing the heavy, ornamented gravestones, and when I thought she had had enough time, walked to the upright marble slab that said 'Sture Vinblad, family grave'. There was a bucket on the grave in front, half full with flowers no more than a day old. 'It's all tidied,' she said, as if she had only been tidying.

'They say it stops hurting,' she said. 'It never does.'

We drove back over the bridge into town. Opposite the church was a substantial three-storey house. 'It used to be the parsonage, but now it is just offices. I was friendly with the parson's wife – she said it was a lovely house, but terrible to run. Imagine how much it cost, and how much time, to put up all the curtains!'

That night, I fished almost until eleven. I wanted to catch one more fish on a dry fly; and so I tried once more the place below the island where I had fished the first time that I came to the river. Almost immediately I hooked a nice fish. I was in a hurry to release him, so I put the rod down and started to pull the nylon directly; just as I noticed he was foul-hooked near the eye

174

he broke free, with the fly still in him. I felt horrible, and rather guilty, and resolved to net everything from then on.

As if to punish me, my own glasses started to steam up terribly whenever I tried to concentrate, so that the fly would vanish as soon as it landed, and after it had floated down for a while, it was all I could do to distinguish the river from the rocks. But I manoeuvred myself into a new position, and managed the long, perfect cast that had eluded me for an hour. The fly had hardly settled on the water before it was taken by a large fish which did not diminish in the water, as so many large fish do, when it approached me.

In the water, it was the biggest grayling I had ever seen, let alone landed; it was definitely too big for my net, and after three or four farcical attempts the net broke away from its frame, but somehow retained the grayling inside – so I could hoist it in and kill the fish on the rock at my feet. I felt nearly as shattered as the fish myself, and walked very slowly home through the liquid light of the woods, thinking about trolls and immortality.

The next day, something strange happened. I walked by the river around noon – wonderful silence, elk tracks in the sand, and a neat pile of yellowing reindeer bone: a skull, a shoulder blade, a bit of a jaw, half of a shin.

After lunch I hauled the armchair into my bedroom so I could sit in front of the window and read. But then I didn't read; I just sat, looking towards the north. I was too low to see anything but sky, the top of an empty flagpole, and round it swallows hunting in the bleak and blue-grey light.

I didn't think, or move much in the chair. I didn't watch in any active sense either: my eyes were not hungry, they were simply clear. It was as if the silence that had been in my ears for so long had finally reached my eyes.

I felt that I was eavesdropping on myself, and when I became aware that I could hear my thoughts, they were all in Swedish, with long vowels stretching out under the sky.

Beneath that sky, I didn't feel small. I felt transient. I knew I would flicker away soon like everything else, a swallow, or a grayling, or one of the large, cautious ants on the edge of the road. Every living thing in the landscape would be dead, hidden, or fled in six months' time; and the river would freeze up more than a metre thick.

In spring the water would return in a flood that tore up boulders the size of cars. As this receded, hundreds of millions of fish would be born in the shallows, and billions of insects in every swamp and pool.

The fecundity of the river, renewed every year, seemed the most powerful force on earth. It had been here long before humans; but even the river was weaker than the ice. Twelve thousand years ago the whole valley was bare rock pressed in the grinding darkness underneath a glacier; one day, the river would vanish again.

Long before that I would die. I'd be as dead as the grayling I had eaten by the river; as dead as everyone I'd loved; everyone I could even remember. Everyone who could ever remember me would die. I didn't want anything else. Up against that huge sky, there was nothing else to want. But this wasn't a revelation for my benefit: there would never be an apocalypse or a reason. It just was.

I thought of the river again and how much more valuable it seemed than human life. So I did want one thing: that the grayling would not die out until after the humans had all gone.

I sat for a long time until the silence was broken by two mosquitoes. I killed them as quickly as I could.

The next day it rained incessantly while I packed to leave. I

176

woke in the middle of the night imagining that the whole landscape was a kind of quilt, soft as unleavened flat-bread, which I
could pull round my giant self, with warm prickly pine trees
like a pelt, and the cooling rivers and smooth, comforting rocks.
My foot started twitching, and I heard its knocking against the
end of the bed as the thumping of a dying perch's tail on the
floor of the boat. Then there was just a huge silence and grief.
I wept a little without any sound, stretched on this abyss, and
when I woke again it was morning and I had to leave.

I walked along the river for half an hour before breakfast,
touching the reindeer skull for luck. It was so sunny that there
was even a hint of yellow in the tips of some wild sprouting rye
on the bank. I have the greens, I thought. Up here, all blues
turn green.

I took a grayling out of the freezer and wrapped it in newspaper as a guest gift for my next stop and then Ulla drove me
into town. At the bus stop I embraced her and promised to try
to return in the winter. Even before the bus moved, the rum-
bling blurry noise and smells had whisked me away from the
forest. Then the journey started, and we were back in the
middle of nowhere: the trees and lakes and rocks outside were
all an undifferentiated smear against the windows that stretched
as far as I could see, and in the middle of the broad daylight I
thought of a line from 'St Lucy's Day': 'I am re-begot. Of
absence, darknesse, death; things which are not.' The radio
hissed and clicked like scorpions in the roof.

Several times we passed cars parked by the side of the road,
with groups of berry pickers beside them, holding white plastic
buckets for their harvest. There, along the roadside, summer
was almost over.

20

Back to Anna

The bus travelled south again, reaching Östersund in the early afternoon, and I was plunged into the juicy sharp-edged delights of early autumn, when all the secret industry of summer appears as fruit. When I walked into Ingela's flat it felt for a few seconds as if nothing had changed in twenty-five years, except that instead of a freshly killed pike I was carrying a grayling, wrapped in newspaper to keep it frozen. I found that the horse-mad adolescent had become a teacher with three grown children and eyes that had known a lot of care. But she was full of joy when I arrived, and she and her family insisted I stay for a while. After several years of wearying domestic excitements, she was at last living in a pleasant flat in the centre of the town with the man she loved.

We spent a confusing few hours trying to catch up with all the various developments in our lives. Anna was living in a modern development a few kilometres away, safe and warm, and she came around for a confused, delighted supper, full of people trying to catch up with decades of absence and ignorance.

Anna was very much older now than I remembered her: the

granddaughters called her 'dandelion' behind her back sometimes because of the way she stood upright with a corona of
grey hair, short, frail, but still tough and oddly radiant. Her
pride was still so fierce as to be indistinguishable from great
humility. One of her neighbours had asked her round for coffee
in the new flats and she had been so impressed by the furniture
and the wealth it displayed that she had never spoken to her
again; she was so ashamed that her own flat had such pathetic
ornaments by comparison. When I pointed my digital camera
at her she made gestures to ward it off until I explained that it
was making a video; then she suddenly dipped in a flirtatious
curtsey: 'Honoured, I'm sure.'

Her grandchildren talked to her across an abyss of change.
Sympathy could bridge it. The youngest granddaughter spent
some time out on the balcony talking to her before supper
about the death of a schoolmate who had frozen to death,
passed out after a party; another of her friends had had a parent
commit suicide. Anna was still a marvellous comfort at times
like that. But the rest of their lives were almost entirely different. Where Anna could only go abroad as a medical missionary,
her granddaughter was planning to go to China for three
months on the money she had saved working as a hotel recep-
tionist in Norway.

At supper, we all made a real effort to get Anna to talk about
her childhood. In all the years I had known her, she had been
too ashamed of much of it to explain. But here, so close to
where she had grown up, and surrounded by her own family,
she was more confident. She even showed off the little fragments of Kikongo that remained from her missionary training:
the word for 'Love'; and what you say to thank someone for a
meal – 'Those were good breads.'

When she reminisced she used the local dialect, which had

words I could not understand at first and just blurred over. Ingela and Jim pointed out that names had strange little gender-dependent prefixes when people talked among themselves in the countryside: *eMoma*, for a grandmother, but *enJim* for a man. Sometimes, Anna said things I couldn't understand at all: her mother, she mentioned, had been the envy of all the neighbours for her skill at washing cows. I thought I must have misheard, but no: at Christmas all of the smallholders would wash their animals: they washed the cows with soap and there was great competition as to who could get their livestock cleanest.

Later we drove her back to the flat where she lived surrounded by souvenirs from her family – small presents from grandchildren; a corner cupboard that Hans had made for her, with a glass door whose frames did not line up with the shelves within. She was still complaining about that, nearly twenty years after he had built it. There was also a picture of her own mother in the nursing home where she had ended her days, sitting at a table. 'See how well she eats,' said Anna proudly, as if to end your days warm and well fed were the summit of human felicity. That's what her childhood had taught her.

I could hardly believe that we were able to see each other, and to talk. All the things that I thought I had abandoned or renounced had been returned to me; conversely, everything I had once clung to had run through my hands like water.

When I left, they pressed on me a copy of Selma Lagerlöf's children's classic *Nils Holgersson's Wonderful Journey*, so that I would have to come back and return it someday. It describes every part of the country in 1903, as it might be seen by a naughty boy who had been shrunk for his bad manners so that he could fly on the back of a great snow goose and learn about the world.

For a while after I came back from Lapland, I told people

that it was stupid to talk about a midlife crisis because anyone with a grasp of arithmetic could see it was more like a two-thirds or three-quarter life crisis. But after that mood wore off, it left me determined to spend as much time as I could of my remaining summers in the north. Huge silence, solitude, and the smell of trees – the very things that had made Lilla Edet torture for me when I first lived there, were now, I understood, necessary elements in my life, without which I could not respire. England seemed for me, once again, as it had been twenty-five years before, a place of failure and of stifling artificiality, from which I might flee to a simpler, less entangled and more honest life.

Soon the daughter whom I had carried on my shoulders round a lake one perfect sunlit day would be grown up. Soon after that, in the way of middle-aged journalists, I would be sacked from something for the very last time. I understood my own life suddenly as that of a hooked fish, pulling with all my strength against a painful and bewildering destiny.

But in this bewilderment I could run north again. I could try to discover what had changed about the country I had once known. I could try to find if there were still the sort of lakes that once had been my sanctuary. And so, the next summer, I put some rods and a laptop in the back of my old Saab and set out to drive as far as I could into Sweden.

21

The revenant

When I rang Anita and said I would be passing through Gothenburg on a trip to find out where the future went, she laughed. It's not the future that changed, she said, it's us. But she was only half right.

The Öresund bridge smelled of sea and wet concrete when I drove across it to Sweden in a blue-gray dazzle of fog. It traverses the fifteen kilometres of strait between Copenhagen and Malmö. Only half of it is airborne: the rest runs through a tunnel and across an artificial island, Pepparholmen, which was built at the same time as the bridge, a little south of the existing, natural island Saltholmen, so as not to disturb the nature reserve there. You could not have a more dramatic, nor more beautiful, symbol of the power and prosperity of Sweden at the end of the twentieth century; nor could you have a clearer statement that the century has ended: the bridge fixes Sweden to the uncontrolled world outside, when through all the years of social democracy the ideal of the country was of a psychological autarky which could deal with the outer world entirely on its own terms. For a while after I had crossed the bridge, only the radio told me which country I was driving through.

To the right of the motorway was temperate countryside, just like Denmark, where substantial farmhouses were set among copses of beech and oak. But the radio news started with an item about a crooked millionaire who had trashed his Ferrari in Beverley Hills. That might not seem in the least bit Swedish, but the millionaire in question came from Uppsala, and the story concluded on a reassuringly familiar note: the important thing about the story, the journalist said, was that it raised Sweden's profile in the USA.

This was followed by the news that the government would open the first treatment centre for overweight children: a professor talked about the need to staple their stomachs in extreme cases. Later, the minister of defence, a woman, was interviewed about a scandal in which members of an elite army unit had celebrated the end of a training course by firing off rocket-propelled grenades while dressed only in their ammunition. A video had found its way on to the television news, and the minister was outraged. 'We must stamp out the macho culture in the army,' she said.

I drove alongside low concrete buildings, one of the satellite towns of Malmö. There is no single good word for these places: the Swedish word is usually translated as 'suburbs', but in English that suggests calm, conventional prosperity. These satellite towns, almost all built in the Sixties and Seventies, function now as ghettos. Rosengård, the satellite town of Malmö nearest to the motorway, has around 18,000 immigrant inhabitants from fifty or more countries, though most are refugees from former Yugoslavia, Lebanon, and Iraq. There are very few native Swedes.

The sleek mercantile prosperity in the university town of Lund, a few miles further on, might have been anywhere in north Germany, Denmark, or even Holland. The chain stores all seemed the same as everywhere else; even the old *Konsum* stores had been renamed to the more international Co-op.

In the centre of Lund there were small cafés selling wine and food so cheap one could imagine eating out every day. This may not be exceptional in other prosperous countries but to anyone who lived in the Swedish provinces in the Seventies, it was unnatural. I had a beer with a salad that contained neither meat nor potatoes. I returned to my hotel room feeling giddy and disoriented, as if I really was in a foreign country; the next morning I fled northwards up the motorway.

Anita and her husband now lived in a renovated house in a renovated village that straggles along a ridge south of Gothenburg; a place of quiet and large new cars driving slowly around speed bumps. It was affluence quite beyond her dreams when she had been married to me. A large red Volvo with cream leather upholstery was parked outside their double garage; a slightly less glossy Volvo lurked inside. The house was what the Americans would call a duplex, running up the side of a hill. In the music room on the ground floor was a white grand piano and two electronic keyboards as well as a sofa and a writing table, all arranged with plenty of space around them; upstairs the rooms were just as large and airy. A studio photograph on the bookcase showed the whole family gathered around the leonine professor: Anita, their two mutual sons, his son by another woman, my son.

The professor walked me around the perimeter of his demesne. The house was surrounded by lawn; a long strip of this, like the handle of a saucepan, ran up at an angle through shaded woodland to the crest of the steep hill behind. It was his partial defence against developers. Once all the land running up the steep hill behind them had belonged to their house, but the grounds had been subdivided when it was sold to them and in the last year the ridge above them had been cleared and a larger, more opulent house than theirs built on it. There was a party on the sun deck going on there as we talked and we could not get away from the noise as we sat on the patio, as if we were on the quayside next to a very large yacht on the Riviera.

Even if the neighbours were richer, Mats and Anita were still deliciously affluent. This wasn't so much a matter of material possessions. Ever since childhood, I have expected Swedes to own more than I do. But their affluence had always seemed confined by society and doled out at its pleasure. What struck me as new was their sense of freedom. I remembered how long I had cowered beneath the imaginary helicopters, and now Mats talked with easy pride about dodging motorway speed cameras: 'It's easy enough to get down from Stockholm in four hours, if you drive down the eastern side of Vättern and tuck in behind someone else who is speeding. That way you can see which of the cameras are actually working, because they will flash at the car in front and ignore the rest. There is always someone happy to drive at 160, but I won't. If you understand about kinetic energy and can calculate, you realize there is a huge difference between travelling at 140 and travelling at 180. If anything goes wrong at 180, you have no chance of keeping control.'

His hair had gone largely white; he had put on both weight and gravity since becoming a full professor; when he turned to talk to his son, he moved like a dancer and hugged him often. In the music room were photographs of the bright-eyed young man with energetic dark hair with whom Anita had fallen in love, standing with her on a boat in the archipelago.

It's a good country to be prosperous in, they agreed; and most people now are reasonably prosperous. 'We call it the two-thirds society, since a third of the country has been left behind,' Anita said. Which third? The uneducated, the unskilled, some of the immigrants, people in the countryside. They felt pity for the poor and for the immigrants; but for the people who stayed behind in the small towns of the interior, they felt a rather superstitious contempt, as if their bad luck might rub off on everyone else.

For years, the farming interior of Sweden had been decaying; all the small towns like Lilla Edet had been losing their industries. There was no reason to live there, nothing to do and no money to be earned. 'We should just close down the whole of the countryside,' Anita said, with as much vehemence as if she still lived in the small town where she had grown up.

Gothenburg was once a noisy town. There were shipyards all along the river, and wharves at its mouth. Fifteen kilometres to the west was Volvo's main plant. I liked it best on a windy autumn night when the rain alternated with sleet, and the massive buildings had some weather to fight. In balmier weather they look muscle-bound and lumpish. The least weighty building in the centre is a theatre modelled on a square wedding cake, with plaster like marzipan icing. This is not a town made for frivolity.

Yet frivolity, or weightlessness, seems its fate. The shipyards and the workshops have all gone. The car industry is dying. The centre has grown both more gentrified and sleazier than it used to be. The centre of the town lies within a zigzag moat, the only remaining part of the seventeenth-century fortifications, laid out by Dutch engineers. It is crossed by a broad street, Avenyn, which leads up to the public library and the art gallery. In all the guidebooks it is listed as the happening place and nowadays it is horrible: shoddy and expensive at once, like Oxford Street but with bars instead of shops.

At the bridge where Avenyn crosses the old moat, there were people staring: in the water were two dark-haired young men in their underpants. One of them had an extravagant mullet hairdo whose tail reached the bottom of his shoulder blades; all his upper back, one arm, and half his chest were covered in tattoos. The rest of him, and all of his friend, were as white as if they'd spent years locked indoors. They were splashing and shouting in the water under the wall on the city-centre side; on the other side was a group of their friends, who shouted something jeering. 'Bugger off,' cried the mullet man, in English with an English accent; the ten or so people on the bank opposite started chanting, in Swedish accents, 'Fuck, fuck, bugger off', while respectable Gothenburg walked across the bridge, or stopped briefly to make comments about their stupidity. No one stopped for long, though. There was too much physical menace coming off the whooping young men.

I wanted to retreat to the decent, reverent atmosphere of a fishing shop. When I was a child, they were dark places with high windows; they smelled of polished wood and leather, with a sharp tang of gun oil on the top. More modern shops smelled of the resins used in fibreglass and graphite rods and of the clear plastic in which rod handles came wrapped. Strömwalls Sportfiske, just inside the old moat, had been my favourite shop in Gothenburg, because it was the oldest, housed in the rounded corner of a massive nineteenth-century mansion block. It belonged to the time when fishing shops were closer to ironmongers than fashionable clothes shops. They sold tools, well made and sometimes beautiful, that did a useful job. People moved in them seriously because they were about to invest important sums of money, and this was true of the adults as much as of the small boys pondering the destination of their pocket money.

But when I returned to Strömwalls it had been turned into a brightly lit science-fiction shop that sold comics and dolls as well as books. You can only dip back into your own childhood. This was one I could not share no matter how I might love science fiction as an adult.

Almost the only place in the centre of town that had not changed was Mauritz Café, a tiny shop in a pedestrian street that sells the strongest and some of the best coffee I have found anywhere in the world. Nowadays everywhere sells cappuccinos and lattes mixed after recipes cooked up with spreadsheets. Mauritz sold cappuccinos when coffee was drunk black and sour everywhere else in Sweden; sugar came not in cubes but in irregular lumps like pebbles, and old-fashioned sensualists would place a sugar lump carefully between their teeth and suck the coffee round it, making an elemental clash of flavours.

Mauritz used to sell some of the most expensive coffee in Sweden, so that a visit there was for us a treat like visiting a cocktail bar would have been, if cocktail bars had then existed in Sweden; but it is now one of the cheaper places to buy a cappuccino. You will find in it bewildered tourists studying a menu which ranks coffees in three different grades of strength, alongside middle-aged women who speak to the counter staff with courteous affection.

Recharged there, I set off to walk across the town – the centre is half an hour's walk at most from side to side. Just outside NK, the smartest department store in Sweden, a light tenor voice behind my shoulder said the English word 'fuck' without any special emphasis. I turned round and saw two young men, one brown, with close-cropped hair, one with blue eyes and ash-blond hair curling round his shoulders where it escaped from a white watch cap. Both men were short and thin; the brown guy was wearing a baggy anorak slightly darker than his skin, and every time they passed a pretty girl he reached into the left-hand pocket and pulled out a short fat spliff to show her, and his friend would snicker. They walked on like this, fast and purposeful, through the slow-moving shoppers, until I lost sight of them past the covered market.

This might not have been remarkable in other countries. There used to be a hippy enclave in Copenhagen where there was a free market in hash and everyone pretended that this was an anarchic vision of a better and more noble future while the dealers strutted up the street with their dogs held on tight chains. In the end the police shut it down. It was all make-believe after all. But in the sunlit, quiet streets of Gothenburg, I felt it was civility that was the sham and that the gentle, ovine creatures all around me were quite doomed.

Sweden has become a very much more violent place since I first lived there. In 1979, violence was so unthinkable that a law was passed forbidding parents to smack their children. There was no penalty for breaking this law: it was thought that if society in general was known to disapprove of it, it would just wither away. The hope of utopia dies hard. I have been assured by a left-wing English journalist that, as a result of this law, Sweden has become a much less violent society; bullying has almost disappeared, and no child has died at the hands of its parents for fifteen years. Of course this is nonsense. If she had bothered to look at the government statistics, she'd have seen that the general rate of violent crime in Sweden has doubled since 1975; assaults on children under six have quadrupled, and on older children they have increased even more. That night in my hotel room I watched on television news as shaven-headed neo-Nazis attempted to riot in Stockholm on National Day, which had been instituted in the Nineties as a way of welcoming immigrants. There weren't very many of them and the coverage was determinedly hostile. But they were young, and lean, with contemptuous angry faces that seemed confident of the decadence of the world around them.

Later the next day I drove down the back roads to Nödinge with a queasy double vision, as if the surface I was driving on was coated with a slippery, treacherous substance. It was my memory, running wide on the corners and leaping ahead on the straights, so that I recognized portions of the road too early or too late. Everything looked wrong. Only when I reached the old settlement of Nödinge did the world come back into focus. The road descends from the farmland on the plateau and the village bluffs, where a church has stood since the twelfth century, and down to the glacial plain along the river where the new estates were built in the Seventies. These hadn't changed at all since we lived there. Three-storey buildings made of brick the colour of dog turds, with white wood facings, as if the turds had dried out at the edges.

I parked my battered, English-registered Saab on the same seamed concrete car park where I had parked the first car I had ever owned in 1978. To one side stood the block of flats where I had came back one winter evening to see a couple waltzing naked in front of a window with the curtains drawn back. Dancing rather well, actually. It was an image that had stuck with me; in my memory the window was larger than the ones I could see.

It's curious what can make you feel lonely. One of the things that made me feel furthest from home when I lived in Nödinge was that there are no Swedish watercolourists, although the skies above the valley are so often full of watercolour clouds with detailed, clear edges between the different greys and blues.

Did no one else notice them? The climate in Sweden is so big, and the revolution of the seasons so great, that the small moments of mere weather seem invisible.

I had returned on another day of watercolour cloud. Once the rain that had sodden me at breakfast time had passed, the day was cool and dry, the light distinct. I walked diagonally through the squares in the middle of the blocks towards the road. A few children were playing in the playgrounds and I passed two young women, one in a hybrid Swedish/Islamic costume, with a white headscarf and white tights under an exuberant knee-length skirt, the other in a tracksuit: she was about four stone overweight, with her hair dragged back from her face in blonde cornrows and a silver dumb-bell piercing her lower lip.

Nobody spoke. That hadn't changed.

I emerged from the estate and stopped dead. The space between the houses and the road had always been a desolate attempt at a lawn. Now it had disappeared under a prefabricated mall, bright with advertising, which ran the whole length of the estate. There were two large supermarkets (neither of them a Co-op), a pet shop, a stationer's, a flower shop, and even a state off-licence. The remaining space was filled with a car park. There were two banks and a pleasant coffee shop, where I sat in stunned calm and ate a pastry. The only thing that seemed to connect this vulgar and extrovert affluence with the old grey Nödinge were the customers in the cafe: by the window three men with the doglike melancholy of retired manual workers, dressed in miscellaneous scruff: grey T-shirts, layers of indeterminate shirts or jackets, jeans, battered trainers.

Two doors along was an entrance to the employment exchange, and beside it a magic money machine. Both had something of the battered dinginess of the shopping square in the Seventies, but what would you expect? The whole place was, by Swedish standards, a slum. People lived here who couldn't afford to live anywhere else. Yet it was airy, prosperous, and clearly cared for, and when I asked in the cafe if there was anywhere with an Internet connection, they directed me to the new school. This was not just new, it was pleasing to look at: perhaps the only building in the whole place that had curves and interesting dimensions. Immediately inside the doors was a high-ceilinged library, apparently made from wood and glass alone, in which the books were much more conspicuous than either CDs or computer terminals.

At the counter, a friendly middle-aged woman urged me to take out a library card. I found myself babbling in Swedish to her like a child of four or five, as if I were recapturing the way I had first learned the language, when no one I knew but Anita spoke English at all, and I had to push myself through the rigid mesh of grammar and intonation to touch the country behind it. I told the librarian I was looking for the history of Nödinge, as it had changed so much since I lived there. She perked up. Had I really lived here myself? She, too, had lived here in the late Seventies, though she had moved away from the estate in the Eighties, and was unclear about what had happened since then. I thought I had read, at some stage in the Nineties, an account of a riot on the estate involving immigrants fighting native gangs. But she couldn't remember any of this. What she knew was that at some time in the mid-Nineties the decision was made to develop Nödinge as a place where people might want to live, and since then everything had got very much better. 'There had been a lot of drinking and people living on social security in the Eighties,' she told me. 'You don't see that now. Of course, these days, they're all on hash and pills, which aren't so obvious.'

I asked if I could walk around the school a little, and she indicated that this would be no problem. The library led to an open social space, with sofas and tables; through that I came to a corridor lined with locked computer labs and then, with a horrible suddenness, I emerged into a cramped concrete square. It looked like a set from a post-apocalyptic video game set in the ruins of civilization but then the scene shook itself into familiarity. This was the old square, where all the shops of Nödinge had been, and the school had just absorbed their concrete shells. Here had been the flower shop, the shoe shop, the labour exchange and the *Konsum*: all of the social and commercial life of the old estate apart from the sausage-and-mashed-potato stand and two petrol stations.

Across the square, towards the apartment blocks, the paving seemed to grow lighter. There had been a few benches here once, and raised flowerbeds; and there, in the far corner, I had witnessed Stig Malm, the metalworkers' union leader, speak to a May Day meeting. When I recognized the place, I felt, for a moment, as if I were walking amid the ruins of a culture as dead and strange to us as the Bronze Age.

In Skepplanda, the village where I had worked for Leif making pallets, the barn that had housed our little factory had completely disappeared. In its place was a tennis court. His house was still there, but when I looked him up online there were no Krügers in the Swedish phone book any more.

The centre of the village seemed not to have changed at all since the Seventies. There was a car park, almost empty, and a low grey concrete supermarket. The stock was meagre and the only customer was a fat woman who was taking a long time to choose an ice cream from the freezer. There was nothing fresh on the shelves, and little of anything I wanted to eat. In the end, I bought flat bread in a polythene bag, and soft processed cheese with bits of ham in it that squeezed, like toothpaste, from a tube. Another fat woman at the till talked to an Indian-looking teenage girl in the back room while she waited for me. The atmosphere of privation was so intense that when I emerged I felt as if the whole shop had been dank, like a cave, though outside the day was hot and bright.

It was only a few kilometres off the main road, and not a long way out of Gothenburg, but here you could sense that the countryside had been shut down as Anita wanted. There was an election campaign just starting, and all through my journey the conservative papers ran reports on the grotesque under-reporting of unemployment. In the official statistics, only about 5 per cent of people were unemployed; but if you added up everyone who was being trained, or had been retired early, or had part-time jobs when they would rather have worked full time, then the unemployment figure looked more like 20 per cent. In a place like Skepplanda, it was hard to believe that anyone worked at all.

The road north to Lilla Edet was less slippery with treacher-ous memories than the roads around the lakes had been. This is partly because it is more boring. There are fewer corners. There is less of anything. The flat alluvial plain is cultivated; the hills around are covered in evergreens. Every ten kilometres there is a little town that the world has forgotten, and they had been easy for me to forget as well, once I was free of the fear that there might be no escape from them.

But when I reached Göta my vision doubled again. This is a township close enough to reach on a bicycle from the house where I had lived our first summer. Much later I had spent part of one Christmas here, when my father-in-law had moved to a bachelor flat on the hillside. The curves to the north of the township – interminable on a bicycle – shrunk to a couple of twitches on the steering wheel, and then the road straightened out for the last run across flat fields towards Lilla Edet. On the left, the old paper factory still stood; but the junction had changed, so that at first I couldn't find my way into the town. I turned up into the hills, instead, trying to find the lakes where I had slept out with Anita. New houses had been built along the old road, and new little tarmacked roads branched off it. I passed a woman walking, very upright, along the verge in a green and brown sari, with granite-grey hair, and a noble face, brown like last year's pine needles. In the end, I couldn't find my way out of the tangle of new roads and turned back down into Lilla Edet.

The town itself had become a meandering backwater. The old straight street that ran through the centre of town, meeting at right angles the road down to the old straight, narrow bridge across the Göta, had been replaced by a curving, wider, slower road. The bus station was still there, but no one needed to go there to order drink for the next day, and the kiosks at each end have shut. The new road winds around it, north of the old crossroads, where once the street had its socialist and its bourgeois side, where ICA and *Konsum* had faced each other from identical concrete bunkers: ICA had shared with an ironmonger's, and the *Konsum* with the Co-op undertakers. Now the struggle was over; the capitalists had won. The *Konsum* was unchanged, but ICA was twice the size and had consumed the ironmonger's. Along the street was a *Systembolag,* instead of the sausage kiosk was a Chinese restaurant. Someone had even opened a pub, but it had gone bankrupt. In the lobby of the ICA store was a gaggle of teenage girls, some of them Muslims in headscarves; inside was a golden light, promising abundance:

shelves filled with delicacies: fresh bread and twenty different sorts of pasta. The magazines and the tabloids had moved on from old-fashioned celebrity to a generalized greasy prurience: 'LAURA'S TRAUMA GAVE HER AN OBSESSION WITH BIG BREASTS (full story and pictures, page 31)'.

Lilla Edet is built by the last rapids of the Göta before it reaches the sea, another fifty kilometres downstream, though they have been tamed by a power station for a century now. The name means 'the small portage' as opposed to the great portage at Trollhättan, where the rapids are immense. The old bridge, narrow and cautious, runs straight across, upstream of the power station, with pillars at frequent intervals. The new one springs in an airy curve across the river half a mile below. There is a hamlet and a petrol station on the far side; beyond them the road runs across a cleared plain. I turned off the road and drove slowly up to Lerdalen, where we had lived in the woods.

I knew that our extended shack – part-cabin, part-caravan – might very likely have fallen down in a bad storm, but when I got to the clearing the whole thing, including the dog-smelling cabin where the old man had lived, had vanished. In its place stood a bright red bungalow big enough for five or six bedrooms, standing in a much-enlarged clearing in the forest. All around was the energetic clutter of rural prosperity. The field when I had practised my fly casting in the snow was now cut in half by a gravel hard-standing on which stood an old Volvo estate car and two boats on trailers, one of them twice as high as the tractor parked beside it. All I could feel from the time that I had lived there was an overwhelming urge to leave.

22

Another country

My old friends Lasse and Kristina still lived in Uddevalla, but they had moved to the old house where she had grown up, on a hill overlooking the town. Lasse was, I think, completely happy there. He had remodelled almost everything when they moved in: rewired, insulated, put in stoves, cladded the walls, painted, papered, built a greenhouse and a little *stuga* for visitors, gardened – he grows grapes, apples, currants, rhubarb. At the back is a place where chanterelles can be harvested in autumn.

Lasse lost his welding job in the mid-Eighties, when the shipyard went bust. Then he found another job as a welder, but a few years later that, too, disappeared, when the firm moved its operations to Lithuania. He retrained as a hydraulic fitter and now, in his sixties, works as hard as he ever did, but further from home, so he is often away all week. The still in the kitchen is a distant memory. He's much more respectable now: indomitable, grave and proud.

He and Kristina have a good, worthwhile life that is in many ways enviable. Their three children delight them, as do their grandchildren. In his shed is a wonderful collection of tools, lovingly accumulated, for making and farming, welding and woodwork. He could probably build the whole house again if he needed to. Despite everything that has gone wrong with their jobs over the years, this is still the kind of spacious, useful and honourable life that he and Kristina and most other Swedes expected to inherit when he was growing up. But no one who is younger now seems to expect it.

One afternoon, while I was staying with them, I was looking for an ice cream in the centre of town, almost wading through the treacly heat, when a man with a notebook and camera accosted me. He had one of those faces on which charm and disillusion had contended for years; charm was losing the battle on the day we met. He was doing a vox pop for the local paper, asking people at random how they survived a heat wave. I saw in him something or someone I might have become if I had never returned to England, so I explained that I was in the trade myself and we arranged to meet: he could tell me everything that had happened there in the twenty years I had been away.

I think I could have cut it as a journalist in Sweden; my language skills were up to it, and there is always a market for smart outsiders. God knows I had not wanted to return to England as a country. I had wanted to go back to the English language, and to make it in London. But if anyone then had told me when I left Uddevalla that I would never again have lived outside England I would have despaired.

Ulf spoke with a melancholy pride about the ruined town around him. Like many journalists, he knew all sorts of things that he could never print, and even when he could print them, no one would take notice. He was a local boy, though he had left town at nineteen for a job lower down the coast, in Kungälv, the home of Club Hangover. 'Two families later, here I am again. The genetic material is back in Gothenburg . . .'

When he grew up, there was no such thing as youth unemployment. 'In this town we had the shipyard, the Post Office, the phone company, the army base, the railways, and the hospital.' All these places would give you jobs and a skill when you left school. They're all gone now. The shipyards went bust. The Post Office has been deregulated and hardly exists any more. The phone company was privatized and has lost money ever since. The old army base here has just about disappeared. The railway is bankrupt and the government is trying to sell off thirty-five stations. Even the hospital is being reorganized into a regional entity, and might lose its A & E department, a story that greatly exercised him. Looking back on the Nineties, he had a terse summary. 'They deregulated everything, and it all went to hell.'

Volvo, which had once made cars for the sort of people who live along Route 45, now made them for Stockholmers, when it made them at all. There is a Volvo factory of sorts in Uddevalla now, which stands on the ground of the old shipyard; it says 'Pininfarina' on the side, because it is a plant run in partnership with the Italians, but Volvo is really just a part of Ford now. Ulf didn't think it would last. 'Both this, and the Saab factory in Trollhättan, to which a thousand people commute every day from here, will probably shut in the next ten years. When Volvo built their factory here, they bought the ground for it from the old shipyard for one *krona*, and a promise from the state to build a motorway from Göteborg. This was built in the face of all sorts of objections on ecological grounds. Now that the motorway has been built they will shut the factory down. That's how big business works these days.'

The only growth industry he could see in Uddevalla was organized crime. As part of the general deregulation and reorganization of society, the police were now concentrated in fewer places, which meant fewer where the criminals might be. 'There is a gang called the Brotherhood of the Wolf Pack, which was formed in prison about twenty years ago, by people from around here. We've had the occasional revolver duel on the street. And this is meant to be one of the more important harbours for heroin smuggling on the west coast.' We agreed that he should write a story about my return to the town, as he thought it remarkable that anyone from abroad should care about the place enough to come back. I set off the next day to see the estates where Anita and I had lived, so that the paper could get a photograph of me there. He told me that our old estate, Hovhult, was on its way up in the world; Dalaberg, across the road, was more like a ghetto.

When I had told Lasse I wanted to go back and look at my old flat he had been shocked.

'Oh, don't do that!' he said. 'It's full of foreigners now.'

Well, I was a sort of foreigner myself, I said.

'No, not like that. Blacks.'

I made a face.

He justified himself. He and Kristina had once been friends with a Palestinian couple. They had shared meals and, he thought, had a relationship of mutual trust. At one stage, Lasse had come into possession of some old, broken video recorders, which the Palestinian said would be useful in Jordan, if he could send them there. So Lasse gave them to him, without hesitation or questions. When he later found out that the man was not passing them on to relatives, but selling them in Sweden, he was furious. The distinction between friendship and commerce was in his mind sacrosanct. To violate it made you a barbarian, and that went for everyone like you, too.

Later, he told me another story that showed how he thought the country ought to work. As a young man, he had been living on the seventh floor of a block in the centre of town, and one night, sitting drinking with friends, they had heard the noise of smashing glass. All of them ran downstairs, to find three youths trying to break into a shop on the ground floor. They chased them, caught two, and handed them over to the police. They were just kids, he said: bored and ignorant. They were not imprisoned for their crimes. In fact a month later one of them was found a job in the shipyard. He and Lasse still greet each other warmly if they meet, and talk about all sorts of things. But never has either of them mentioned how they first met. Lasse thinks this is a wonderful example of how the system ought to work: a brief shock, and the young man rescued from a life of crime.

The story made sense of something that had puzzled me almost every time I opened a paper. The country seemed full of horrendous crimes – any newspaper in any country can make you feel like that – but no one was complaining about the low sentences imposed on violent criminals. Christer Pettersson, who was almost certainly the murderer of Olof Palme, had murdered a stranger before then – with a bayonet – yet had been set free to wander Stockholm by night, his life sentence served after five years. This was not unusual. Mikael Hagelin, a young man who killed his mother with a kitchen knife, was sentenced to two years in a young offenders' institution; I came across the story because he was appealing against a later life sentence imposed for knifing to death a girlfriend after his release, when he was twenty-two.

Gangsters, pimps and rapists could get away with sentences of two or four years and even these were quite notional figures: you would have to be a very consistently troublesome prisoner to serve out your full sentence in a Swedish jail. The normal time served is half the official sentence. Yet no one seemed to think that criminals were cheating justice. To anyone used to the British tabloids, this is difficult to explain.

One might say it was just the conformism, verging on self-censorship, of the Swedish media. That certainly exists. Talking to an old friend – another journalist – I remarked how strange it was to see the Swedish television news, in which there is never any doubt which are the villains and which the heroes in any story. 'And why not?' she replied happily.

The unanimity of the press, and its deep respect for its own judgement, is reminiscent of America rather than Britain. One veteran columnist on the national tabloid *Expressen*, Ulf Nilsson, wrote as a British journalist might about a country where schools were constantly burning down, when they weren't being theatres of macho bullying by dark-skinned immigrants – 'Is there anywhere where Swedish girls aren't screamed at as white whores?' he asked. Where ten rapes a day are reported? Where the crime rate in general is worse than in New York, and where, he claimed, there are at least a million people unemployed? – that is, 25 per cent of the working population, more or less. But his seemed an isolated voice. Although his crime figures are the government's, the official unemployment rate is still 5 per cent and there is still enough make work to go round for almost everyone, even if real jobs are scarcer on the ground.

If you are an outsider, the optimism of the 'official' press seems to be part of a soft conspiracy. But this is to underestimate its force. It isn't just an expression of fashion, and a herd mentality. It's a belief that herds are good: that the natural state of a human being is as a part of a harmonious society. That is why even a short prison sentence is held to be enough: what's needed is to shock the criminal out of their bad habits, not to cut them off from redemption altogether. A lot of the time, this is actually true. But for shock and shame to work on ordinary criminals, unwritten rules are required, which are understood and enforced by almost everyone in the community. Immigration is certainly not the only threat to this process, nor even the greatest. But it is the most visible. The behaviour of the immigrants themselves need not be destructive. The belief in foreign scroungers can be destructive even when they don't exist, just as the belief in the gallant Swedish army was constructive when that, too, was a myth.

Hovhult and Dalaberg estates are about a kilometre and a half north of the centre of town; the broad road lies in easy curves uphill all the way from the hospital tower. I walked up slowly in the heat, meeting only two or three people. Hovhult, too, was almost deserted when I reached it, though it looked more open, even prosperous, than I remembered it. The spaciousness was explained when I noticed that many of the squares were now three-sided. Four or five whole blocks of flats had simply vanished, their foundations grassed over. The playgrounds in the middle had been renewed, and the vile, spiky berberis bushes that had been planted in front of the buildings had all been grubbed up and replaced, so far as I could see, by real flowers.

Passing some of the ground-floor flats I saw Kurdish-looking women in scalloped pink and cream headscarves watching the desultory play of grandchildren in the sun. When finally I reached our old flat, there was no one in sight at all, though the day nursery beyond it had clearly doubled in size. I walked up the stairs. My breath caught at the sour and suddenly nostalgic smell of concrete and disinfectant. On the door, the plastic letters above the letter box now said 'Ahmed'. I waited a few moments. What could I say if I knocked? There seemed to be nothing that would make sense, coming from a stranger. I walked back down the cool dark stairs and into the glare outside. There was no one on our balcony, and thick patterned curtains were drawn across the windows behind, as they were across the windows of the downstairs flat.

Across the road, between the blank walls of Dalaberg, everything felt different. Even when we lived opposite, it had a scummy reputation, and seemed an unfriendly place. The houses are in rows, not squares, and six or seven storeys high, not three. These very small changes seemed to set the character of the place as somewhere to escape. All these things are relative. When you compare life in Dalaberg to poor life almost anywhere else, the delights of poverty in Sweden become apparent: for £400 a month, the tenants get a three-bedroom flat and a properly equipped kitchen, and the whole thing is connected by frequent buses to an agreeable small town over a distance that could just as well be walked. In fact, to judge by the prices, this offer was more desirable than our old flat in Hovhult, which now rented for 4,647 *krona* a month – say £350.

But it still felt concrete and inhuman; it had changed much less than Hovhult. Almost the first thing I saw walking into the estate were signs to the social services, and to an 'international women's club', both of which I remembered from twenty years before. The centre, where these facilities were, along with a library and a few shops, reminded me why Oskar, Felix's friend, talked of the old Sweden as being something like East Germany. It was clean, and safe and tidy. But people seemed to be an afterthought, and commerce an embarrassment.

The appearance of prosperity might be misleading. In the little pizzeria beside the entrance to an underground car park – a more depressing place for a restaurant can hardly be imagined – a can of fizz costs about 6 *krona* (40p) as opposed to the 15 *krona* charged down in town, even in the sleazier establishments. A father and daughter were speaking in Arabic to each other while I sipped my Coca-Cola. Anywhere else they would be classified as white – she in particular was very fair-skinned – but I could see that in Uddevalla they would count as 'black'. Their knowledge of immigration seemed infinitely distant from mine, and the Sweden that they had moved to seemed a place about which I knew nothing. The bus I caught back down to town in the middle of the day had ten other passengers. Only the driver spoke Swedish to anyone, which he did with a thick foreign accent.

In the evening, after supper and stories, Lasse and I sat up late watching fishing porn: a DVD of three men fishing their way down one of the great rivers of Lapland. It was a very familiar comfort – in fact he knew all the exciting moments by heart, and would announce them in advance. But I couldn't stay to fish. The 45, the road which runs up the valley of the Göta from Gothenburg past Nödinge and Lilla Edet, continues for nearly 1,300 kilometres northwards, long past Sorsele, until it comes to the Finnish border, high above the Arctic Circle.

23

Far north

The deep country along Route 45 does not start until the road rears away from Trollhättan over a superb, spirit-lifting bridge to the west bank of the river and then runs up the apparently endless shores of Lake Vänern. The country is still largely flat, and not even entirely wooded. The lake extends northwards for a hundred kilometres; towards the end of this stretch is Åmål, a town known only for a film about the boredom of life there, which was called 'Fucking Åmål' even in its Swedish version.

Actually, it was called *Jävla Fucking Helvetes Kuk Åmål* in the original, which makes the point even more strongly, and I shouted the whole name as I came across the signpost to the town's short, official name. I had a little digital recorder on the seat beside me, so that I could take notes without stopping, and also so that I could work on my Swedish accent without causing pain to strangers. The further I drove, the more I started talking in Swedish for reasons that were not pedagogic, and the less sense any of the things I said could possibly have made to anyone else. To discuss my own life with myself in Swedish was a curious experience, as if I were allowing my younger self a privileged, disheartening glimpse into what I had become. He didn't have anything very useful to say, either. But all his gleeful loathing of the provinces rushed back and made me feel very much better.

From Åmål on northwards is a string of small towns from which people sometimes emerge to fame in the outer world, but to which, if they are lucky, they never return. The next town is Säffle, the home of an authoritarian policeman who is murdered with a bayonet as he lies stricken by cancer in one of the Sjöwall and Wahlöö books; another two hours' driving and I came to Torsby, where the former England football manager, Sven Göran Eriksson, grew up.

Torsby has a curiously Texan feel: it reminds me of the dying small towns in Larry McMurtry novels. The forests around are no longer economical to farm, any more than Texan prairies are: it's cheaper to shift the timber in from Lithuania. The town's hopes are pinned on a single prestige project – a chilled tunnel nearly a mile long in which one can practise cross-country skiing in summer. But the most vivid evocation of *The Last Picture Show* comes from the cars, and the blondes.

All through the afternoon, and long into the bright evening, five or six huge American cars drove slowly round the centre of town, crammed with whooping young people whose parents can hardly have been born when these Chevvies and Oldsmobiles were made in old Detroit. Torsby is one of the centres of the Swedish working-class cult of owning gigantic American cars. This is one of those aspects of the country quite invisible from the outside, though you can get a suggestion of it in the films of the Finnish director Aki Kaurismäki.

I remembered this *passeggiata* from the first time I came here, in 1992, when there were many more cars; even then the tradition was in decline. The glorious freedom and wealth that these cars celebrated and depended on could not survive in a world where petrol grows steadily more expensive and spare parts are no longer made.

In the evening I went in search of a bar where I could watch some football. The game bores me most of the time, but this was the World Cup. England was in the grip of some kind of national neurosis, and it was managed by a Swede who came from Torsby. For a long time, the English Football Pools were about the only widespread legal form of gambling in Sweden, so there is a lot of knowledge about the English game. One might think, then, that the town would be full of excited fans on a Saturday evening, especially as Sweden was also playing (and heading for the same predictable ignominy: the two teams actually played each other, and drew, before both being knocked out by the first good teams they met).

I walked out looking for a crowd around a television set. The pizzeria was almost deserted, and the Hotel Björnide, whose name translates, not unfairly, as the Hotel Hibernation, was quiet in anticipation of the disco that night, where we were promised a celebrity – one of the participants from the previous year's Swedish version of *Big Brother*. A few blocks away was a 'Sports Bar'; the main room was quiet and almost empty. Off to one side there were tables arranged, as in a classroom, facing the magisterial television on the wall. Around thirty people of both sexes sat around the tables, most of them facing the screen, in an atmosphere of attentive good humour, as if they were at an interesting evening class. No one sang or shouted; hardly anyone swore. It was as unlike an English pub showing an England football game as a Labrador is unlike a pit bull. I sat and drank a beer for half an hour. Hardly anything more happened on the pitch than in the room, and it didn't seem worth the price of another beer to find out how the match ended. I returned to the Hotel Hibernation to find out what the disco had to offer.

There were three people waiting in the hotel bar. The disco room next door, about the size of a walk-in freezer, was pulsing with green, red and yellow lights. But there was no sound, and no DJ. The three men, all with moustaches, in their thirties or forties, drank beer and talked quietly at a table. I walked to the balcony and looked down.

In the bright midsummer daylight of ten in the evening I could see a cream-and-chrome-finned Cadillac wheeze away from the pizzeria, driven by a glorious blonde, so that her boyfriend, with an Elvis quiff, could drink in the passenger side. It looked like the most majestic transport since the *Queen Mary* was turned into a casino, but unfortunately the engine kept dying. In the bar, the three men were joined by a younger one, without a moustache. Perhaps this was the celebrity. He drank with them for a while, waiting for the girls to arrive and the music to start. After a while, the music started up in the room where the coloured lights were, but there didn't seem to be any DJ, and there certainly weren't any dancers. By midnight, no women had arrived, and there were seven men drinking quietly but seriously at two different tables. At some stage, the bouncer came in to check that everything was in order. He, too, was drawn into one of the melancholy conversational circles. I left the disco around one in the morning. By that time there were only five men left. There had been no dancing at all, and no women.

Picking a forest at random, I drove out of Torsby towards the Norwegian border behind an Oldsmobile convertible about nine feet wide that lumbered sedately at the speed limit. Between the driver and the passengers' heads hung something that might be a stuffed hippopotamus, but resolved itself, when the car lumbered off down a gravel side track, into the biggest pair of furry dice I have ever seen.

The frontier was marked by a lake, a camping ground and a

shop selling tobacco that was cheap if you came from over the border. It was a bright, hot day and the forest smelled of dust and resin. A small, stony river ran back from the lake into Sweden, and after a few miles I followed a dirt road down to it. I was standing on a wooden bridge, watching for trout in the water – slivers of green and violet wavering against a grey-and-gold ground – when a dirty red Volvo 240 saloon came down the track. It was a boxy model that had been an object of desire in the late Eighties; a strip of plastic trim hung down behind the radiator and trailed in the dirt. The driver was a dusty blond man of early middle age, but I didn't notice anything more about him until he turned round, drove back to the bridge, and stopped beside me. He wound down the window and placed a pouch of snuff inside his lower lip.

'Yerr-man-y?' he said, confidently enough. I looked and smiled, bewildered. 'Yerr-man-y!' he repeated, enthusiastically. 'Yer-manny? *Kommer du ifrån Deutschland?*

No, I said, in Swedish: I was English. Since I spoke Swedish, he offered me a portion of snuff. I declined, but we talked a little about fishing.

'I was a good fly fisherman once,' he said. 'One of the best in the country, when I worked in Motala. But I had to stop. I got arthritis in my wrist.'

On the front seat beside him was a child of about three who hadn't said a thing in all this time. He seemed entirely preoccupied with a length of fluorescent green string he was playing with. He was blond, like his father, lean and gangly.

'Do you tie your own flies?' asked the driver.

'Yes. Do you want to see them?'

'Why not?'

I brought him a couple of boxes from my car, thinking he would be amused by the mayflies, but he appeared shocked.

210

'Come home and I'll tie you a proper fly for round here,' he said. 'We could have a drink. I only live around the corner.' He gestured, and drove off. I followed, wondering if, and by how much, he was drunk. His car barrelled down the dirt road through farmland, for about five kilometres, until suddenly he pulled off at a large, beautifully situated house on the side of a hill above a couple of barns. In one of them a radio played old-fashioned dance music as we approached, though it was empty; the other was a garage, with low rafters above our heads and fifteen or more fishing rods of every sort lying across them. I followed him in. When he now turned to talk to me, his breath smelled like rotting apples. The child, still silent, played with his bright green string around our feet.

The man pulled down the butt joint of an old fawn rod, with faded scarlet whippings holding on dulled rings. It had a long cork handle, lovingly worn down above the reel seat. 'This was a wonderful rod. You could catch trout up to eight kilos on it. I lost the top, though. It was a wonderful rod. Look at it.' After I had admired this, down came a fly rod. This was complete, but old and drooping. He laughed to see the dust on the reel seat. Then he moved suddenly to the shadows by the wall and stooped. 'But this is the treasure chest!'

From down on the ground he lifted a weather-beaten wooden box. Ancient feathers from pheasant, duck, and rooster mingled with stiff, furry skins inside it. The lid was piled anyhow on top of it with the brass hinges flapping loose. The smell of dust was even stronger here.

'Now I will tie you a proper fly!'

He set off towards the house. 'I'm sorry if I'm hung over,' he said. 'I'm badly hung over, but you know how it is. We Swedes – we're like Finns. Once we start drinking, we never know when to stop.'

We climbed the trim lawn. At the porch, he kicked off his clogs neatly. 'Would you like tea or coffee, or – something to drink?'

Coffee would be fine, I said. Inside we came into a large, neat kitchen, with a big table laid with five white plates, and knives and forks and glasses. 'Damn,' he said, as if shocked by the sight he had left. 'I was expecting company. But they never showed up. I don't know what it was. I was just on my way out to see them when I saw you.'

He whisked the plates and knives and forks away, and cleaned up the table with a cloth. On the counter in the background I could see two frying pans full of congealing slices of fried sausage. The house was completely empty.

'Have you ever had coffee from a percolator machine like this?' he said. 'I bet they don't have real boiling coffee in England – and this is Gevalia brand, not Löfbergs Lila. There's no taste to that.'

The child started to make inarticulate noises of discontent. There was something wrong with the way his green string had become attached to a cart full of wooden bricks. I walked into the next room and sorted this, while the manufacture of coffee continued in the kitchen, with clanking and commentary.

In this room was a television showing the start screen of a Disney DVD, with all the text in English. The child pointed at trees on the screen and said something monosyllabic and unintelligible. How old is he? I asked. Three and a half.

The coffee percolator was finally plugged into the mains, and while it worked, we all went upstairs, so that he could show me a letter he had written on the subject of wolves. They had been exterminated in Värmland a hundred years ago; in those days, peasants who did not show up for the organized wolf hunts could be fined. Now you were fined if you shot them. What was the sense of that? His letter would explain more, he said.

'But don't they compensate farmers?' I asked.

'Oh, yes. You get compensation for every animal they eat. And there is special wire that the wolves are supposed to be unable to get through, with five strands that they can't get over or under neither. But they are destroying the valley. They'll drive the people out.'

'Are they here, in this valley?'

'Oh yes. All over the place. If you look in the garage, you can see a dog bed. The wolves killed my dog. Now, you tell me: should I get another puppy? And what happens if they take the little boy? Then you'll see riots. But nobody lives here, only pensioners. The Dutch and the Norwegians buy all the houses, because they are so cheap.'

We returned downstairs for coffee and a lesson in fly-tying. He gave us both mugs and started to tie a sorry sedge fly: a reddish, shaggy thing with a flat wing made of fawn speckled mallard feathers. His commentary grew increasingly enthusiastic. For a man who had not tied a fly in twelve years, he did pretty well: the result would certainly catch fish, and his hands hardly shook at all.

The little boy sat at the table like a well-trained dog – playing with stuff until told to stop, largely silent, never spoken to except by me. I let him play with the torch in my little penknife, which he loved.

After a quarter of an hour the fly was done. He gave it me and opened a beer to celebrate. I placed the fly carefully in a film canister. It would catch fish. He wanted to show me his photographs but I insisted I had to return to Torsby so I left him and his son in the kitchen with the two frying pans full of congealing sausage for the visitors who never came. All the way back to Torsby I wondered whether I should have stayed, and whether the little boy would be all right. Then I realized that when I had lived on the edge of the woods with a small son myself, I might have struck a visitor in much the same way, except that I never drank. When I walked around Torsby in the evening I looked this time in the windows of the estate agent's, and saw my host had been right. I could buy a small house out towards the Norwegian border for £15,000.

The next morning, the promise of peace and chilled, anaesthetized desolation still seemed to echo round me as I took a last walk through the broad, quiet streets.

I reached the ski resort at Sälen in the blazing heat of lunchtime, with the car's thermometer registering 36 degrees, only to find the whole place shut. There was a small low mall on one side of the road, a couple of supermarkets and a pizza restaurant in a wooden cabin on the other side. The pizza place was run by a family of Iraqi Kurdish refugees. They had set up a wireless Internet network, which customers were free to use, though I never saw anyone else pull out a laptop there. It is one of the marks of modern Sweden that you cannot find anywhere so remote that it does not have a Kurdish family running a pizza restaurant.

Sälen lies at the foot of the mountainous border country, where the billowing forested hills of the interior break into rock and bare heath. The lowest limit of reindeer cultivation lies a little further north. The river Ljöra, which runs across the Norwegian border here, is the southernmost place for really good dry-fly fishing, because it is the first place where the food chain consists mostly of carnivorous insects. Everything grows more carnivorous as the vegetation grows sparser. Even the oyster mushrooms in the forest exude from their filaments a poison that paralyses the nematode worms they subsequently absorb, while the mussels in which freshwater pearls grow spend their larval stages as parasites on the gills of small trout. The air makes humans glad to be alive.

Along the Ljöra valley there is a large, modern, purpose-built youth hostel. It was open, although almost deserted. Downhill was a clearing, a stretch of forest, then a bog, and then the river. Uphill, across the empty road was another clearing, and a sign proclaiming the arrival of a 'wilderness village: 50 houses coming here'. There was a yellow bulldozer that I never saw moving, and beyond it, the scrubby forest stretched up into the mountains. But some weeks before, I was told, the bulldozer's driver had seen an elk lurch out of the forest and hurry across the clearing, and, a minute or two later, a wolf ran after it, and into the trees again.

The youth hostel was bright and warm in that empty landscape; the nearest house might have been a kilometre away; the nearest shop was half an hour's drive. On my second night there was only one other guest, a large man in late middle age with a determined young man's face besieged by jowls and wrinkles. We ate in silence, at separate tables, but when we were finished he introduced himself, invited me to share his bottle of red wine and started to tell his story.

He had come here to plant flowers on his mother's grave. He did this every year, as soon as the danger of frosts had passed. Rolf talked of himself as a geologist, and that was how he had trained, but for much of his life he had been trying to find water for poor people rather than metals for rich ones. With his wife, he had started one of the earliest aerial survey businesses in Sweden, and flown for hours up and down the country in small planes looking for minerals. It was hard, profitable, high-tech work, the sort of thing that Sweden was meant to be good at. He had gone out to Africa, and at first it was minerals he was searching for there, too. But soon he had turned to searching for water, since that was what poor people needed, and in his quiet practical way, he was, I realized, a considerable philanthropist.

He was not a religious man, he told me, but there was one place he really believed in, which lay a long way north of almost every settlement on earth.

'Lannavaara is not a beautiful place. There are swamps all around; it's dark in winter, and full of mosquitoes in summer. But it has something. People move there from all over the world. If ley-lines existed that's where they would cross.' He laughed here, excited and ashamed all at once.

The twilight beyond us stretched like gauze, letting the starlight through. Rolf talked on. In Lannavaara, he said, there was a man named Agne Söderström, who I should meet. He was not the easiest man to talk to. 'But he is admirable. He has made the life he wanted, and he has done so with his honour intact.'

The next morning he urged me again to travel to Lannavaara; then, in shorts and sandals, shouldering his little red haversack, he stumped out to the car to visit his mother's grave before driving through the mountains and on to Stockholm.

In the evening, I sat out on the veranda that ran the length of the front of the hostel, and talked with Kjell Röngård, who had built it in the mid-Nineties. Kjell was a retired policeman. He could easily have been one of the constables pounding the beat under Martin Beck: he had joined the force in 1963, the year after *Roseanna* was published, when he was nineteen. He had ended up as the police chief in Sälen, before taking early retirement on a very generous pension in 2004. He had worked on murder investigations, of course, he said. But most of his time had been spent on the two types of crime that undermined society rather more. From 1970 until 1982 he had worked on the county drug squad and seen the problem steadily increase. Then he moved into what is in Sweden known as 'economic crime', which is mostly tax evasion. Here, too, the rate of crime had grown since the Seventies as the economy grew more open and people had become more individualistic.

He had sympathy for some of the criminals he'd had to deal with. A self-employed carpenter, he said, might earn 25 or 30,000 pounds a year: but since more than half of that would go in taxes, he would obviously do a few jobs for cash. He also felt it undermined the sense of interdependence, which was the foundation of society. But in small communities everyone depended on everyone else: the teacher depended on the lumberjack, the fisherman, the hunter. Solidarity was forced on them. 'But as society has developed, and people have become more mobile, they move to Stockholm, and then they don't know each other. The social bonds disappear in a large city.'

This wasn't a very cuddly vision of society. The social bonds he was talking about are just that – bonds – and I could still remember feeling that the sky above Lilla Edet was made of iron, riveted down to hold us all in place. But something like this was at the root of social democracy, and the old policeman, talking about it, sounded a lot kinder than policemen usually do. 'I think the social control is important in society – that we care about each other as children, and as adults. Take such a little place as this: it is tremendously important that we work together, socially, economically, and culturally. We must look after one another. If we have that, then the social control is one hundred per cent.'

His wife had been a social worker almost all the time that he had been a policeman, and in retirement, the two of them had helped out with their church's social work in Russia. They had visited a home in the provinces there, where thirty-five abandoned old people shared one outside lavatory and a cracked bathtub in the house next door, and to him it was clear that such a hell arose from a society where all relationships were voluntary and none could be compelled or regulated by society. Under the written law he had enforced all his life was the unwritten foundation of the *Jäntelagen*, the Scandinavian code of egalitarian conformity, which absolutely forbids anyone to feel superior to their neighbours. Only then can true neighbourliness flourish.

'I believe in integration, absolutely. I have been a civil policeman for the United Nations. I worked in Cyprus, for example, and there you see how the Greek Cypriots and the Turkish Cypriots do not really regard each other as human. Even in Sälen I have noticed the schoolchildren screw around with the Turkish children – and why? Because their parents have not understood how important it is to talk well of them.'

There was a silence. Swallows hunted around our heads as we sat; over the mountains to the north-west, the clouds were purplish-blue and grey, like the mother-of-pearl inside a mussel shell.

'What a privilege it is to live out here,' he said, 'after so many years in towns.'

The youth hostel in Sälen was not at all the sort of quiet place I had dreamed of writing in, but I stayed there for nearly a week. It was cheap, and for the most part deserted, since I had come between the main fishing seasons. The travellers who did arrive were few and strange: Lithuanian forestry workers,

218

middle-aged parties up from the south for a holiday, lean mountain walkers who moved carefully and said little; even a travelling salesman of superglues who wanted to know why Sven Göran Eriksson had all that trouble with women when he could afford any whore he wanted.

After the salesman was gone, a deep melancholy and revulsion from the world took possession of me. I worked until about two without feeling that I had accomplished very much, and then went for a walk by the river. Nothing seemed wrong there: clear water, a sandy bottom; a sizeable pike startled; but there was nothing right or enjoyable about these moments either. Back at the hostel I lay down for a sleep and then woke, gasping and frightened, like a fish leaping into a world of fright. Some terrible hook from the world I had hoped to leave behind had been set inside me. My hands shook. I dashed cold water on my face. I had not felt so awful, so unutterably lost, since my first summer in Lilla Edet, when sometimes I would abandon my rod and box of spinners by the lake and hurry unburdened through the woods until no sound from the world below could reach me, and I could just sit huddled in the rocks and leaves, right at the end of my tether.

Now I rushed out to the car instead and lifted my fishing vest from the boot. The weight of half a dozen clanking fly-boxes was soothing, and so were the compound summer smells of cloth, damp wader, mosquito repellent and tobacco. My panicked run was checked. I could breathe normally. With the weight of the vest to keep me down in the normal world, I walked back into the hostel and spent half an hour at a table by the window, sorting through the flies in every box and throwing away everything that I would never use. The meticulous process of destruction steadied my nerves enough to drive, and I set out north, driving slowly as if I were looking for the right turn-off, but I was on a road that had no exits; I just wanted to be in motion. After about fifteen minutes on an empty road I realized that this wouldn't do and turned back south towards the town. A few kilometres before I got there, a single-track wooden bridge stretched across the river, which was so clear that I fancied I could see the shadows of fish moving over the pale stretches of the bottom. On the far bank, the steering felt soapy and vague on the dirt track: it was hard to remember that there was a ton-and-a-half of steel on top of these wandering tyres. A few logging tracks ran up the hill, but I stayed on the lowest road, which gradually lost its gravel and became an earthen track, hummocked and potholed, until it descended almost to the level of the river and stopped. The path beyond was blocked with a gate, and led to a nature reserve. There were two more cars parked there, but no sound or sight of living human beings. I changed into waders amid the mosquitoes and walked past the gate, up a fairly steep hill to the top of a bluff overlooking the river.

On the far side, the path dropped unexpectedly into a kind of paradise. There was a broad meadow, fringed with birch trees along the riverbank; at the far end, a sheepfold and an unpainted wooden barn the colour of soaked driftwood. There were a few sheep on the grass, which turned out, as I walked across it, to be tough and fibrous, growing out of a tussocky bog. Upstream and downstream of this clearing, the river broke into braided channels around wooded islands, but for the length of the meadow – perhaps half a kilometre – it was smooth and inviting. The sun was still well clear of the trees on the ridge to the north-west. I fished for two hours in a waking trance. There is a moment in every fly cast where your hand has stopped, the rod has straightened. It is a kind of judgement on all the preceding movements. If they have been performed exactly right, then the line will be drawn in a loop unrolling above the water for twenty metres or more until it settles almost gently, and the fly itself whips over the tip of the line and wobbles on to the water like a leaf. It hardly ever happens like that, but that evening almost every cast straightened exactly as I wanted it to: I felt that I knew where each fish would rise next. Sometimes, when I hooked one, I would laugh out loud. I didn't really care whether I netted them or not. After two hours, I had caught eight grayling. The river was in shadow by then, and the wind, which had swung round to the north, was bracing, its gusts invigorating. I was waist-deep in water as cold as a plunge pool. I couldn't feel my arms because they were perfectly obedient to my will; I couldn't feel my legs because they had gone numb. I shuffled slowly to the bank and stumbled across the meadow, the sensation returning to my legs as my feet banged into the ground. Even the mosquitoes were chilled into a stupor. Back at the car, the thermometer read four degrees; it was three by the time I returned to the hostel. The next morning, I woke up quite sane. Whatever pulled me had broken loose, or at least the line had gone slack.

The next morning I set out to drive north until I was out of the forest. Four hours later I was in Östersund and then the journey began in earnest. The long run from Östersund to Sorsele is the flattest and dreariest part of the journey. I had thought, when I rode up there in a bus the previous summer, that it would be faster by car, but there was just enough traffic to ensure that it was not. At least on a bus you can sleep or watch the passing landscape. This time, I settled after some hours into a rhythm; I would drive for a couple of hours, then stop to wash and scrape the crushed mosquitoes from the windscreen, drink dreadful coffee, and drive on. But after three of these stops, somewhere north of Sorsele, my spirits lifted. The

landscape seemed to inflate; the hills became more mountainous and the views of the forest zoomed and then cut back to
wide. After the bridge over the Pite, the last big river before the
Arctic Circle, the whitish grey road rose straight towards the sky,
which was already slightly darker than the road. There would be
a storm. The car was filled with exuberant drumming from the
CD player. As I left the flatlands and climbed I felt the thrill of
a plunging river. Everything seemed turned upside down.

North of Jokkmokk, the town where the road crosses the
Arctic Circle, I drove into a rainstorm intense enough to produce an illusion of dusk, even at six in the evening. Bubbles
bursting all over the road shone silvery in the headlights. The
tarmac had deep wheel ruts worn in it down which the water
streamed. I squinted to keep sight of the car in front, and hoped
the car behind was not too close. At Porjus, the whole procession dipped steeply into a valley towards a huge power station
on a river. I glimpsed a forest of transformers rising out of the
scrubby trees. The silver cage around them glittered in a pale,
milky light. This, far more than Jokkmokk, felt like the
entrance to the real north.

The squall lifted, leaving tendrils of cloud trailing down the
mountain like the paws of a Chinese dragon. There was a little
sign by the side of the road, proclaiming that we had crossed the
boundary of cultivation. From here on agriculture was officially no longer possible. Only nomads and miners could live
off this land. Above the low trees, the rocks and the swamps, a
line of pylons stood like gunslingers shining with their arms
akimbo in the overcast. We were approaching Gällivare, the
first great mining town of the Swedish arctic.

The traffic thickened until there were seven cars visible at the
same time: the most I had seen at one time outside a town all
day. The pines and the birches were almost the same height

beside the road. Then, as the clouds drew back and the road approached Gällivare, a large smooth hill rose to the right, and the greater part of it was treeless. I had almost emerged from the forest. The trees would never entirely vanish, however far I drove, but above the boundary of cultivation they were sparse and shrunken, standing further apart on the flat ground where they grew. Instead of fields, there were flat stretches of swampy ground, often covered knee-high in a close, entangling myrtle.

In the middle of all this, the town of Gällivare was surreally normal. Since everything had to be brought up by road and rail, it was almost exactly the same as any other town in Sweden. I found the good hotel by the railway station, where businessmen watched football in the bar. By the time I had eaten supper and settled in, the ferocious rain had stopped. I took some photographs of the bright evening, leaning out of my window. The horizon across the lake was about fifteen kilometres away now. The midnight sun is not a settled condition, but a constantly changing one, in which horizons expand and contract without pattern or very much warning.

24

Gold

Lannavaara was about another three hours' drive the next morning. At a sign for Nedre Sopporo, the nearest settlement, I turned off the road just after a bridge and drove ten kilometres south down a concrete track along the flat, swampy valley of the Lainio river. At last there were a dozen houses, a white-painted wooden church standing on a low rise, and a signpost directing me out of town to the prospecting camp. I don't know what I was expecting. What I found were two rows of low modern buildings faced with exactly the same pale cladding as the council blocks in Nödinge. Variously dilapidated cars and buses were parked on the beaten earth strip between them, some looking a lot older than the houses.

I had been propelled here by Rolf Larsson's enthusiastic belief in the spirit of the place; after he had left the youth hostel, he had rung Lannavaara to say that I might be coming, and then rung me back to explain what he had done. That had been enough to decide me. I had travelled just enough in the high north to know that it is a country unlike any other in the world, and certainly distinct from the parts of Sweden that lie 800 kilometres or more to the south. The chance to meet someone who was at home here, to the extent that anyone can be, was not to be passed up.

When I introduced myself the first thing I noticed was the unwavering way that Agne Söderström looked at me. It wasn't prurient or rude; it was just a distinct weight of attention common to people who spend a lot of time alone. 'You have to see the mountains that aren't there,' he said, tracing an invisible hill on an invisible horizon with a hand broad and hard like a badger's. 'Only then can you understand the rocks that remain.

'You have to decide, when you see a rock, how it was formed, and how it has been tilted since.' Against the wall was a polished slab of stone showing a V-shaped pattern of striations, and as he talked these stopped being a decoration and turned into markings of an imaginable history, showing the way that the stone had been created in layers, and twisted halfway through. He was talking as he showed me around his little museum of rocks and gems in one of the older buildings.

It was just a room opening off the small café, where there were pine tables and chairs. In one corner hung a quartzite axe-head the size of two fists, stained with reddish fat along its faceted edge. It had been recently whipped with leather thongs on to a wooden haft, but the axe-head itself was about ten thousand years old, and had been found by Agne Söderström in his rangings around Lannavaara. This region had, he said, been settled even in the last ice age, when much of the land to the south was crushed under glaciers originating from Kebnekaise, the largest mountain on the Norwegian border.

The rocks in the museum were very much older. Even the water was millions of years old: one of the displays was of a lump of quartz about the size of a pineapple, sliced cleanly across its midsection so that it had a dark and indistinct interior within the glittering outer rind. The whole thing was mounted in a sort of gimbal ring to hold it upright; when this was tipped, the darkness within could be seen to fluctuate, as a paler shadow moved slightly within it. This was water, he said, trapped there since the crystal formed; and he had shaved the rock so that it could be seen.

In the cases on another wall were ores of silver and other metals and some dust and crumbs of gold, but his passion extended to every kind of stone. The monetary value of some of them was to be respected – it had built this house and all the others – but there was beauty in the composition and history of every kind of rock. As he talked, I began to see the inversion that I have previously sensed, when the sky was darker than the shining road in front of me, continued all the way down into the ground, so that here, where the earth was too poor to farm, the rocks must be harvested instead, and the fawn and grey monotony of the rocks around was only a skin hiding their true and almost liquid nature, which would appear when they were caressed with hammers.

Agne Söderström had been brought up in the hamlet around the church, which had started up in 1870 as an offshoot of the older settlement at Nedre Sapporo, where I had turned off the road on to the concrete path across the flats. Though the older settlement had been inhabited for hundreds of years, agriculture was impossible there. You could live only on fish, berries, and game, as well as what might be smuggled or traded from the coast. One summer, as soon as the snow had gone, the men went out and scattered handfuls of barley seed around the region, a form of enquiry that can't have changed since Neolithic times. The only place where anything would grow was on the southern slopes of the low hill where Lannavaara church was later built – the name means 'the mountain of the settlers', as opposed to the mountain camps of nomads. The first house was floated whole down the river from Nedre Sapporo that summer.

'It was all desolation then,' Agne said. 'There was no government at all.'

We talked at a table in the large refectory that was part of the newest building in his settlement. There was also a gallery area, displaying jewellery and silverware made by students and craftspeople of the region. It was all very fine and none of it cheap. The floor of the refectory and the counter top in front of the bar or kitchen area were made of the same stone, black polished to such a gloss that it seemed to be hollow, varied with glowing flecks of mica in yellow and green as well as the usual silvery white. This came from a deposit that he had found in the trenches of a battleground of the Finnish–Russian war. He walked behind the bar to a fridge and came back with two beers. Now we could talk. He told me how his family had come there.

His grandfather, August Lundberg, had been a missionary sent up from the south to civilize the natives. He had married into the family of Lars Levi Laestadius, who had been the John Wesley of Lapland, and who founded a strict and powerfully puritan sect, distinguished by ecstatic services and iron temperance. Laestadianism was a frontier religion. It was spread by preaching in Finnish and Lapp, rather than the official Swedish, and it still persists across Finland and Swedish and Norwegian Lapland. Lundberg is reckoned to have been the founder of the milder of two main Laestadian sects, the one that allowed women with uncovered heads into church, and which did not preach against bicycles as vehicles of whoredom (the justification for the prohibition was that bicycles made it possible to go courting over longer distances).

Among Lundberg's descendants was Agne Söderström's

uncle, a Finnish-speaking smallholder during the First World War. He wasn't just a farmer – no one could be up there, where the growing season is only a few weeks long. He was also a hunter, a fisherman, a small trader, and a prospector. In the summer of 1917, he was out on a long hunting trip, somewhere near the Finnish border, many miles from home. He was caught by a storm, and finally made camp by a stream. When he woke the next morning, the weather had cleared, and he noticed something strange about a rock on the other bank. So he crossed the stream, chipped off a piece, and, because he was a careful man, he covered up the evidence of what he had done. If the rock turned out to be valuable, he would know where it was.

When he came home, a week or two later, he told his family about the curious rock he had found, and had half of it sent off to a laboratory for analysis. Shortly afterwards he went off on a grouse-shooting trip. While he was stalking, he climbed down into the icy tributary that runs into the Lainio river just south of Lannavaara. He kept on hunting all that day, soaked through. When he returned he fell ill with pneumonia, and died. He never had told anyone where he had found the ore.

When the news came back from the laboratory that the rock he had found was full of gold, there were plenty of prospectors and geologists who followed his route into the wilderness to find the lode. None did, and the outside world forgot the story. But Agne's uncle had a much younger sister, who all her life remembered the excitement when the hunter came home, and the way everyone crowded round to hear the news. Much later, she would tell her own children the story, and so it was that Agne Söderström learned about his uncle. Of course he wanted to find the lost treasure himself.

But in those days the state owned the rights to all the mineral wealth of the country. There was no work in Lannavaara, so he moved to Kiruna, 150 kilometres to the south west, married, and took what work he could, as a lumberjack, a mechanic, and a telephone technician. 'But all through that time, I spent every weekend and every holiday in the wilderness, prospecting for gold, and when I found it, I started digging it up, and learning to work with it. So when the day came, I knew where I would start mining. In 1976, it became legal to prospect again, and to stake claims here. So in 1981, I moved back here.'

He built a weekend cottage first, and spent as much time there as he and his family could; then they sold their house in Kiruna and moved back for good. 'Everyone thought we were crazy: that there was no chance of being able to give up two full-time secure jobs – my wife had a job at the school office. She gave that up, too. We had two small children, and we moved to – nothing. We had no salary. But I have never registered as unemployed, or taken a *krona* from the state. I mined gold, and collected rocks, and then we sold the jewellery.'

Once he was seen to be a success, the business expanded. He was asked to teach others how to work in stone, and how to prospect. Anyone who had found a new way to make a living up there was expected to share their skills, and he progressed from writing the syllabus for a course in Torne valley to putting up the pupils himself, and then building the workshops where they could learn, and then housing so they could stay.

Behind the shop a door led into the industrial regions, rooms that seemed full of dust and fluorescent light, with grinding machines and, in one room, tall power-saws in green-grey housings. Sheets of sawn rock were stacked like plywood against the wall. I gripped one and a friable piece about an inch thick broke off ragged in my hand. In other rooms we came upon moments of clean and calm, mirrors and microscopes, where students were learning to judge gems by their refractions, and little forges and ovens for the metal-workers. There were classrooms full of computers, with pale beech and pine panelling. The telephones had stopped working while I was there, perhaps destroyed by the storm of the day before, and mobile phones did not work at all; but there was still a broadband connection to the Internet.

As he conducted me through these rooms, accepting the unobtrusive homage of his students, Agne seemed like the king of some dwarf kingdom. But when he talked of the wilderness, sitting down in the beautiful clean refectory he had built, I could hear his preaching ancestors. He had shared his camps with eagle owls and bears, and spent weeks at a time on his own out in the beyond.

'There aren't four seasons here. People say there are eight, but even that's not enough. Something is always happening. In Africa, or Australia, everything is the same' – he banged the table in a steady rhythm here, as if it were a funeral drum. 'But here – here I can lie by my campfire and watch the buds opening. I can't see that anywhere else. You can feel the sky. You feel like a radio receiver, as if you're getting signals all the time. But if I walk in the pine forest, or among spruces, I am shut in. I can't feel anything; I feel jailed.

'If you're in the wilderness, you have no problems because you have to struggle the whole time. You have to see that the fire stays alight, so you have to collect wood all the time. You have to get food: catch a grouse, or a fish, or a hare, something edible. If you don't have warmth, then you freeze to death. Nature is hard as rock. It has no compassion for you at all.

'Then, when you have been out for three weeks – and in all that time, when you lay down, you knelt, you ate, you did everything on the ground beside a fire – when you come back from there and can sit down at a table like this! What a feeling! You feel like a king. I don't think even kings can feel that good. It's a fantastic feeling to sit down at a table. Everything is put on plates, and a new heaven opens for you. To lie down in clean sheets in a bed: that's really fantastic.'

The love of wilderness and of solitude that he talked about was not the source of his power, though. That came from the gold. There is a paradox here. Gold has no value to the man on his own. You can't eat it or use it for anything other than social purposes. It is found by men who have moved, for a while, beyond society. But it is worthwhile only when they return to it. Perhaps gold changes its nature, like a trout when pulled from water, for no fish is ever as beautiful in the air as it was when free.

Agne Söderström talked about these heavy clumps of gold as if they had a spirit of their own and had to be hunted: 'Mostly you don't know where the gold is. Really, it is everywhere up here, but gold is difficult. It teases you. It can be found in some places – then it finishes. It's gone. And then, in the next place, it can appear again, and vanish . . .'

Yet the prospector could never entirely lose his human self in the hunt, nor escape the desires of other human beings. Agne's uncle, lost in the freezing wilderness in 1917, had been the same. The only animal that could frighten him then was another human, and when he had found the gold-bearing rock, he had taken the trouble to conceal it from any other man who might come along.

By now, rich and respected, Agne could watch the workings of gold fever in other men with detachment. The Söderströms were, in one aspect, an international business concern, prospecting now in Africa, South America, and Australia. Gold might tease them, but they could charm it back, and this gift was recognized in sober boardrooms around the world. Carl Bildt, the former prime minister, sometimes came to stay in Lannavaara to accustom his sons to the wild. Later in the evening I was talking to Agne's son on the porch outside the shop when we were interrupted by a metallic Volvo saloon with aluminium allow wheels, driven by a lean, sharply dressed young man wearing large, amber aviator shades. He stopped the engine. The driver's side window whirred down and he called from it: 'Drinking on a Monday? That's what I call being a millionaire.'

He came to drink and talk with us. Agne's son said that he personally would not worry very much if civilization were wiped out. He hoped in any case to retire to a hut by a lake. 'So long as I have an axe for firewood, a net for the lake, and a warm place to shit, I'll be all right.' He spoke as if he had given the matter practical thought. 'I'll have a woman come up from the village once a week. I won't want it more than that by then.'

It was difficult to concentrate entirely on what they were saying. I kept thinking of a story Agne had told me about a mosquito-squishing contest that had taken place here one August, played out, perhaps, exactly where we sat. The rules were simple enough: the winner was the man who could count the most corpses on his hand after a single slap against his thigh: the winning score was sixty-eight. I no longer found this incredible.

The last I saw of Agne was at about half past eleven that evening, as I prepared to go off to bed in one of the student blocks opposite the shop and refectory building. He had lain down for a moment on the ground so that he could study where to put the patio that would open out from the refectory. He had received an official letter demanding that he put up railings all around it, since the refectory was licensed to sell alcohol and there must be a barrier against passing trade. He seemed almost to jump to his feet when he was finished, as large hunting dogs will do, and then passed out of sight across the tracked and trampled ground towards his own house.

The next morning I was gone as soon as I could be. I had promised to be in Dalarna, 1,200 kilometres from there, in three days' time, for midsummer, to meet some Swedish friends I knew from England. For a few hours, I drove in quiescent silence, hardly speeding, slowing only for a group of three reindeer who trotted unhurriedly in front of me until a car appeared from the opposite direction to disperse them. In Gällivare I stopped for breakfast. Fresh orange juice, lightly foaming; croissants, cars parked neatly on tarmac; the cappuccino smelt faintly of bitter chocolate. There were newspapers scattered around the table. All these things had a glossy, hallucinatory solidity after the mining camp at Lannavaara. The sense of being overwhelmed by prosperity summoned a memory of a restaurant in Finland, where I had stopped with my family after a week in a very small cabin in Karelia, on the Russian border, where the water came from a well and the only way to have any sort of bath was to make up a sauna in the outhouse and afterwards empty well water from a plastic washing-up basin over your head while standing in the porch. The mosquitoes were less assiduous that far south. When we had left it and stopped in a restaurant converted from a former manor house, I had thought three things as I entered the lavatory: how extraordinary to build a room just for peeing in; how wonderful that hot water gushed from an open tap; and why was this one room larger than the whole building in which my wife and daughter and I had just lived for a week?

As I followed the long road back down from Gällivare there was no trace of the storm that had made the passage into the high north seem like a dark and glistening tunnel. When I paused at the bridge crossing the Pite Älv, the view to the west was almost unendurably glorious. It reminded me of Aldous Huxley's writings about mescaline. I thought, looking up the river bank, that all jewels of heaven were only invented in an attempt to describe those birch leaves mounded like diamonds, the clarity of the distant horizons, and the distinct lines of hills like ribbons heaped on one another, pale green, dark green, violet, diamond-coloured again.

25

Midsummer feasting

South of Sorsele the brightness drained from the air. I grew oppressed by the sense that I had begun to travel not on an ordinary road, but on a Möbius strip, and that gravity was hauling me down the other side of the road I had driven up, a side on which the world had grown harder to recognize but not really changed at all. I had travelled to the end of the country, more or less, and had still not found my lake. The nearest I had come to it was the idea that there might, after civilization had ended, still be a place for a man who knew how to fish with nets in the remotest reaches of the high north. I don't know how to use a net.

A day or two later, I drove through a chill grey rain to the town where I had been invited to spend midsummer by a Swedish couple – he was in telecoms, and she was in biotech – who had emigrated to England for business purposes, and fetched up in the Essex market town where I live. The wife had met my wife while waiting for a bus when they were newly arrived in England, and still assumed that public transport worked. I had ended up giving them both a lift to the station in my car, and the friendship had developed from there. That life in England now seemed very far away as I drove the last few miles in Dalarna.

The forest around was close and dank, and rarely opened to show lakes. When I reached the outskirts of town there was one hotel, or roadhouse, open over the holiday, where I had been booked into a small, simple room. Then I was driven off by my friends from England for twenty or thirty kilometres down the main road, off on to smaller and smaller tracks, across a single-track pontoon bridge, and finally down a pot-holed earth track to a clearing by the river where two small red houses stood. They had flowers round their white-framed doors.

These were the homes of two aged patriarchs who had married two sisters. Both couples were somewhere in their eighties or early nineties; both husbands were limber and clear-eyed, with ferociously tangled eyebrows. Children, grandchildren, and now great grandchildren had been coming here to celebrate midsummer for sixty years, and the gathering of the tribe this year had brought at least thirty people. Some branches of the family were prosperous businessmen: one had a flat in Stockholm just down the road from where my parents had lived as diplomats; another brother was a provincial school-teacher: 'Borås, Borås', he sang, to the tune of 'New York, New York' – the point of this was that Borås is a town only marginally more vibrant than Lilla Edet. If you can't make it there, you can't make it anywhere. At midsummer, all distinctions of wealth just vanished. Everyone queued for the earthen closet. There was a water scoop, a washing-up bowl, and a squirt of soap outside. Everyone drank water from the well, or if they wanted to wash, swam in the river. There was one petrol generator for electricity, but it was seldom switched on; the cooking was done at a wood-fired range. Almost everyone slept in tents and no one had any choice about singing.

The singing started with the very first meal. This was described as schnapps and herring; in fact it was a small smörgåsbord, with really good home-made pickled herring, crispbread, potatoes, meatballs, three cheeses, a dish of potatoes and anchovies. Both the rooms on the ground floor of one of the cottages were full. We sat around tables beneath plain, off-white walls, drinking beer or juniper cordial, until the son of the house, my friend the middle-aged businessman, came round with bottles of Akvavit, putting an inch into every shot glass, and since there weren't enough shot glasses, some of us had small tumblers instead.

Then his father, the clean-shaven younger of the two old men, who carried himself with jaunty concentration, like a finch, stood up in the doorway between the two rooms, where he sang in a clear bright voice the first verse of a drinking song. We drank. We sang an antiphon of thanks. The glasses were refilled. Someone else rose and sang a slightly less respectable song. We drank. The glasses were refilled. It would have been a frightful solecism to drink without a toast proposed, but the family was extremely musical and four or five people had risen to sing these toasts before the meal was over and I realized that in the name of high culture I had been drinking Boilermakers – beer and Akvavit chasers – for an hour, and so had nearly everyone around me.

When this bout was through, there was a disorganized period of conversation in the garden; then more relatives arrived. At once, huge cakes were produced, covered in whipped cream and sliced strawberries, to be eaten with black coffee. There were buns and five sorts of biscuits, too. So we ate, and drank many cups of black coffee. I noticed that an electric piano was being dragged from one of the cars, plugged into the generator, and set up on the porch of one of the smaller outlying cottages, but before I could appreciate the significance of this, one of the old men shouted that all the beautiful young girls must go out into the meadow between the two houses and gather wild flowers.

All the beautiful young girls turned out to mean every woman under the age of seventy. One woman, who lived in one of the grandest addresses in Stockholm, just down from the embassy flat where my parents had lived, wore a stretchy white T-shirt with diamanté details, which seemed a little too young for her; her teenage daughter wore skinny white jeans, with, low down on each buttock, large pink diamanté crowns appliquéd. Almost everyone else was dressed for the forest, rather than the regatta. Laughing and calling to each other, sometimes still singing, the women gathered armloads of wild flowers, blue, red and yellow, while the men attended to the maypole. This was a cross about four metres long, already lying on trestles. Sheaves of fresh birch branches were on the ground around it. The handier men dressed the pole with these so it was completely covered. The useless ones – me and an uncle – hacked away the thinner branches to form the garlands that hang from the pole. Later, the girls bound these and their bunches of flowers on to wire rings about a metre across, which were hung from the cross-pieces. Finally the whole thing was raised and set in the ground.

Then the piano started up and everyone younger than seventy joined hands to dance around the maypole, singing or, after a while, just gasping out loud as we stumbled through a series of elaborate games for which no one knew all the words, or the rules, after the first one, which required mime to a nonsense song about frogs: 'The little frogs look silly, because they have no ears!' (At this, the company directors and teachers place their hands beside their heads and waggle them.) 'The

little frogs look silly, because they have no tails!' (Assembled dignitaries waggle their hands behind their bottoms, while running
around in a circle.) 'The little frogs can only go brekekekek
koax koax.' At this we all made croaky noises and jumped in a
circle until it was time for the next chorus. Just the thing to
settle a stomach full of Boilermakers, coffee and two sorts of
cake.

Eventually there was no one left standing who could remember even fragments of another song and the dancing died away
in exhaustion and some laughter.

After a pause there was a new organization. We queued to
collect clipboards and pencils for a sort of treasure hunt through
the woods – a gentle walk among the midges, answering thirteen questions that were pinned to trees. There were strict rules
about not consulting, which everyone ignored. It did them no
good. Since the quiz had been set by the patriarchs, who had
been teachers, the questions were difficult and detailed: identify
a particular kind of eagle from its picture; what is the Latin
name of a common anemone; name the author of this six-
teenth-century poem. When all thirteen had been found and
answered, the trail brought us circuitously to the other cottage,
outside which, under a small marquee, a table had been spread
for supper and the completed answers to the treasure hunt were
to be marked. No one got every answer right, but we all agreed
that the midges had never been worse than this year. We stood
around for ages, slapping our necks and rubbing itching ears
and eyebrows, until the food appeared – more crispbread,
cheese, smoked pork in slices, potato salad, red wine in copious
boxes – and then the more midge-bitten returned to the barn
where we could watch swallows nesting above the beams of the
roof and eat and talk until it was time to sing again.

While we were talking, the rain came down hard and drove

away the worst of the midges. Then the sun came back, and back-lit the birches outside the barn door, so that every hanging raindrop shone and the leaves just glowed. It was by then about nine in the evening, and the party was just getting into its stride.

Before the singing came the solemn prize-giving ceremony, which was obviously something that had been going on for thirty years or more, ever since the younger generation of parents were children. There was a table loaded with prizes of the sort you find in upmarket crackers: plastic tape measures, plugs for pike fishing, notebooks, a wallet, a little laser thing for measuring distances. These were given out in ascending order of age, so that the two pregnant women were called first; then by divisions ('Girls under thirty' and so forth). I picked up a little 'gold' cup in plastic, the sort of thing you would get for wining a darts tournament. It watches me as I write.

After the ceremony we were summoned into the second house, where the bearded patriarch lived. Thirty or so people were crammed into one room around a large table. The petrol generator had been carried over to where the meal had been, and a thick flex was run through to the Yamaha stage piano, which earlier had been directed at the dancing around the maypole. But the piano was not played yet. Instead, two local men turned up, each with his *nyckelharpa*, an autochthonous Swedish instrument, a cross between an auto-harp and a violin, which has been made in the valley of the Dalälv for around four hundred years. It has eleven steel strings, arranged in four groups. Along the bottom of the neck are three banks of keys that stop the outermost strings. It is held like a violin, and scraped with a bow, while the left hand manipulates the keys. It sounds like an accordion on the verge of tears.

We heard three duets, of varying accomplishment, but the

skill hardly mattered. I felt as if I was watching pterodactyls mating.

Another giant cream-and-strawberry cake was produced, with more coffee, and a litre bottle of whisky, which was drained quite rapidly in inch-deep slugs out of paper cups. By this time I had switched entirely to water and juniper cordial. If I hadn't, I would never have believed what I heard next.

A thin and extravagantly drunk cousin took his place behind the piano, and another, not at all thin, was called forward to sing. He had a powerful tenor voice and delivered a series of camped-up songs that stunned the room. There was a gloriously silly and self-mocking version of 'My Way' to loosen us up, but the point at which I lost seriousness completely was when he launched into 'Borås Borås', sung with as much feeling and volume as if he had been in an opera house. It turned out both men were semi-professional musicians. The pianist had spent most of his weekends for the last twenty years driving around the country wearing ludicrous costumes for a dance band; the singer was seriously considering music as his career, but he had been advised to wait a couple of years for his voice to mature.

Gradually the singing became more general. The pianist conducted a four-part round, which, though largely tuneful, degenerated into a thirteen-part round as the singers found it increasingly difficult to remember at which section of the table they were sitting. A completely sober student, Janna, sung a comic song whose comedy I have now forgotten, then very sweetly drove me back to the hotel at midnight.

When I returned next morning, there were people having breakfast at 10.30 who told me, speaking softly and with exaggerated care, that the evening had broken up some time after two.

The healthier survivors then gathered around freshly picked

plastic tubs of worms for a traditional midsummer's day fishing session. Equipped with pole rods, we drove off to a shallow lake set on the margins of heath and forest some miles away. All the bait fishers hauled up large quantities of tiny perch, ranging in length from a hand-span down to large man's finger. Every one of them was killed. They would be rolled in flour and fried and served for lunch as a kind of freshwater whitebait. I caught nothing, since I wanted to try fly-fishing, but had left the necessary fly box at the cottage where I had been showing it to someone. Janna turned out to be easily the best at fishing, and did sneaky things like actually wandering off to where the fish were. She put about twenty-five into the communal carrier bag where all the booty was collected.

Back at the cottage I sat with her for a while at a table on the lawn and we cleaned the fish. Perch have such a tough and supple skin they might be the waterborne form of dragons: if you almost behead them and then slit the skin carefully down the back and loosen it from the flesh, you can peel the glittering skin away in a sort of pouch with the head and guts attached. A brisk chop across the tail and fish is ready to roll in flour and fry. Inert, skinned, headless, gutless parcels of grey flesh, they seemed to represent to me my English state, from which only the flickering animation of travel had briefly released me.

I left before lunch, and before the football match, for which the whole country was waiting: Sweden against Germany. The men had been quite confident their country would win. The roads were deserted and the progress of the match came to me in fragments of commentary from the radio as I checked it intermittently over the next couple of hours, picking up the story about eight minutes in: 'Not the start we wanted! Not at all the start we wanted, to go a goal down after four minutes!'

Each time I checked, the news was worse, and the commentator's optimism more determined:

'You have to admire our courage – two nil down after twelve minutes. There's still all to play for!'

'Henrik Larsson is the last man you would have expected to miss a penalty!'

'The referee is not on our side at all!'

'That was a very harsh sending off!'

The match limped towards its conclusion and the countryside around me turned into domesticated plains. I thought about Swedishness. There was nothing distinctively Swedish in the demented nationalism of the radio commentary. You would have heard that anywhere in the world where football was taken seriously that summer – it should be possible to make a decent profit on any World Cup by betting against every team in its native country. But the midsummer festivity was a different matter. It was certainly distinctively Swedish; perhaps it seemed, in a rather self-conscious way, essentially Swedish, too. Yet a good half of the participants lived outside Sweden, and no one but our hosts actually lived in the countryside where there were poles to dance around.

My current, English, wife used to talk a lot about the strangeness of the Swedes, and find it curious that I did not notice it, or appear to. But 'strangeness' can mean either unfamiliarity or mystery, and the two are very different. I was little surprised by anything that seemed to me particularly Swedish, but this didn't mean that I could understand it: merely that it was mysterious to me in the way that certain aspects of Britishness might be. When Anita and I had been married, the difference in nationality and in culture had been an apparently essential way to understand the differences between us, and between what we wanted and could tolerate. But now we no longer were married to each other, she just seemed a person whose history was not as strange to me as it once had been.

Yet there is a distinction between life as it is lived and life as newspapers can represent it. As a journalist I had made my living from the supposition – shared by me and my readers – that there was something called 'Sweden', or 'Swedishness', which could usefully be defined. But now I find that it is something that I can recognize without being able to define it at all. I know it when I see it, and all I can hope to do when writing about it is to let other people see it too.

26

Gringo

The great change in the last thirty years is that Swedishness doesn't look like Swedishness any more. I mean that literally. In the past, the most visible thing about Swedes to the outside world was always that they were blond, although in fact there were *two* very recognizable physical types in Sweden – the tall willowy blonds, and the shorter, dark-haired Swedes, found mostly in the north, such as Anna in her youth, whose skin would weather in summer to the brown and faded crimson of old boats.

These two light and dark colour schemes were so ubiquitous as to be invisible. Only when I came to London would I notice people who were black, brown, yellow or fat. So it was a visceral shock to come down to Stockholm and be shown a copy of *Gringo*, a glossy magazine for and about new Swedes, the ones whom the rest doubt are really Swedish at all. The cover showed a grinning young man, Turkish or Greek, with a pelt of black hair all over his chest. It was shocking, and it was meant to be; it looked exotic and intimate at once. If integration is going to happen, it will involve a lot of sex across racial and social boundaries; and, if it doesn't, there will be bad times ahead.

There are about a million people, that is, one in nine of the population, in Sweden today who appear exotic – or just foreign – to the rest. This is a large immigrant population by most European standards, and it seems even larger in a country that was, historically, a place that hungry peasants left. The first and still the largest single group were Finns, throughout the Fifties and Sixties. Then came labour migration from Italy, Turkey, and the former Yugoslavia; that more or less stopped in the Seventies, but increasing waves of refugees poured in, as if to compensate. There were South Americans, fleeing from dictatorships; Kurds, fleeing from wars and oppression; Lebanese; Bosnians; Somalis: the less the rest of the world was willing to take in refugees, the more important Sweden has become to them. The change happened gradually, and largely unremarked by the rest of Sweden, partly because the areas of heavy immigrant settlement were satellite towns, which are out of sight of the rest of the country, except for the upper reaches of their tower blocks.

I am not Swedish, and I was once an immigrant; yet I can write, I think, much more truthfully about being Swedish than about being an immigrant, because immigration is a process both individual and irreversible. I can remember once seeing 'Sweden' as a single, impermeable monolith. But I cannot see it that way any more. I lived there. It is a world, with its own frame of reference. It can stand for many things, even when seen from the inside. But none of them are more real to me than the rocks and water, or the flickering of sunlight and fish.

That Swedes could be unaffectedly racist was something I learned very early. A relative of mine by marriage had a boyfriend who had served time in jail for drunkenly attacking a Yugoslav immigrant, just because the victim was dark-skinned and ahead of him in a fast-food queue. Among the working classes, there was not just the sense of unreflecting superiority felt by all Swedes in the Seventies towards almost everyone else on earth; there was also a particular distaste towards the olive-skinned, whom the British, fifty years before, would have called 'Wops', or 'Dagoes'. *Svartskallar*, they were called: 'black skulls', as if the dark hair on their heads marked them off as separate forever.

Because of the generally undemonstrative nature of Swedish public life, in which good manners demand that everyone ignore everyone else, it is easy to miss the degree to which olive-skinned immigrants are specially ignored – and easy for them, too, to overestimate it. But one story here is illuminating. On the west side of the Göta Älv, outside Gothenburg, there is a suburb, not as distinct as one of the satellite towns, but socially very similar, where in 1998 a disco full of young Muslims – Somalis, Iranians, former Yugoslavs and Turks – caught fire and sixty-three of them were killed. Three young Iranians were among those accused of setting the fire. A friend of mine, sent over from Brussels by his newspaper to cover it, remembers the next morning: the burnt-out shell, with grief-stricken relatives around it – right next to a supermarket with indifferent native Swedes going about their business as if it were any other Monday.

But at the same time, and sometimes among the same people, there was a deep sense that racism was wrong; that the benefits of equality and prosperity should be spread around the world, and that Sweden should set an example, but also behave well for its own sake. Tolerance was one of the things that every-one had to believe in.

There has not been any labour immigration for a long time – the unions complained and effectively stopped it in the early 1970s. But the belief that Sweden has a duty to refugees remains strong. Even at the height of the racist backlash of the early Nineties, which coincided with a stream of refugees from the wars in former Yugoslavia, there was never less than 30 per cent of the population who believed that Sweden should accept more refugees than it did. This was a far more generous attitude than the English one, though there is still a majority belief that Sweden has accepted far too many. There is a very clear and measurable discrimination against Swedes with Levantine-sounding names. In the summer of 2006 *Svenska Dagbladet* reported that such people could greatly increase their incomes by changing their surnames to something Swedish. Lower-paid workers could find jobs at nearly double their current wages this way; and the effect persisted – though with a diminishing effect on salary – almost up to the highest levels of society.

But of course these people are not immigrants. The majority are Swedes; most of them were born in Sweden and so were many of their parents. They are what the future is going to be, and the country they live in will to a large extent be shaped by the understandings that are reached about Swedishness.

Emerging from the tube at Skärholmen, a suburb about half an hour south of Stockholm city centre, I found myself in a square transformed. It must once have been one of the feature-less concrete spaces, like the much smaller square in Nödinge, in which nothing seemed to happen that was neither planned nor alcoholic. Now it was a market. There were stalls and small shops around the edges, as colourful as summer lichen on a rock. They sold clothes, food, electronics, travel; everything you might need except books; and on the far side was a massive yet graceful concrete building that housed the municipal theatre.

Gringo's offices were at the side of the theatre in a suite of rooms that looked cluttered and unfurnished at the same time, as if everything was half-built and had not yet been humanized:

the walls were smooth and grey but there were strings of cabling all over the floor linking the desks where people worked. It is a magazine, an idea, and a political programme all at once. The programme has no party, because all the respectable parties in parliament could sign up to it: it is simply to get new Swedes and old Swedes to understand themselves as citizens of the same country. The idea – again shared, I think, by all the governing classes – is that this is vitally important, because the consequences of failure could be terrible.

The magazine is large, glossy, and written in an argot full of American words: a story about flats in the outskirts of Stockholm was headed 'HOODENS FRESHASTE CRIBS' – 'The newest cribs in the 'hood'. there are words in new Swedish that come from Turkish and other immigrant languages, but most of the argot has been taken from MTV and wedged or hammered into the templates of Swedish grammar.

The founder and editor of the magazine, Zanyar Adami, is the son of Iranian Kurds. He came to Sweden in 1987 at the age of five, as a haemophiliac child to be treated on humanitarian grounds. His parents, who had been active in the guerrilla war against the Iranian government, were allowed in a year later. He is a young man of great force and self-possession. He trained as a civil engineer before founding the magazine in 2004, and since then has won prizes for it. 'I want people to see, in twenty years' time, that Swedishness is broad enough for there to be many ways of being Swedish.'

In some ways, this has already happened. The minister for integration in the non-socialist coalition government that took office in 2006 is an African woman, born in Burundi – one of her first actions was to sack her own uncle from another government job. There are prominent sportsmen, academics, and intellectuals of obviously foreign descent.

Still, the idea that Sweden should be a multifarious society is an odd one. (Tolerance, of course, is another matter: tolerance can be compulsory.) The great distinguishing characteristic of the society as I knew it was its narrowness. It was narrowly liberal, or narrowly socialist within its different net cages, but that there should be two acceptable views on matters of real importance, such as the treatment of women, or racism, was not a Swedish characteristic, and I can't really believe that anything has happened to change that. A narrow society is not necessarily inflexible: everyone can always change their minds, provided they all do so at once, and together. But it is very different from a genuinely plural one.

Zanyar Adami knew what I meant about the narrowness of Swedish society – how could he not? It was what he had set up his magazine to fight. He agreed, I think, that it would be hard to disrupt. But he feared for a future in which the society could not expand. Already one Bosnian Muslim who grew up in Kungälv had been caught and sentenced to fifteen years in jail after planning a series of suicide bombings in Sarajevo.

I remembered a social worker from Los Angeles whom I had talked to on a story about prison reform who had showed me photographs of some of the young men he visited in Californian jails. They were pictures from a society that was happy to disintegrate. The young men were serving absurd sentences for tiny crimes – twenty or thirty years without hope of parole for being in a car in which someone else had a gun. Yet even after he had explained all these things to me, I hadn't seen what was to him the most obvious fact about these pictures: that all the prisoners in them were black. They weren't. They were Latinos, to my eye no darker than a surfer. Yet neither their crimes nor their punishments made sense without the understanding that they were, to a Californian eye, not white at all.

It is one of the known unspeakables of Swedish life that the crime rate among immigrants and their descendants is at least double that in the native population. The most recent figures I could find on this subject came from 2005, when the Criminal Statistics Board produced a report it had been dithering over for years: characteristically, the section with the hard figures in it is introduced by saying it is important to realize that most Swedes, whatever their ethnic background, aren't criminals at all. But of those who were born to Swedish-born parents, 95 per cent have never been convicted of a crime. Swedes with immigrant parents are twice as likely to have been convicted, and immigrants born abroad two and a half times as likely. This is true even after the figures have been corrected for age, sex, social class and so on. The figures are further skewed in that violent crime of all sorts and rape are crimes of which immigrants are disproportionately more likely to be convicted. Immigrants are more than four times as likely as Swedes to commit a murder, and more than five times as likely to commit a rape. Their children, who have grown up in Sweden, are somewhere in between the two figures: two and a half times as likely to kill someone; less than twice as likely to rape. This isn't Armageddon: in general Swedish crime figures are about in the middle of the European range and much lower than England's. But it is not the promised land to which the world was tending in the Sixties either; nor the promised land into which Swedes hoped, or assumed, they could welcome the deserving, grateful wretched of the earth.

Zanyar Adami was optimistic about integration when I talked to him. But he certainly didn't think it was an inevitable development, and he thought it depended, above all, on work. Without employment for the young people of the satellite towns, their estrangement from the society outside them will increase, as will its estrangement from them.

But he really didn't want to generalize, which was one of the things that made him trustworthy. In some of the satellite towns the schools were fine, the government's policies were working as they should. In others, and here he mentioned two districts north of Gothenburg, things were very bad. The schools were run down, the children disaffected, gangs building up. No one who had a choice would want to move to there. There is some hard evidence for this, in as much as you can buy a house in those places for a quarter of what the identical model would cost in somewhere more salubrious.

Reading about the country from the outside, especially in the work of American hyper-nationalists, you would suppose that the whole place was on the verge of a *jihadi* uprising, that the satellite towns are slums full of disaffected Muslims. This is clearly exciting to believe, even for some Swedes: in April 2007, when there was an outburst of arson attacks in Rosengård, the largely Muslim satellite town outside Malmö, there were newspaper articles asking whether this was Sweden's equivalent of the French rioting in the *banlieux*. It wasn't.

There are now 400,000 Muslims in Sweden, and, among children in Malmö, the most common new boys' name is Mohammed. Of course, anyone born in Malmö is by definition not an immigrant; that doesn't make them welcome, and it need not make them feel at home. It seems to me that one of the distinctive marks of Swedishness is the ability to feel completely excluded from the society around you, precisely because it is so conformist and close. But this is not the kind of Swedishness to encourage among the children of immigrants. Meanwhile, hostility to the dark-skinned Swedes grows where they are most numerous, whether you measure it by attitudes in opinion polls or by votes for anti-immigrant parties.

The one partial exception to this rule is Stockholm, which has satellite towns full of olive-skinned Swedes, but a low vote for anti-immigrant parties. Stockholm, though, seems like a Sweden all to itself, distinct both from the back-country where I had travelled and lived, and from the satellite towns around it. On the buses and in the tubes there are posters urging young people to move out to the satellite towns precisely because they are not like their parents' Sweden but, rather, 'edgy', 'urban', and other hackneyed or Hackney-ish terms.

Parts of Stockholm are genuinely sophisticated, cosmopolitan, and almost weightless. It is a place where I have to make an effort to speak Swedish; where many of the people I meet will have been educated abroad. It is Stockholm-Sweden that politicians talk about abroad, and that is the lens through which visiting foreign dignitaries and journalists look at Sweden, unless they make a real effort. When foreigners write in praise of Swedish policies, it is from Stockholm that they get their information or their understanding, and this is always influenced by the very great confidence of the ruling class that still run the place. This is in some ways the country that Tony Blair would have liked to run. When the prime minister says something should happen, it does; or at least the newspapers agree that it has happened, which is just as good.

On my last trip there I did meet one inhabitant of this exotic country, who was not at all the same sort of immigrant as the poor or visibly different. Francis Strand is an American who moved to Stockholm some years ago to be with his Swedish husband, because gay marriage is recognized in Sweden. He is middle-aged, friendly, stubbly, fashionably dressed. He wrote an amusing blog about his experiences – 'How to learn Swedish in 1000 Difficult Lessons'. But for the first three or four years that he lived in the city, towards the end of a high-tech boom in the late Nineties, he knew no Swedish at all, and needed none to work at his publishing job.

We met just round the corner from Mary and Keith's old flat, where I had spent so many delightful hours lamenting the dreary stolidity of Sweden. The restaurant was decorated to suggest plain rural prosperity seventy years ago, with a menu of peasant or primitive food made light and fresh. I ordered a *salade niçoise* which came with a slab of seared tuna; he ate potato cakes, made as if woven out of straw, with sour cream and orange caviare. We drank tap water from large glasses, but that's because fashionable people don't drink at lunch. He had never once heard the word *nykterhet*, or temperance; nor the other word under whose sign I had lived, solidarity.

27

Still water

Driving back towards Gothenburg, I found myself shouting at the radio even more than usual. It was not terribly hostile shouting: more like a drunk cheering on his team. For though I was sober, I was listening to the grave silliness of *Ring P Ett*, a phone-in programme which reveals a country almost invisible from the outside, full of polite and earnest eccentricity. It is hosted with unobtrusive skill by a woman who listens to her callers sympathetically so that she can cut them off so quickly and politely it is almost painless. There was a man who thought that the problem with Sweden – the overwhelming problem – was that the country did not do enough to nourish and appreciate the badgers in its midst. He was given the time he needed to explain. As I listened, I was reminded of a sequence in Armistead Maupin's *Tales of the City* where a television hostess interviews a woman who has had her pet freeze-dried. The skill that makes the hostess marketable is that she can laugh at her guests and encourage the audience to do so without the victim realizing that this is the game. The Swedish version was quite without that cruelty. It tended to enlarge sympathy rather than diminish it, and in this sense it was close to what the Swedes mean by democracy:

not a voting system, but a recognition of common humanity. This was the spirit that had lain behind all the craft circles and evening classes and even the passionate fishing clubs of which I had been a member.

Nowhere in England seemed more false and corrupted than some of the places I had fished. This wasn't just because there is no wilderness in England, so almost all the fishing, and certainly all the very best, takes place in manicured surroundings. In England, river care is a form of landscape gardening. In Sweden it is about whether to use the river for hydro-electric power or as a giant chute to run logs down to the coast. None the less, the complex and artificial ecology of the water meadows along English chalk streams has had its own integrity. At one of my schools was the remains of an old water meadow system running down to the Kennett: a geometrical maze of small ditches, sluices and ponds in which I caught sticklebacks without a hook. They are so greedy that if you tie cotton thread around a worm and lower it into the water the fish will grab the worm and cling to it all the way out of the water and into a waiting bucket. Nothing wrong there.

The water meadows are all gone now, partly because they are no longer economic: the farm workers who maintained them no longer exist, and the sheep that graze on them have also been replaced. Even the water that filled them has largely vanished from the aquifers beneath the chalk downs, so that the head-waters of the Kennett, which were waist deep, are now a succession of dry gulches writhing across empty fields. The wild trout of the rivers has largely been replaced by implanted rainbows, not because the native fish are all dead from acid rain, but because rainbow trout grow more quickly than the natives, and so are more profitable if you are running the river as an upmarket fish farm.

This is what most of the trout streams of southern England have become. In the case of one stretch of the Itchen, a little upstream of Winchester, I saw this happening. When I first went there, as a journalist in the Eighties, it was still run by a drunken advertising man who had left the wild trout in place. They were small, and very shy, but easy to catch if you hid from them scrupulously. Then it was bought by an American company, which put in barrel-bellied stock fish that were not in the least afraid of humans on the bank. They were very finicky – you might say neurotic – about what they would eat. But they were never allowed to get too neurotic, for it was well understood that if none were caught, no stockbroker would pay £200 a day to fish there. There was really nothing left of the experience but the knowledge that you had spent a lot of money – or, in my case, been given a valuable freebie on the understanding that I would write something that increased the value of the property I was allowed on. I gave up fishing journalism almost as soon as I had started in it. It felt like reviewing porn videos in which one was oneself an actor.

In the years since I left Sweden I had managed to fish in quite a lot of desirable and even some expensive places, from Montana to Slovenia. I had even watched the broad agricultural reservoirs of the English Midlands appear in Swedish fishing magazines as exotic and desirable destinations. It's true that they hold very large fish, some of which might as well be wild. But they are still suburban, and the largest wild animals on their shores are probably rabbits.

In Montana there are bears and wolves, but the fishing itself is preserved by catch and release, so that in one place we hiked to each fish is caught on average seven times a year. In Slovenia, too, the beauty of the surroundings, the rivers, and the trout could not rid me of the suspicion that I was playing in the world's most delightful aquarium. In one river I waded so close to a grayling that I could see the yellow-gold rim all round the great dark eye watching me through three feet of clear water as I trundled nymphs down towards the fish. The eye seemed infinitely wise and weary. I felt better about catching the despised wild chub further upstream.

Only in the scruffy forest lakes of Sweden could I recapture the sense that I had stepped into a better world when I reached water, and even there I found myself reluctant to kill anything I would not eat, or to catch what I knew I would not kill.

I seemed to have driven for days and days. I needed a dank, grey-green shade; I needed silence and still water. So I found my way from memory towards the lakes where I had used to fish, so tired and road-lagged that when I passed a clearing in the forest full of ostriches I didn't register it as oddness. A few minutes later I passed a sign advertising a one-room cottage for the night: in a gentler climate it would have been a substantial garden shed. Inside there was a bed, a table, and a small refrigerator. I took the room and slept like a brick until four in the morning, and then I dreamed with exceptional vividness that I was sharing my pillow with a pair of cats. When I woke in the morning, the cats puzzled me long after I had remembered the ostriches.

Beyond the red curtains was a bright grey morning, too chilly for mosquitoes. The ostriches, as I drove past them, looked as if they had been rained on. Just past them I turned off the metalled road and took a track through the forest to Aborrevatten, the lake where, twenty-five years before, I had caught my first trout on a fly. A quiet, steady rain began as I left the car with a plastic carrier bag of breakfast. The lake was further away than it had been, the hummocks and hillocks guarding it were steeper; but what I had really forgotten was the intense prickling greens of the forest which no drizzle can quench, though this fiercest season lasts only for a couple of weeks. The birches are vivid all year round. They seem to hold the light inside their trunks, but as the summer wears on, their leaves grow dull. When their new leaves first appear there is no grey in them at all. Even the evergreens are caught up in fierce spring. The last few inches of every spruce branch wore a thick green ruff of fresh needles tipped with a soft yellowy bud, almost like a catkin, which would swell and harden over the summer until it became one of the old, erupted cones which hung further in on the trees.

The old pine needles, collected in drifts along the side of the path, seemed russet rather than their usual exhausted yellowy brown. They smelled, though, much as they had always done, of loneliness. When I had walked for long enough I sat down at the foot of one of the casting jetties, under a spreading pine tree, and watched the drizzle hunting across the lake. I heard very occasional greedy trout noises; a mallard duck prospected along the edge of a weed bed. Long-legged water boatmen ran in circles over the water. I watched the rain for a long while; after that I walked back to the car carrying my still uneaten breakfast.

I drove instead to the fly-fishing-only lake where I had always fled when I could from Nödinge: a rounded, shallow lake where the margins are so thick with water lilies in summer that it seems you could walk across them. The rain had cleared but I walked around the lake anyway to the shelter where I had sometimes spent the night. It had three walls, a roof, and a raised sleeping platform. Everything there always smelled of ash and burnt stone from the fireplace in front, and if I ate chocolate in my sleeping bag last thing at night the field mice would wake me, running over my face while it was still much too dark to fish.

Here I sat and ate and watched the water, trying to spot old wading routes to underwater boulders. I knew this lake as intimately as anywhere in the world. My feet remembered how to climb around the ridges. I knew where the crayfish lurked. They were almost invisible, but if you cleaned a fish in the right place, and dropped the pale guts into the water, they would rest and settle for a while, then start to shake and quiver as the invisible crayfish pulled at them, and sometimes they would be pulled into the depths or crannies of the rock.

When at last I assembled my rod and walked out along the casting jetty I thought my hand would know exactly where to place the back-cast between the trees behind. But it did not. The cunning it had once had was bound up with the rod I had then used, and though the one I now had was better by every measure – longer, lighter, more powerful and more responsive, as well as very much more expensive – it did not have the cunning that the older one had acquired in my hand, and several times I cast the fly decisively backwards into a stand of birches, where it stuck. When this had been the best, the nearest place to fish for me, I had cast beautifully. All those hours of practice in the snow at Lerdalen had been experiment as well as drill. Because I could not afford a fancy scientific line I had made up my own from a cheap one with a Monofil running line. The weighted portion was exactly the greatest length that I could hold in the air before shooting the rest, and with that outfit I could cast further than ever before or since.

The olive-green American lines that I now use cost more than my first rod and reel together. I still couldn't cast them as far from the jetty. But I could cast just far enough; and now that I care less, I fish better. When a trout moved somewhere near where my fly ought to be I just lifted the rod enough to tighten the line if he was there, and he was. I never for a moment supposed that I would lose this fish, and as it approached through the water lilies I saw it was a brown trout of about two pounds with black and red spots on his flanks the size of my fingernails. A fish like that, caught from there, would once have made me so happy I could have somersaulted straight into the lake, but instead I knelt first, then lay down at full length so that I could unhook it without even lifting it from the water. I understood I had no business there any longer.

None the less, I went there one last time before the long drive back to England. It was early evening; I sat at the foot of one of the wooden casting jetties and watched a wagtail at the other end. The lake was quite calm, as I always remember it, and completely deserted. The wagtail finished whatever it had been doing, climbed on to one of the posts and, when I made a move to photograph it, jumped up and then flew across the still lake on a completely straight course, bounding exultantly through the air. The lake glittered like pollen. I thought about it often on the dirty grey circuitous route back home.

Acknowledgements

This book owes a great deal to the kindness of friends, some dead; others have had their names changed. At the very least I should thank Agne Söderström, Alvar Alsterdal, Anita, Caroline Brown, Cecilia Steen Johnsson, Christer, Gunilla, Hans, Hasse, Ian Jack, Ingela, Lars Ryding, Lasse and Birgitta Anderström, Leif Krüger, Oskar Kollberg, Ray, Rolf, Rolf and Gunnel Larsson, Rosamond Brown, Sigrid, Ulla, and Zeynar Adami.

Three people are owed special thanks: Caroline and Rosamond for putting up with me, and Liz Jobey, my thoughtful and tirelessly encouraging editor.